Sports in International Politics

Between Power and Peacebuilding

Timothy D. Sisk
University of Denver

ROWMAN & LITTLEFIELD
Lanham • Boulder • New York • London

Executive Acquisitions Editor: Michael Kerns
Assistant Editor: Elizabeth Von Buhr
Sales and Marketing Inquiries: textbooks@rowman.com

Credits and acknowledgments for material borrowed from other sources, and reproduced with permission, appear on the appropriate pages within the text.

Published by Rowman & Littlefield
An imprint of The Rowman & Littlefield Publishing Group, Inc.
4501 Forbes Boulevard, Suite 200, Lanham, Maryland 20706
www.rowman.com

86-90 Paul Street, London EC2A 4NE

British Library Cataloguing in Publication Information Available

Library of Congress Cataloging-in-Publication Data

Names: Sisk, Timothy D., 1960- author.
Title: Sports in international politics : between power and peacebuilding / Timothy D. Sisk, University of Denver.
Description: Lanham, Maryland : Rowman & Littlefield, [2024] | Includes bibliographical references and index.
Identifiers: LCCN 2023051515 (print) | LCCN 2023051516 (ebook) | ISBN 9781538187104 (cloth) | ISBN 9781538187111 (paperback) | ISBN 9781538187128 (ebook)
Subjects: LCSH: Sports—Political aspects. | Sports—Social aspects. | Sports and state. | Peace-building.
Classification: LCC GV706.35 .S5154 2024 (print) | LCC GV706.35 (ebook) | DDC 306.4/83—dc23/eng/20240125
LC record available at https://lccn.loc.gov/2023051515
LC ebook record available at https://lccn.loc.gov/2023051516

PRAISE FOR *SPORTS IN INTERNATIONAL POLITICS*

"Accessibly and with deep insight, *Sports in International Politics* provides an exploration into key trends in the relationship between, on the one hand, sports and global politics and, on the other hand, the 'everyday' dimensions of sports in the nurturing of peace and tolerance. By offering the reader a conceptual toolbox and mapping empirical trends, it is essential reading for understanding the double-edged nature of sports in promoting peace and driving conflict, locally and internationally."

—Kristine Höglund, professor of peace and conflict research, Uppsala University

"In this insightful and comprehensive book, Timothy D. Sisk explores the intricate connections among sports, power, and global governance, as well as peacebuilding, within our ever-changing and turbulent global landscape. An essential resource for those seeking to understand the transformative potential of sport in promoting international peace and sustainable development."

—Dr. Fred Tanner, Swiss ambassador (ret.); visiting professor at the Graduate Institute, Geneva (HEID); senior adviser, Center for Strategic Analysis (CSA), Vienna; and former director of the Geneva Centre for Security Policy (GCSP)

"In this extremely impressive analysis of the impact of sports on global politics, Timothy D. Sisk goes straight to the heart of the matter: power. The book lays bare the complexities and politicization of sports and punctures a number of myths about the healing power of sports. I highly recommend it."

—Roger Mac Ginty, Durham University

"Timothy D. Sisk critically explores the complex relationships among sports, politics, and peace. He shows how the same drivers that boost social unity have been used to promote ideologies of hate. He finds, however, that with care, sports can be a powerful catalyst for peace."

—Cedric De Coning, research professor, Norwegian Institute of International Affairs (NUPI)

Contents

List of Illustrations, Tables, Concept Boxes, Case Studies, and Documentary Insights

ILLUSTRATIONS

TABLES

CONCEPT BOXES

CASE STUDIES

DOCUMENTARY INSIGHTS

Preface

International sports create global culture within and beyond the borders of the countries of the world. As such, sport is unmatched in the extent of cross-cultural engagement among peoples beyond borders. The international market for global sports-related economic activities is estimated to be as much as $700 billion annually, or about 1 percent of global GDP (Collignon and Sultan 2014; Russel, Barrios, and Andrews 2016). Each year, more than 3 billion viewers tune in to watch the Tour de France, 3.3 billion watch World Cup soccer's quadrennial tournament, and billions more tune in or stream on their smart devices to watch cricket, golf, and boxing. That's just to begin with: millions more watch UEFA Champions League, the NFL Super Bowl, or Major League Baseball World Series, as the reported most-viewed sports according to market research (Gough 2023).

The most prestigious arena in international sports is without question: The Olympic Games. The International Olympic Committee (IOC) reports that the Tokyo 2020 Summer Games (held in 2021, postponed due to COVID-19) reached a broadcast audience of 3 billion, or roughly 35 percent of the world's total population (IOC 2021), and that the Beijing 2022 Winter Olympic Games reached a global broadcast audience of more than 2 billion people (IOC 2022a).

Because of its transcendent reach to populations, and its symbolic value to people globally in some ostensibly universal way, sports are regularly said to have special power to unite as it is a venue for the diffusion of global values reflected in sports, especially excellence in physical activity. Sports are highly symbolic as they reflect narratives, myths, individuals, music, objects, and art that evokes strong emotions. Symbols come in a package—they can evoke and convey a collage of sentiments, beliefs, and values. As the pioneering sociologist Pierre Bourdieu observed, symbols have a seemingly magical power to "produce ideology," or to present to individuals a compact set of ideas, beliefs, and orientations—such as sentiments of national patriotism or ethnic unity—and to convey a holistic cognitive message to those who understand the meaning-making of the symbolism (Bourdieu 1989; Tomlinson 2011; Kaufman 2001; MacGinty 2003).

Sport, as a nearly universal transnational culture, is exceptional in our highly interconnected, globalized world. Sport is ostensibly a *universal* cultural language of symbolism, and in the very origin of core global sports organizations such as the Olympic Movement there is an explicit mission, and empirical claim: global sports contribute to international peace through activities and events that are constructed to symbolize peace. The Olympic Charter, first published in 1908, defines the universalist aims of international sport to advance these aims in terms of *Olympism*, the guiding philosophy of international sports.[1] In the Charter's lofty language: "The goal of Olympism is to place sport at the service of the harmonious development of humankind, with a view to promoting a peaceful society concerned with the preservation of human dignity" (IOC 2020: 11).

That sports have such ethereal, transcendental, power to contribute to peace is a common claim of advocates who see sports across and within the borders of the countries as a stark symbol of the ability of countries to unite around a set of shared, universal values. Nobel Peace Prize Laureate Nelson Mandela, speaking at the inaugural Laureus "sport for good" awards in 2012, prophetically expressed a common belief that informs both the global public mind and core mission of global sport organizations:

> Sport has the power to change the world. It has the power to inspire, it has the power to unite people in a way that little else does. It speaks to youth in a language they understand. Sport can create hope, where once there was only despair. It is more powerful than governments in breaking down racial barriers. It laughs in the face of all types of discrimination. (Mandela 2000)

That sports contribute to peace through their unifying effects and inherent universalistic view of the human condition—grounded in the philosophy of humanism, or common dignity which in turn is the basis of "human rights"—is the secular religion of international sports. The Mandela Laureus-awards quotation is the go-to cliché for many in the world of international sports, and has been written into many mission statements, speeches, and platitudinous mottos of sport organizations by diplomats, politicians, celebrities, athletes, and sport officials around the world. This is perhaps with good reason, for if anyone speaks with some authority on the putative power of sports, it is Mandela who in his presidency of South Africa employed sports as an instrument of his regime's policies of postapartheid racial reconciliation. (This book will return in chapter 11 to Mandela's contribution to social cohesion in South Africa, at the 1995 Rugby World Cup, a moment well-known by the way Mandela himself strategically used sports to further reconciliation in the wake of apartheid in South Africa.)

Yet Mandela's claims need critical inspection and "unpacking" for exploring its alleged causal connections. We must inquire *why and how* sport can unite, how its symbolic power can contribute to peace, and how that power can be equally employed for nefarious aims by those who would use sports to advance particularistic aims—such as the grandeur of a nation—in contrast to universal goals of unity and collective action given a common or shared destiny.

The problem with the clichéd claim that sports are a unifying basis of peace is that there is no systematic or directly empirical (observable) evidence of a direct, consistent, or enduring contribution of sports to the ebb and flow of war and peace around the world in aggregate. While more than 120 years of Olympic Games may have contributed to peace in some indirect or globally symbolic way, there is no scholarly research that would affirm an observable and verifiable, systematic relationship between the Olympic summer or winter events of a significant effect on achieving international peace and security. At best it might be said that sports' contribution to peace is evident, just that it is highly indirect. Would international relations be even worse if there weren't international sports that symbolized global universalism?

An alternative view must be taken seriously: sports don't, and can't, contribute to peace because they are too closely associated with the idea of nations, nationalism, national interest . . . hence political power. Quite contrary to contributing to peace, international sports reinforce historically determined national identities that inhibit international cooperation and human rights. Because international *sport organizations like the Olympics are so tied to the national idea*—that international sports somehow reflect organic "nations" of the world—and the notion that athletes and teams symbolically represent nations, is precisely what prevents sports from realizing its potential to unite.

Many an example from deep and near history reinforce the regrettable reality of international sports' entanglement with authoritarian regimes, corruption and cheating, citizenship scandals, and exploitation by autocratic elites for washing human rights abuses away using the putative "power" of sports. The 1936 Olympic Games, a festival of fascism in Nazi Germany, leave an indelible stain on the reputation of the games. Later in this book, we'll look at the 2014 Sochi Olympic Games and 2018 FIFA World Cup in Russia as modern examples.

Between the 2022 Beijing Winter Olympic Games and the beginning of the 2022 Beijing Winter Paralympic Games, Russia launched its war of aggression against Ukraine (more on that in chapter 1) even as the Chinese hosts asked Russia to hold off on the military action until after the peace-emblemizing Olympic torch had been extinguished (Wong and Barnes 2022).

If national-interest politicization and geopolitical contestation—power—trump peace-through-sports, then one should look elsewhere for contributions to peace.

This book presents the author's point of view: there is in fact no convincing scholarly evidence of a robust corollary or direct causal relationship between international sport competition at the elite levels and the overall pattern, trajectory, or termination of armed conflict. At best, as described later in this book, sporting events like the Olympic Games have reflected the ebb and flow of geopolitical tensions (or détente) in the 20th century and the entanglement of sports in international political polarization and geopolitical contestation continues into the present.

Scholarly research in international peace and security lends insights into these relationships and to the overall puzzle of sports' apparent inability to directly contribute to peace. Increasingly, the drivers of conflict and the causes of peace in societies globally and in the international arena are known from experience (World Bank and United Nations 2018). A peaceful international order rests on inclusive, peaceful societies. In turn, such societies are grounded in human rights, inclusive growth, and social cohesion. In countries emerging from war, it is clear that priorities of peace are humanitarian action and preventing extremism, peace processes to end conflicts and to yield progress toward more inclusive societies and strengthening social cohesion through a shared or common destiny.

This book explores the complex role of sports in international politics, asking the most critical question:

> *How can sports more effectively contribute to sustainable international peace and security in a turbulent, uncertain, and intractably violent world?*

To identify what contribution sports can make to peace, we must look beyond the anthems, tearful spectacles, dove-releases, national medal tables, costumed parades, and chest-beating victories of the Olympic Games and other elite, televised, sporting events. While entertaining, international sports at their most prestigious and far-reaching levels present at best an *entertainment-oriented façade of peace*, a carnival-like spectacle that draws excited viewers, reinforces their own nationalistic identities, but does not directly relate to or contribute to the drivers of peace as they are experienced within and across the borders of the world.

In looking elsewhere for sports' contribution to international peace, this book aims to present the direct and indirect ways that sports can or do contribute to the ultimate drivers of peace in today's turbulent world: in providing respite from conflict and fostering reconciliation through humanitarian action and transitions from war, and in advancing human rights, inclusive development, and social cohesion. If international sports are to ever realize their ostensibly magic potential for contributing to peace, a more inclusive, democratized, and participation-focused system—or global "regime" of sports—must be imagined and created through widespread reform of the current system for the global governance of sports.

OBJECTIVES

The *objective* of the book is to provide an overview in the highly diverse and interdisciplinary knowledge base that links the field of sport and related research in sociology, together with knowledge and reflective practice from the field of international peace and security.

Sports in International Politics: Between Power and Peace:

- Provides a *framework for inquiry* to analyze and explore the complex relationships between the international world of sports, both between and within countries, and the urgent need to find new solutions for strengthening peace in a turbulent world.
- Situates and features analysis of the sport, power, and peace relationships *through the lens of the United Nations* and its specialized agencies in serving as a hub of knowledge, international norms and organizations, state policy and practice, and implementer of programming as a partner with international civil society organizations.
- Presents *a scoping review of the principal concepts, findings, and implications* of important scholarly and practice-oriented resources on key topics at the nexus between international politics, sports, and the conditions for sustainable peace.
- Proffers the author's view that there is need to define sport inclusively and recognize that *sports have powerful symbolic value, for power or for peacebuilding.*

The principal objective is to guide readers to important knowledge and examples of sports' contribution to peace, and to enable readers to reflect, discuss, and debate sports' historical and possible role in peace. The hope is that readers ask themselves whether and how the broad reach of international sports can more directly related to preventing conflict, building peace, and expanding trust into the 21st century. In their own discipline, specialized role or position, how readers may advance the opening of new arenas and avenues, improve practice and evaluation, and develop new curricula and approaches to sport-for-knowledge-driven and evidence-based peacebuilding practice in humanitarian action, development, and peacebuilding professions.

AUDIENCE

The book is designed for those with interest in how sports affect politics internationally, and vice versa, with a view toward interest in exploring pathways for potential professional practice in public policy (at various levels), sport science or policy, or in international organizations and nongovernmental organizations (NGOs). It is designed for upper-division undergraduate and graduate-level professional classes in the sociology of sport, sport science, international studies, and political studies. It is designed with an interdisciplinary perspective in the spirit of international studies' relevance across the social sciences and public policy.

APPROACH

In the chapters that follow, these elements appear to guide the reader through theory and research, international organization and practitioner literature, case studies, and resources for further learning and practice.

- *Chapter highlights* provide a summary of each chapter's principal objective and themes.
- *Concept boxes* highlight important theories, knowledge bases, or principles.
- *Case studies* offer examples of key events, athletes, resources, or rules and guidelines and illustrate and elaborate on concepts or evidence-based claims.
- *Documentary insights* point the reader to some of the most engaging documentary films produced on the themes of international sports and peace.
- *Questions for consideration* are offered to stimulate discussion and debate about some of the most critical or contentious issues related to the chapter's theme.
- Readers are pointed to *further information* in research, policies, and practice.

OVERVIEW AND GUIDE

Part I and chapter 1 develop more fully sports in the contemporary international context, how the onset of the Ukraine war in 2022, together with other persistent and structural factors, leave sports ensnared in global power politics and underscore the vexed relationships between sports and peace. We live in a turbulent world post-COVID and given climate change, or "uncertain times," and international sports are swimming in these global currents.

The chapter provides a starting point to orienteering through the complex universe of institutions, networks, and organizations that together comprise the global sports regime and the challenges of doping, corruption, sportswashing, and gambling with which they must contend. It argues that the Achilles' heel of international sports is politicization and political power and presents the case for looking to sports in human rights, development, humanitarian action, and peacebuilding for sports' potential contribution to peace.

Part II, "Situating Sports in a Globalized World," steps back to explore the wide world of sports globally and the social relevance of sports. The chapters here collectively address the question *What is the so-called "power" of sport, and where does it come from?* Chapter 2, "A Wide World of Global Sports," begins with the foundational conceptual understanding of defining sport, and especially how do sports, physical activity, and play relate. These concepts are important for understanding the notion that access to sports is a fundamental human right. Chapter 3 explores sociological and psychological perspectives to provide essential knowledge for evaluating when and how sports are so politicized, and, too, to the theories of change that sport-related intervention to further human development and human security rely upon.

Part III, "Comparative and International Perspectives," investigates sports' deep and ostensibly abiding relationships with nationalism as performative social identity, national mythmaking, and pursuit of the national interest. It investigates the history of the Olympic Games as reflecting, not shaping, international politics. Part III focuses readers' attention on the question *How are international sports compromised by the pursuit of power, nationally and as a disingenuous instrument of foreign policy and "soft power?"* Chapter 4 explores the nefarious capture of sports for power-seeking aims and national identity consolidation, and the presumably more benign use of sports diplomacy in "soft power" projection by states for advancing their culture and ideals globally through cross-cultural sport exchanges. Chapter 5 provides an overview of the evolution of the Olympic Games in the currents of history, from the early days with its association with circus-like spectacles through to the perhaps most globally significant institution, network, and "movement" (those who subscribe to Olympic ideals) that is at the center of international sports into the 21st century.

Part IV, "The Basis of Peace: Human Rights and Sustainable Development," turns to how sports contribute to the underlying basis of peace: human rights and development. Here, the organizing question is *Under what conditions can sports contribute directly to human-rights advancement and to sustainable development?* Chapter 6 investigates sports' long association with human rights. Sports provide a theater of opportunity for claiming rights and mobilization and have also been a forum for pushback against claiming human rights as sports organizers seek to keep sports "neutral." Chapter 7 explores the role of sports in development, beginning with the potential to offer pathways to development, the work of the "sport for development and peace" (SDP) sector and evidence for sports in individual capacity development, local and national development, and in pursuit of the UN's 2030 sustainable development agenda or Sustainable Development Goals (SDGs).

Part V, "Sustaining Peace: Humanitarianism, Peacebuilding, and Social Cohesion," considers sports' specific and direct contributions to peace: *How can sports contribute to reducing the drivers of conflict and violence and support humanitarian action, peacebuilding and strengthening social cohesion?* Chapter 8 considers the use of sports for humanitarian action for protection and psychosocial interventions, peacebuilding and social cohesion, and social inclusion in conflict-affected contexts.

Part VI, "Imagining a Better Sports Regime," concludes the book by addressing an important question: *How can a system of international sports be imagined that more effectively, directly, and consistently contributes to international peace and security?* Chapter 9 explores the imagination of a better global sports regime: rethinking and re-prioritizing sports for peacebuilding and reforming international sport organizations to increase participation, reduce toxic nationalism, promote inclusion, and—most importantly—further integrate harm reduction and accountability in the transnational management of global sports.

NOTE

1. The current text of the Olympic Charter, in force from October 15, 2023, is at https://olympics.com/ioc/olympic-charter.

Abbreviations

ABS	Australian Bureau of Statistics
AFP	France Press Agency
AIMS	Association of Independent Recognized Members of Sport
AIN	Individual Neutral Athlete
AP	Associated Press
ARISF	Association of IOC Recognized International Sports Federations
ASC	Australian Sports Commission
ASOIF	Association of Summer Olympic International Federations
AWOIF	Association of Winter Olympic International Federations
BAA	Boston Athletic Association
BAL	Basketball Africa League
BBC	British Broadcasting Corporation
BRICS	Brazil, Russia, India, China, and South Africa
BWB	Basketball without Borders
CAS	Court for Arbitration for Sport
CISM	International Military Sports Council
COVID	Coronavirus
CRPD	Convention on the Rights of Persons with Disabilities
DRC	Democratic Republic of Congo
DSD	Differences of sexual development
EOR	Olympic Refugee Team
EU	European Union
FC	Football club
FIBA	International Basketball Federation
FIFA	International Football Federation
FIG	International Gymnastics Federation
FKT	Fastest known time

GIZ	*Deutsche Gesellschaft für Internationale Zusammenarbeit* (German Development Cooperation)
HRC	Human Rights Council
IBSF	International Blind Sports Federation
ICC	International Criminal Court
ICRC	International Committee of the Red Cross
ICSSPE	International Council of Sport Science and Physical Education
DCM	Internal Displacement Monitoring Centre
IEP	Institute for Economics and Peace
IHF	International Handball Federation
ISCF	International Sport Climbing Federation
ISSA	International Sociology of Sport Association
IOC	International Olympic Committee
IOM	International Organization for Migration
IPC	International Paralympic Committee
IPF	International Parkours Federation
IHF	International Handball Federation
IWF	International Weightlifting Federation
ISW	Institute for Women Surfers
KNVB	Netherlands Football Association
LGTBQ	Lesbian, gay, transexual, bisexual, queer
MINUS-TAH	United Nations Assistance Mission in Haiti
MLB	Major League Baseball (US)
MMA	Mixed martial arts
NAIG	North American Indigenous Games
NATO	North Atlantic Treaty Organization
NBA	National Basketball Association (US)
NBC	National Broadcasting Corporation (US)
NCAA	National Collegiate Athletics Association (US)
NGO	Nongovernmental organization
NOC	National Olympic Committee
OHCHR	Office of the High Representative for Human Rights (UN)
S4D	Sport for Development
SEA	South-East Asia Games
SDP	Sport for Development and Peace
SDGs	Sustainable Development Goals (2030)
SHA	Sport for humanitarian action
SLASA	Single Leg Amputee Sports Association

SRSA	Department of Sport and Recreation, South Africa
OAR	Olympic Athletes from Russia
ODA	Official development assistance
OECD	Organization for Economic Cooperation and Development
OFFS	Open Fun Football Schools
OIA	Independent Olympic Athlete
OER	Olympic Refugee Team
PIN	Peace Initiative Network
PGA	Professional Golfers Association
PFL	Professional Fighters League
PVE	Prevention of Violent Extremism
RCT	Randomized controlled trial
RFE/RL	Radio Free Europe/Radio Liberty
ROC	Russian Olympic Committee
RTP	Right to Play
TWIF	International Tug-of-War Federation
UCI	International Cycling Union
UEFA	Union of European Football Associations
UFA	Ultimate Frisbee Association
UFC	Ultimate Fighting Championship
UK	United Kingdom
UN	United Nations
UNDP	United Nations Development Program
UNICEF	United Nations Children's Fund
UNESCO	United Nations Economic, Social, and Cultural Organization
UNGA	United Nations General Assembly
UNDESA	United Nations Department of Economic and Social Affairs
UNHCHR	United Nations High Commissioner for Human Rights
UNHCR	United Nations High Commissioner for Refugees
UN HRC	United Nations Human Rights Council
UNICEF	United Nations Childrens Fund
UNODC	United Nations Office of Drugs and Crime
UNSC	United Nations Security Council
UNMISS	United Nations Mission in South Sudan
US	United States
USOPC	United States Olympic and Paralympic Committee
USSR	Union of Soviet Socialist Republics (Soviet Union)
USWNT	US Women's National Team (football)
V-DEM	Varieties of Democracy Project
WADA	World Anti-Doping Agency

WAWF	World Arm Wrestling Federation
WHO	World Health Organization
WPA	World Players Association
WSAG	World Scholastic Athletic Games
WWE	World Wrestling Entertainment

PART I

Sport, Power, and Peace
in a Turbulent World

Chapter 1

Sport between Power
and Peacebuilding

CHAPTER OVERVIEW

Into the 21st century, the world faces a troubling context of new geopolitical rivalries, climate-change disasters, and social polarization exacerbated by the unprecedented COVID-19 pandemic that broke out in 2020 and which continues to reverberate with economic, social, and political effects. Global challenges have left a pattern of polarization in societies around the world, and the return of cross-border, state-driven war in the international system that was the Russian invasion of Ukraine in 2022 has deepened uncertainty. We live in highly turbulent times.

In this global context, international sport finds itself where it was in much of the 20th century: mired in a world of geopolitical competition among nation-states, ineffective global institutions, profit-based incentives, and national capture of putatively autonomous sport institutions in many countries. There is a large gap between the rhetoric of sport's potential contribution to human development and peace and the present crisis of legitimacy that besets international sport organizations as they navigate the complexities of issues such as citizenship, gender, and how to respond to human rights violations in and beyond sport.

The book seeks to shed light on the now century-long puzzle of why the Olympic Games and international sport more broadly is hamstrung in striving toward the aim of peace through sport in a world of power politics. Rather than contributing to peace in a tangible or direct way, international sport is best characterized in international politics terms as a set of global governance institutions and processes that evolved to coordinate and manage international sport as a transnational issue, but which are deeply constrained and ensnared by international politics.

Where should we look to find sport's oft-claimed contribution to peace?

CHAPTER HIGHLIGHTS

- The global context of international sport into the 21st century is one of turbulence, characterized by uncertainty and new challenges that affect international sport and to which sport's more globally altruistic aims of development or peacebuilding must contend.
- The invasion of Ukraine by Russia and the ensuing war have once again ensnared peace-seeking efforts in international sport in an existential crisis: whether Russian and Belarussian athletes should be allowed to participate in the Paris 2024 Summer Olympic Games and Paralympic Games as neutral athletes not formally representing the country.
- To begin the search for sport's contribution to peace, an introduction of the expanding sector of international development practice captioned "Sport for Development and Peace" (SDP) and initial exploration of how the SDP has developed incipient but compelling evidence to support the sport-based interventions contribute to the underlying factors that sustain peace.

TURBULENT WORLD, UNCERTAIN TIMES

At the end of the Cold War in 1989, as the post–World War II global context of superpower rivalry gave way to a new era of change in international politics, the rules, relationships, and interactions among the countries in the international system saw a period of "turbulence" or uncertain shifts: as old empires disintegrated, new countries emerged, long-standing civil wars such as in Angola, Cambodia, El Salvador, or Mozambique were ended through UN-guided peace processes, and a wave of countries around the world shed authoritarian regimes for newly founded democracies based on human rights and personal freedoms. Scholar James Roseau captured this fundamental change in international politics, contrasting the growing interdependence among countries in the international system while at the same time seeing increasing fragmentation within societies and new relationships that can't be well described the long-standing theory of realism prioritizing national interests over collective interests—in the international system (Rosenau 1990).

Today we live in a similar period, and Rosenau's post–Cold War observations about global interconnectedness and societal fragmentation ring true some three decades later. The COVID-19 pandemic has increased focus on the authority, legitimacy, and capacity of states to effectively govern complex, transnational challenges, and in many countries where the pandemic has led to restricted public space, inclusive governance has been further constrained and inhibited. The pandemic, UN Secretary-General António Guterres recently admonished, "continues to unleash a tsunami of hate and xenophobia, scapegoating, and scare mongering" (Guterres 2020). The pandemic crisis appears to have exacerbated inequality, marginalization, and socioeconomic stressors around the world, heightening fragility or vulnerability to conflict.

The toxic mix of increasing enmity and inequality between and within states and socioeconomic and environmental stressors present grave risks to international peace and security (World Bank and United Nations 2011). Identity-based tensions, such as ethnic and religious enmity, xenophobia, and resurgent, exclusive nationalism contribute to today's historically high number of armed conflicts (Pettersson and Öberg 2020). In April 2019, Guterres decried how hate speech, social polarization, and intolerance accelerated this "disturbing groundswell" of strife, polarization, and authoritarian populism (Guterres 2019). See Concept Box 1.1.

International sports reflect today's globalized world: relationships, organizations, and activities defy international borders drawn on a map. Money, people, and organizational reach go well beyond the local. There is a need for understanding how sport is organized internationally, and the historical and contemporary dynamics of sports' role between and within states in the international system. Commensurate with globalization and the widespread

CONCEPT BOX 1.1. A TURBULENT WORLD

The 2010s and into the 2020s sees growing and multiple pressures that hamper contemporary institutions of international cooperation be they on critical issues of climate change and sustainability, preventing and ending violent armed conflicts, or reducing levels of interpersonal violence globally. New major conflict escalations internationally in Ukraine in 2022, and internally in Sudan in 2023, put a damper on claims the world is becoming more peaceful.

The Sydney-based Institute for Economics and Peace, which tracks global security through its global peace index, reports that security—peacefulness has remarkably declined in recent years with "significant deteriorations in political instability, political terror, neighboring country relations and refugees and IDPs indicators. . . . Other indicators to deteriorate were deaths from external conflict and intensity of internal conflicts" (IEP 2022: 8).

The world is also beset with increasing incidence of civil war and armed conflict, well beyond the Ukraine imbroglio. New wars have broken out in recent years in countries such as Ethiopia and Sudan. All told, in 2021 there were 54 armed conflicts in countries around the world, and global monitoring organizations reported a 46 percent increase in fatalities from armed conflict (Davies, Petterson, and Öberg 2022).

Too, since 2008, the gold standard of academic democracy-tracking organizations, V-DEM (Varieties of Democracy) report that in 2023 political transitions in countries globally have continued (also since about 2008) toward autocracy and restriction of human rights autocratization—rather than in the post–Cold War era which saw widespread processes of transitions toward democracy, inclusion, and human rights (Papada and Lindberg, eds. 2023).

The socioeconomic effects of the pandemic, and the drivers of global stress that came before the pandemic from conflicts and their effects such as migration, and growing threats of the consequences of climate change, have been now well-documented. Case Study 1.1 offers a look at the latest reporting from UNDP on development, and the interlocking pressures faced by societies around the world with lingering effects from the pandemic.

The implications of the global uncertainty complex for sport are clear. New approaches and redoubling of effort are required for strengthening social cohesion and improving resilience globally—at individual, community, national, and international levels—in the face of these long-term stressors and current conditions of uncertainty and fear. If the high-flying rhetoric about sport's magical powers and properties to promote peace are plausible, a new orientation toward sport and peacebuilding is required. If the global crisis of uncertainty and insecurity is to be overcome, it will require a redoubled international effort to enable individuals to make the choices for themselves, and societies that contribute to peace. Can sport be a catalyst toward that end? See Case Study 1.1.

CASE STUDY 1.1. UNDP HUMAN DEVELOPMENT REPORT 2021–2022: "UNCERTAIN TIMES"

The United Nations Development Program (UNDP)'s 2021–2022 Human Development Report documents the effects of global turbulence on development and socioeconomic conditions around the world. Its theme is uncertainty: that a strained international system is combined with local stress dynamics from transnational pressures such as climate change and migration, rapid technological change, and deep economic uncertainties such that global crises have "piled up" (UNDP 2022: 4). More than six in ten people report that they feel insecure and that their well-being is affected by inequalities, social polarization, and lack of trust in governance.

The UNDP's landmark measure of human development, the human development index, for the first time, has shown retrenchment or declining measures of development globally: even during the 2008 global financial crisis, sum total index scores continued to show rising education, incomes, and health. Ninety percent of countries saw declining human development scores in 2020–2021 (UNDP 2022: 11). Insecurity and vulnerability to violence are rising in both poorer and wealthier countries alike.

As a result, the UNDP team points to a new "uncertainty complex" in societies around the world, fueling the dynamics of political polarization (deep differences along ideological lines), and a crisis of confidence. As UNDP Administrator Achim Steiner observed, these uncertainties hit youth around the world the hardest: today's youth are deeply uncertain about their future prospects, distrustful of governments and authority, and suffer a deep feeling of distress (see Steiner's remarks on YouTube at https://www.youtube.com/watch?v=GoiJoC3WIl0).

expansion of trade and finance, information and communication, human migration, worldwide public health, and global environmental interdependency and climate change, the concept of "global governance" as a concept to capture the extent to which in any transnational issue area is governed, and by whom. International sport, centered around the Olympics and now reaching virtually around the globe, is an under-studied and under-analyzed transnational issue and associated global-governance regime.

Sport, like other aspects of international interactions, is a transnational issue that can't be managed by states acting alone. Like other areas such as climate, health, and migration, international sport is a transnational issue. The structure of contemporary international relations is that global sport is a complex "regime" of institutions, organizations, and advocates with mandates to promote peace, foster development, and advance human rights.

The challenge to which this regime is called upon to respond is stark: globally, there is a rolling demographic crisis of youth vulnerability, evidenced by the UN in its second major report on the "global youth crisis" described in Case Study 1.2.

CASE STUDY 1.2. THE 2ND UN YOUTH, PEACE, AND SECURITY REPORT 2022: A ROLLING CRISIS

The COVID-19 pandemic was doubly devastating to the world's "next generation," youth. In 2022 the UN published its second landmark report on the global crisis of youth and its relationship to security, especially the vulnerability of youth to potentially violent political extremism, or to their social withdrawal and vulnerability to depression, anxiety, and alienation. Climate change, insecurity and threats of violence, ethnic and racial discrimination, and the effects of COVID and responses have had a devastating effect on youth globally.

The report finds:

The COVID-19 crisis has significantly exacerbated the root causes of conflict and has magnified existing socioeconomic and political vulnerabilities and inequalities experienced by young people, especially in contexts in which conflict and crises have undermined institutional capacities and limited access to services. Young people with specific needs are at a heightened risk and are particularly vulnerable, especially if their identities are intersectional, for example, young women, young lesbian, gay, bisexual, transgender, queer and intersex (LGBTQI+) people and young people living with disabilities.

This is further compounded for refugees, internally displaced persons, migrants, young people who are homeless or out of school, young people living in informal settlements or rural areas, young people living with HIV/AIDS and young people from ethnic minorities or indigenous groups. The gendered effects of the pandemic have been particularly severe and the risk is that they will reverse gains made in the area of gender equality. (UN Security Council 2022, 2)

ORIENTEERING THROUGH THE
GLOBAL SPORT UNIVERSE

International sport is a highly complex arena of international cooperation, such that it can be accurately described in international-studies terminology as a global governance network. That means that understanding the world of global sport requires a broad knowledge base on an exceptionally wide range of issues, from the historical institutionalist or "path-dependency" origins of the modern Olympic Games through to knowledge about how puberty affects male physical development. The global regimes perspective allows for a framework for this varied understanding in that it provides a clear framework for sorting through a wide range of issues such as human rights in sport, whether "mega-events" contribute to urban development, or conversations about which sports have evolved from countercultural "urban guerrilla" sports like skateboarding to Olympic events aimed to bring youthful new fans into the brand's fold.

As a predecessor to evaluation of sport in global comparison, and how it might be harnessed for nefarious purposes such as political gain or global power projection, and, similarly, how global cooperation can implement sport to achieve gains in education, health, livelihoods, and building peace and social cohesion. The concept of a "regime" in the global-governance framework provides a critical look at the contemporary set of organizations and associated networks for global sport. Scholar Holly Thorpe examines the transnational nature of sport networks in action sports such as skateboarding for development (see chapter 7) and finds an active "imagined transnational action sport community" that reflects a local-global dialectic or perhaps polar relationship (Thorpe 2014, 277). With the International Olympic Committee at the center of this universe, together with the sport-specific roles of a multitude of sport federations, national Olympic committees (NOCs), global civil society organizations, the sport-product private sector, global broadcasting and broadcast-rights companies, and the evolution of new institutions to manage "noncompliance" in sport such as the World Anti-Doping Agency (WADA) . . . international sport is a highly complicated network.

Since the 2020–2021 COVID-19 pandemic, the underlying global interdependency and transnational nature of public health is now widely understood and appreciated—some 5.5 billion people globally had received at least one dose of vaccine by 2023—and there is new understanding about the roles of international organizations such as the World Health Organization (WHO), national authorities, the private sector, scientists and researchers, the media, and local civic organizations. While COVID-19 is an unambiguous harm, sport is argued by norm-makers to be an unambiguous catalyst for good.

Global regime theory seeks to explain management of transnational problems—such as corruption in sport—as well as creating the enabling conditions for realizing the potential contributions of transnational interactions.

At the center of the universe are the *core governance institutions* of international sport. Figure 1.1. seeks to present a heuristic overview of the global sport regime as a planetary system, meaning that *relatively autonomous or separate entities are dynamically interrelated in a series of concentric circles*. In international sport, this puts the powerful IOC at the center of the universe, with bands of organizations and institutions orbiting in close proximity and reaching out on a global-local level and continue through to the sport federations, states, and local community organizations and, for example, city-level governments.

While not all more than 100 global sport federations, or innumerable set of sport-related organizations, can be depicted in such a sky full of stars, the planetary organigram seeks to provide a visual framework of analysis to reflect a highly complex set of relationships that spill across borders and can't be managed by countries acting alone. See Case Study 1.3.

The IOC in in relational orbit with some 82 *international sport federations* that are themselves nongovernmental bodies that regulate various sports from skeleton to skiing to surfing and which must be recognized by the IOC, or in the case of para sport, by the International Paralympic Committee, IPC (based in Bonn, Germany), in order to be recognized by these entities. The relationships between sport federations and the IOC and IPC differ: some para sports are organized separately from able sport federations (such as in athletics;

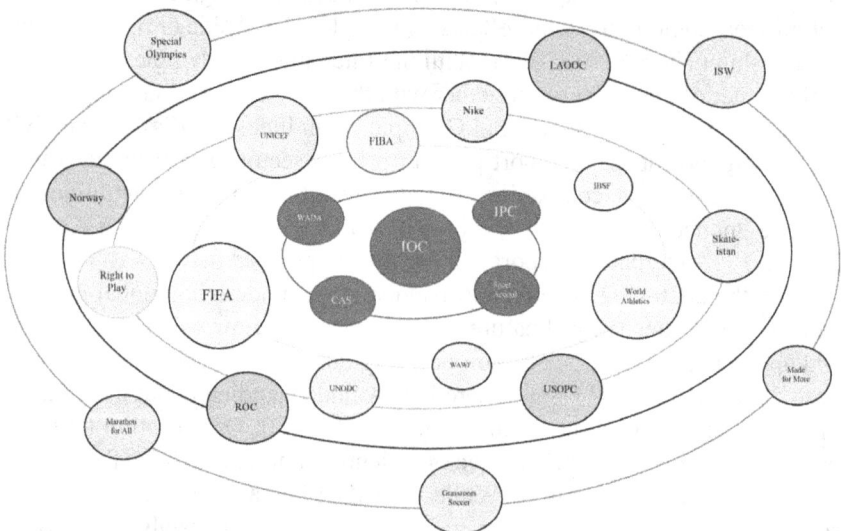

Figure 1.1.   Context: The Global Sport Universe, a Representation

CASE STUDY 1.3. THE SUN IN THE GLOBAL SPORT UNIVERSE: THE INTERNATIONAL OLYMPIC COMMITTEE (IOC)

The organization with the largest gravitational pull in the international sport universe is, rather indisputably, the IOC . . . it's not actually the largest sport organization in terms of budget, but it derives its authority from the prestige of the Olympic brand and trademarks (ownership of the symbolism of the most prestigious events in international sport), and this historical trajectory which has elevated the competition in the Olympics above other competitionsin the collective mind of athletes, the media, and publics the world over.

In close orbit to the IOC are, since 1989, the International Paralympic Committee (IPC), the World Anti-Doping Agency (WADA), Court of Arbitration for Sport (CAS), and the associations of Sport Accord, the umbrella body of sport federations.

Among the most important sub-elements of the IOC are its General Assembly, or the "IOC in Session," the role of the president (presently, Dr. Thomas Bach, a one-time Olympic fencer for Germany and medical doctor), and consultative bodies such as the Athletes Commission and the Ethics Commission.

The IOC organizes and convenes summer, winter, and youth Olympic games. Important in comparison to other global governance regimes, 92-member IOC are not representatives of states; rather, flipping the script of international diplomacy, they are representatives of the IOC in their home countries.

The IOC—based in Lausanne, Switzerland and ultimately subject to Swiss law—operates as a "quasi-official" international organization. As such, it presents an impeccably created website: https://Olympics.com/ioc.

para-athletics is not organized by World Athletics), whereas in other sports cycling federations such as the UCI manage both the para and able-athlete competitions.

The role of *national organizing committees*, or NOCs, is central to the essentially planetary, federalist-type structure of the international sport regime. IOC recognition of NOCS varies, and varies dramatically, from representation of states in the UN. In the context of Olympic geography, or recognition of various NOCs, for example, the IOC has recognized 206 NOCS including states such as Kosovo which has limited recognition in international competition. For example, a Kosovar athlete won the disputed territory's first gold medal at the 2016 Rio Games. In other instances, dependent territories such as the British Virgin Islands are separately represented in Olympic competition, but do not have member-state status at the UN.

Organizations such as the WADA, created in 1999, and the CAS, to settle disputes (notably, doping allegations, athlete biological passports, and issues of gender determination) which are subject to appeal to the Supreme Court of Switzerland and with ultimate appeal to the European Court of Human Rights.

The application of global governance regime theory explains currently *operating norms, institutions, nature of social networks, and global-local nature of an integrated, and highly complex, system* of international sport. In international sport, the role of states in the global-governance network is as determinative, that is holding final authority, as is the case in other networks (such as participation in global environmental agreements). While there is supranational authority (law and compliance above the level of national state authorities—as in the suspension of formal representation of Russia and sanctions by the IOC)—at the end of the day international organizations are constrained in monitoring or affecting and policing sport.

In other words, in international relations, the *principle of state sovereignty* remains an absolute and underlying theory of realism, rational action by states, and state authority are fundamental, even though the system of international interactions can at times constrain or shape state behavior (Houlihan 1994).

With this ultimate-authority idea in mind, it is clear that the institutions of global sport, even though they are essentially large global corporation-like nongovernmental organizations (NGOs), operate in essence as international organizations. The close embrace of the IOC by the UN—see the reports referenced in chapter 1—underscore that these private organizations operate essentially as the normative, institutional, monitoring, and policing functions of a worldwide global regime or set of rules of the road.

While most depictions of the global sports network feature hierarchical organigrams (organizational charts), for heuristic purposes this chapter and Figure 1.1 seek to provide a planetary-system view of the world of global sport to spark consideration of the relationships, power dynamics, and core-periphery relationships in the world of international sport. See Concept Box 1.2.

In global governance, it is typical to evaluate key aspects of such as interrelated system, such as the effectiveness of the interaction, linkages with other global governance regimes (such as international public health) and institutions (viz., the relationship between the IOC and the UN). Evaluating interactions between the periphery of the regime and the core might evaluate how, for example, prevention of doping in sport requires top-level consistent

CONCEPT BOX 1.2. WHO REPRESENTS WHOM?
THE NORM OF NATIONAL AFFILIATION
AND RECOGNITION IN SPORT

Thus, among the bedrock principles of international sport is *the norm of national affiliation and national recognition*. Athletes are not diplomats, at least not formally and, thus, do not join diplomatic immunity. The arrest of US women's basketball star and two-time Olympic gold medalist Brittney Griner on a drug possession charge in 2022 illustrates this; Griner was sentenced to a penal colony and only freed after a prisoner exchange between Russia and the United States that returned notorious arms dealer Victor Bout to Russia in late 2022.

As Jedlicka finds, "The semiotic entanglement between sport and national representation in turn suggest that the association between athletes and teams with state is unavoidably involved in the projection of state identity within the international system" (2018: 292).

While the advent of the Olympic Refugee Team (EOR) is possibly an initial erosion of this norm (see chapter 7), that there is no pathway to participation in the highest levels of elite sport absent national affiliation and recognition is a fundamental design flaw in the global governance regime of sport. As it highlighted in the 2015 FIFA corruption scandal, the norm of national recognition also leads to decision rules within sport organizations that set the stage for graft, rent-seeking, and national political manipulation of high-profit elite sport (Bensinger 2018).

rules and medical knowledge outwardly to building the capacity of local sport bodies to comply. Equally, one might think about the nature of relationships across "nodes" or areas of common interest and action between and among global sport organizations, like addressing issues of gender inequality or best practices in partnering with global and local corporations and governments.

With dispersed authority and complex relationships, it is helpful to conceive of the governance regime of international sport as a planetary system, with a myriad of organizations and entities (including those of the UN, which typically lead in other global-governance regimes) as a planetary system . . . all revolving around the self-appointed "supreme authority" of international sport's most prestigious, the Olympic Games, as well as the organizations in close orbit to the IOC such as the IPC.

The global governance regime for sport, like other international regimes, has struggled with monitoring and noncompliance of both the broader principles and legal frameworks (or "hard law"), as well as compliance with the overall values of Olympism that serve as a philosophical lodestar for international sport.

Among the most significant and recurring areas that have proven challenging in "policing" the global sport regime are the challenges of *doping, corruption, misogyny and racism, and gambling* in sport. The challenges of misogyny and racism in international sport are returned to in this book as issues of discrimination and human rights, as is corruption and gambling in sport where sport is ensnared in illicit financial interests and networks. Doping in sport is a major concern of the global sport regime, and doping can be highly politicized as the case of Russia's state-sponsored doping in relation to Sochi 2014, described in chapter 4. So, too, the problem of gambling and sports betting is monitored by the UN Office of Drugs and Crime (UNODC), which regularly monitors the ill social and individual harms of sports-betting and on the integrity of sport when athletes and coaches face monetary inducements to fix sport outcomes (UNODC 2021).

The global governance regime that has arisen historically is a classic case of "historical institutionalism." That is, *initiatives, choices, and institutional designs created in the past leave legacies of rules and order* that reflect the interests and considerations at the time of their inception . . . but once in place tend to develop their own incentives structures and endure. In the case of the global governance regime for sport, which is in comparison to other global regimes designed to manage international interdependencies—such as in global trade, or international public health which is highly unique and differently evolved—the regime is highly complex, lacks clear authority and autonomy boundaries, and struggles with policing noncompliance with norms such as corruption, doping, or political capture.

As Jedlicka finds, the international sport regime is commonly described as "structurally inchoate," or disorganized and inconsistent in terms of authority of organizations, autonomy, and transparency and accountability. As he observes, the governance of international sport is a transnational governance system which can be defined as "nongovernmental regulation [that] occurs across state boundaries but is nonetheless performed within existing international political frameworks" (Jedlicka 208, 289). As such, the global governance regime for sport seems ill-suited to either its main functional objective, to coordinate global sport consistent with the regime's norms on human rights and "sport for all," or to realize in a consistent way the benefits of global cooperation in maximizing sport's potential to contribute to global goals. See Documentary Box 1.1.

DOCUMENTARY INSIGHTS 1.1.
COPING WITH CORRUPTION IN
GLOBAL SPORT: *FIFA UNCOVERED* (2022)
AND *THE TWO ESCOBARS* (2010)

Persistent corruption, patronage, patriarchy, and relentless profit-seeking at the highest levels of the world's most popular sport, FIFA World Cup Soccer, is the subject of *FIFA Uncovered*, a four-part docuseries released by Netflix just prior to the Qatar tournament in 2022 (https://www.imdb.com/title/tt22872838/).

In deep detail and with compelling evidence, the series documents how the "one nation, one vote" voting system within FIFA led to rampant corruption that undermines any pretense that the global sport organization somehow serves the interest of its global fandom for ever-popular games.

In 2015, the United States Justice Department indicted 14 officials of the organization on bribery, racketeering, fraud, and money laundering with officials dramatically arrested in Switzerland and extradited to the United States; in 2020, U.S. officials alleged that FIFA decision-makers were bribed to award World Cup tournaments to Russia and Qatar (Gonzalez 2020).

The Two Escobars explores the nexus among sports, crime, and politics in the context of war-ridden Colombia in the 1990s, featuring drug cartel boss Pablo Escobar and Andres Escobar, a footballer who infamously scored an "own goal" that led to the country's defeat at the 1994 FIFA World Cup in Los Angeles. The film portrays how crime, football, and politics interacted in an era in Colombia where the country's national identity was on the line in the success or failure of the national soccer team (https://www.imdb.com/title/tt2700330/?ref_=ttpl_ov).

SPORT LIBERALISM IN A REALISTS'
WORLD: A UKRAINE STORY

International sport in the 21st century resides between rhetoric and reality. The rhetoric of sport's promise as a catalytic force for good is negated by the stark reality that liberal international aspirations for sport's contributing to peace are subject to the realities of a world controlled by powerful nations and powerful political elites. The symbolism of peace through sport is just as easily the symbolism of international competition and enmity. A Ukraine story illustrates the disassociation between the rhetoric and reality of international sport in today's turbulent and uncertain world. The country's fight against Russia has played out widely in the world of sport, for example through the courageous mid-war representation of the country by the club FC Shakhtar Donetsk, based originally in Donbas, which plays in the Champions League and Europe League. The club has emerged as a stark political symbol of resistance and resilience by Ukraine; in 2022, it played a series of friendly matches in "Global Tour of Peace" to raise money for the fight and to assist the victims of war (Brück 2022).

The potential political symbolism of Russian athletes participating at the 2024 Olympic and Paralympic Games in Paris while the horrors and war crimes unleashed by Russia in Ukraine and documented by a United Nations independent commission (UN HRC 2023) is an unacceptable symbol to the victims of such war crimes. Addressing a February 2022 meeting of 35 foreign ministers convened to consider a boycott if Russians were to appear in the Olympic arena, he said, "If the Olympic sports were killings and missile strikes, then you know which national team would occupy the first place." He continued, "If representatives of a terrorist state appear at international sports competitions, will it matter if they are there without their national symbols? . . . The mere presence of representatives of the terrorist state is a manifestation of violence and lawlessness" (Zelensky 2022).

That sport's power is harnessed for ill intent by political elites is plausibly one of the reasons why sport's contribution to peace remains at an ethereal, unmeasurable, and unverifiable level. Sport's symbolism has been subject to capture and manipulation by power-seeking and power-retaining political regimes and used in sinister ways for the putatively higher-order goals pursued by political ideologues seeking to create similarly minded societies of "cohesive" nations. It can be an instrument of realism, realpolitik, or furrowed-brow pursuit of national interest and security in an untrustworthy and anarchic world. Or sport can equally add to liberalism, that is global cooperation through international institutions, rules, and agreements, consistent with the principal UN missions of human rights, humanitarian action, sustainable development, and inclusive rights (Houlihan 1994).

When Russia launched its invasion of Ukraine during the interim period between the Beijing 2022 Winter Olympic Games and the Beijing 2022 Winter Paralympic Games, it once again violated the letter and spirit of the origin myth that is in essence the ideology of modern international sport: *Olympism*. The military onslaught unleashed February 24, 2022, on Ukraine, featuring missile strikes on civilians including in the capital, Kyiv, together with an artillery and tank attack, which occurred after the end of the Olympic Games in Beijing, but *before* the start of the Paralympic Games; Putin announced the invasion one day after the closing ceremonies of the Olympic Games but before the Paralympic Games had even begun.

Russian president Vladimir Putin's "Special Military Operation" was a clear violation of international law as an act of aggression against a sovereign state. Specific to sport, the invasion was equally an unambiguous violation of the putative "Olympic Truce." The Olympic Truce is a resuscitated element of the Olympic Games of ancient Greece; following the declaration of the truce which conflict would cease among the city states of the realm—and among the gods that oversaw mankind—during the period of the Olympic celebrations sufficiently to allow safe travel of athletes to the games.

In the case of the Beijing Winter 2022 Olympic Games, the United Nations General Assembly (UNGA) had just months prior in late 2021 adopted, by consensus, a resolution captioned "Building a Peaceful and Better World through Sport and the Olympic Ideal." The truce-like resolution calls upon member states to "use sport as a tool to promote peace, dialogue," and reconciliation in areas of conflict during and beyond the period of the Olympic and Paralympic Games (United Nations 2021).

When the Paralympic Games commenced March 4, 2022, in Beijing, a historically unprecedented event occurred in the annals of world sport and international politics. Andrew Parsons, president of the International Paralympic Committee, denounced Russia from the podium of the opening ceremonies of the Paralympic Games. "I am horrified by what is taking place in the world now," he said, citing the UN's 2021 Olympic Truce resolution; "It must be respected and observed not violated," he said. "The 21st century is a time for dialogue and diplomacy, not war and hate," Parsons forcefully implored, "We aspire to a better and more inclusive world, free from discrimination, free from hate, free from ignorance and free from conflict" (IPC 2022).

Russian's ROC athletes had easily evaded the athlete-representation sanctions that had them competing as OAR (Olympic Athletes from Russia). The uniforms of the ROC athletes at the Beijing 2022 Winter Games were fashion-forward black splashed with the colors of the Russian flag. Moreover, sport is infused into the pinnacle of power in the Russian state; journalist Nancy Armour reported that in Tokyo in 2020, 45 of the Russians' 71 medals were won by members of the Russian Army's Central Sports Club, according to the Ukrainian foreign ministry (Armour 2023). After the invasion, Russian gymnast Ivan Kuliak was sanctioned by the International Gymnastics Federation (FIG) with a yearlong ban for "shocking behavior" for sporting on his chest the invasion-related "Z" symbol on the podium standing next to a Ukrainian athlete (Kuliak won bronze; the Ukrainian, Illia Kovtun, won gold) (Ingle 2022; Patil 2022). The "Z" was a symbol used on the tanks and trucks of the invading troops.

The Ukraine imbroglio introduced an existential crisis for international sport organizations. A subsequent 2023 row between International Olympic Committee (IOC) president Thomas Bach and Ukrainian president Volodymyr Zelensky over potential Russian and Belarussian athlete participation at Paris 2024 exposes the Achilles' heel of the Olympic Games: the peace-promising celebrations are inescapably ensnared in nation-state power politics.

The IOC had announced on January 25 a proposal to facilitate participation in the 2024 Olympic Games for individual athletes from Russia (and close ally Belarus) individually and neutrally in the Paris games (IOC 2023) under the category of "authorized neutral athlete" (Individual Neutral Athlete [AIN]). The statement reversed an IOC Executive Board decision from February 28, 2022, to impose more sweeping participation sanctions on Russia following the Ukraine invasion (IOC 2022b). The International Paralympic Committee announced on January 23 that it would "follow" the IOC decision for the Paris paralympic events, with president Andrew Parsons noting that "We wish to reiterate that we hope and pray that the conflict comes to an end, that no more lives are taken, and that we can run sports and politics separately" (IPC 2023).

In a slope-side appearance at the World Alpine Skiing Championships in Courchevel, France, days later, Bach defended the IOC's position: "No, history will show who is doing more for peace" (Dampf and Dunbar 2023). The IOC's approach to addressing the thorny question of Russian participation in the 2024 Games is similar to the sporting world's response to the sprawling Russian state-sponsored doping scandal and cover-up when it hosted the 2014 winter games in Sochi. In December 2019, the World Anti-Doping Agency imposed a set of four-year sanctions on Russia, including banning Russian teams from Olympic-related events, barring use of its flag and anthem, and imposing diplomatic and other sanctions. Athletes could participate but could not represent Russia as such, but rather the Russian Olympic Committee (ROC) (WADA 2019).

The staging of the FIFA World Cup in Russia in 2018 underscored that in international sport's effort to be inclusive and politically neutral, it enables autocracy, corruption, and rights-denying autocratic regimes. The images of FIFA president Gianni Infantino celebrating cozily with Russian president (and now International Criminal Court [ICC]–indicted war criminal) Vladimir Putin evokes cries of hypocrisy: "By allowing their crown jewels to be used to burnish Russia's image," journalist Kieran Pender observes, "the IOC and FIFA have been complicit in Putin's wanton acts over the past decade" (Pender 2022). When the IOC presented an Olympic Truce resolution for the 2024 Paris games in November 2023, for the first time the resolution was not adopted unanimously: Russia and its ally Syria abstained, alleging that the truce resolution politicizes sports (UN News 2023b).

SYMBOLIC POWER: THE ACHILLES' HEEL OF INTERNATIONAL SPORT

The integrated theme that runs through this book is a conceptual perspective of sport providing the opportunity for political symbolism: symbolic politics. An integrated theory helps us understand the vulnerability of sport to capture for national power-seeking and for power-wielding purposes: Sport provides a theater of opportunity for powerful symbolic politics. *The very conditions that give sport its power as a social force is precisely those which have led to its capture and manipulation for political ends.* Despite efforts to remain neutral or indifferent to international politics, sport organizations are faced with a deep "neutrality paradox" between the objective of national-representation universalism and their dogged protection of their internal autonomy and authority, and the global peace-promising objectives of respecting, fostering, and enabling human rights (Næss 2022).

The disassociation between sport and peace has historically been the result of a broader quest by regimes to harness the symbolic power of sport for power-demonstrating and prestige on the world stage, and that success in global sport was a function of a country's projection of hegemony and place in an anarchic international system.

Historically, many observers of international sport have concluded that, ultimately, that sport can't contribute to peace. In 1945, in the immediate wake of World War II, a set of "friendly" football matches were organized to bring former the Moscow-based FC Dynamo club to play a series of matches with teams such as Arsenal. The visit was chronicled by journalist George Orwell, who penned his reflections in the editorial "The Sporting Spirit." After the four-match friendly tour, which included solely club-to-club play, Orwell opined caustically in reflection on the friendly tour:

Sport is an unfailing cause of ill-will, and if such a visit as this had any effect on Anglo-Soviet relations, it could make them slightly worse than before. . . . Nearly all the sports practiced nowadays are competitive. You play to win, and the game has little meaning unless you do your utmost to win.

On the village green, where you pick up sides and no feeling of local patriotism is involved, it is possible to play simply for fun and exercise: but as soon as the question of prestige arises, as soon as you feel that you and some larger unit will be disgraced if you lose, the most savage combative instincts are aroused. Anyone who has played even in a school football match knows this.

At the international level, sport is (sic) frankly mimic warfare. But the significant thing is not the behavior of the players but the attitude of the spectators: and, behind the spectators, of the nations who work themselves into furors over these absurd contests, and seriously believe—at any rate for short periods—that running, jumping, and kicking a ball are tests of national virtue. (Orwell 1968)

Perhaps little has changed since 1948. Sport's potential to contribute to power-seeking and polarization continue—clearly the most egregious example is the Sochi 2014 Winter games, which cost $54+ billion to stage, $30 billion of it "stolen" (BBC 2019), and which was characterized by a massive state-sponsored doping scandal. Sochi 2014 is yet another low point in Olympic history in its quest for sport to be politically neutral.

In June 2023, a referee in Las Vegas, Nevada (belatedly, in some views) terminated a U.S.-Mexico football match over fan fanaticism, in this case not a nationalistic slur but the tendency of some Mexican fans to taunt foreign goalkeepers with homophobic slurs (the termination cut short a 3–0 U.S. win). The concern is doubly strong because Canada, the United States, and Mexico will jointly host the 2026 FIFA World Cup. The problem of Mexico's homophobic fan chants is a long one, and prior U.S.-Mexico events weeks earlier did not see such chants; FIFA has sought to discipline Mexico's soccer federation and in two matches in the 2022 World Cup Mexico was not allowed to have fans in the stands (Borg 2023). See Case Study 1.4.

CASE STUDY 1.4. A PUZZLE, HISTORY BUFFS: WHY HAVE THE OLYMPICS NEVER WON THE NOBEL PEACE PRIZE?

The convening of the first modern Olympic Games in Athens, 1896 marks a pivotal moment in the evolution of sport internationally: as the first in a now 120-year tradition, the Olympics has sought over time to symbolically represent international peace (or, at least, cooperation) among nations of the world.

At roughly the same time historically, just a few short years after the first Olympics in 1901, Swedish industrialist Alfred Nobel established through his will what has become the world's most "prestigious prize" for peace: The Nobel Peace Prize. Established in the last will of the chemist and industrialist, Nobel's wish was the Peace Prize should be awarded by Norway—through the measured decisions the Norwegian Nobel Committee—while the other Nobel prizes, for example for physiology or medicine, are awarded in Sweden. It is the world's most prestigious prize for peace (Lundestad 2019).

Thus, the Olympic Games as the world's most unambiguously prestigious international sport event, explicitly dedicated to strengthening peace, and the Nobel Peace Prize have unfolded historically over the same 120-year period of the war-ridden 20th century and still deeply war-torn 21st century. Given this history together, a puzzle emerges.

Why over more than a century of concurrent evolution has the International Olympic Committee (IOC), which organizes the games, nor any organization, individual or athlete, nor host-city organizing committee ever won the world's most prestigious prize for peace?

It might be surprising that the Norwegian Committee has not recognized the Olympics' historical efforts at peace, given that Norway as a rich country of six million is seen globally as a "sporting superpower," has high rates of sport participation, and was the first country (in 1984) to adopt sport-related interventions in its development assistance policies. Today, Norway is a significant contributor in the so-called "sport for development and peace" (SDP) sector.

If over 120 years of the prestigious prize for peace, the learned and generally well-intentioned members of the Norwegian Nobel Committee have not ever been convinced that a directly or explicitly Olympic-related organization, individual, or effort should win the prestigious prize, we must ask ourselves more explicitly: if the Olympic Games aren't seen to contribute to peace, what explains the deep disconnect between the rhetorical aims of sport organizations that they contribute to peace through the Olympics or FIFA World Cup soccer (the world's most popular single sport)?

Note: The Nobel Peace Prize was won by an Olympic medalist in 1959—UK diplomat Philip Noel-Baker—but not for his Olympic achievement; the Norwegian Nobel Committee cited his humanitarian and disarmament efforts. The presentation speech by Norwegian Nobel Committee chairperson Gunnar Jahn does not even mention Noel-Baker's Olympic medal nor his prowess in sport; see the Jahn speech at https://www.nobelprize.org/prizes/peace/1959/ceremony-speech/.

While the 1936 Berlin Olympic Games in fascist Germany have long been identified as an example of sport's susceptibility to political manipulation, the problem of sport being considered nothing more than "war minus the shooting" (Orwell, 1948) is omnipresent. From Salt Lake City 2002 to Sochi 2014 to PyeongChang 2018, for example, even the ostensibly more benign Winter Olympic Games—with less popular sports globally, and fewer participants from fewer countries—remain vulnerable to political influences. The Beijing 2022 Winter Olympic Games were about heroic performances on ice and snow, but equally about China's domestic strife (e.g., Hong Kong, Xinjiang and Uighur repression), COVID-19 "zero" strategy, regional dynamics and tensions, and global power politics.

The unfulfilled promises of international sport's contribution to peace are because sport, as global culture, both reflects, and shapes, international politics. Sport reflects, and at times shapes, international politics and can contribute to both conflict and peace. Through the 20th and into the 21st century the universality and inclusivity of participation in international sport such as the Olympic Games has ebbed and flowed with the vicissitudes of great-power relations in the international system. Whether sport between the Soviet Union and the United States during the period of the Cold War (roughly, 1948–1989) directly contributed to the war staying "cold"—meaning, no nuclear Armageddon—is a forever-open question. Yet the promise of sort contributing to international peace has typically reflected the extent to which there is cooperation or competition among great powers in the international system. See Concept Box 1.3.

Sport aspires to and should contribute to peace, but its contribution at the global level remains constrained to the superficially symbolic: international sport as elite sport is, at best, a façade of peace.

CONCEPT BOX 1.3 "SPORTSWASHING"

When *sport is used to detract from social conflicts, human rights abuses, or environmental irresponsibility*, is it aptly described in colloquial terms as "sportswashing" of these ill behaviors and their consequences? Sportswashing has been used both historically to provide a veneer of goodwill and purity in contexts in which human rights are being deeply abused and to cover up corrupt practices, exploitation of labor, and political suppression.

Because of sport's seemingly universalistic appeal, and the way in which it perhaps superficially presents a picture of peace and common values, it has become a preferred tool of many regimes to shape society, project an image of internal cohesion, and to distract from regime abuses and nefarious behavior abroad.

Too, the pursuit of sportswashing has led to abuses in the context of sport, such as suppression of dissidents and opposition prior to mega-events. In the run-up to the 1968 Mexico City Games more than 300 protesters were killed by police in the Tlatelolco Massacre in the dirty war of the Mexican regime against a student- and union-led protest movement.

Abuses directly related to sport, such as the state-sponsored doping of athletes, were committed by the former East German regime during the Cold War to show its socialist-system superiority to the unjust system of the capitalist West.

Global sport is politically ensnared at global levels and at national levels as governments seek to project "soft power." And it is constrained nationally in cases where the purpose of national sport is to advance the national interest. The prophetic claims about sport's catalytic contribution to peace are deeply disassociated from a world aflame with the return of international war which had ostensibly been "tamed" since the end of World War II, intractable violent conflicts such as the Israeli-Palestinian imbroglio, state failure as in Sudan as infighting leads to millions of displaced, permanent statelessness such as Rohingya in Bangladesh who are permanently without a state, and recurring end-of-time nuclear stalemate on the Korean peninsula.

We will return to the relationships between sport, national power, and national-interest projection later in this book.

ABOUT THIS BOOK: FINDING SPORT'S CONTRIBUTION TO PEACE

To find sport's contribution to peace, we must look elsewhere from elite competition along the lines of national representation as the principal manifestation of what constitutes international sport.

The most challenging question about sport's relationship to peace is whether international sport can shape or *directly affect* international politics, ostensibly in the direction of peace and its essential companions, human rights, and development. Sport's contribution to the underlying drivers of peace in turn leads to inclusive, peaceful societies that provide an environment, an environment of safety and trust, or social cohesion. This book explores these issues in searching for sport's contribution to peace beyond the façade of peace represented by global international sport events and their implicit or explicit celebrations of national identity and national representation as the underlying norm for global sport cooperation.

Where can we instead find sport's contribution to sustainable international peace in a deeply conflicted and violent world?

In roughly the last 20 years, there has been the parallel development of the use of sport as an approach to international development cooperation to foster human rights, advance sustainable development (notably, the 2015–2030 Sustainable Development Goals and agenda), and for humanitarian action and peacebuilding initiatives in fragile and conflict-affected contexts. The sector of "SDP" or development-project intervention for sport-related or sport-enabled gains in human development began as early as the late 1940s with initial work by the International Labor Organization (ILO) with antecedents in the evolution of sport for social good in 19th-century sport societies. Accounts of the evolution of the SDP community of practice point to the innovative work of Norwegian development assistance providers who designed and implemented some of the first sport-centric programs in Tanzania, and today Norway continues to invest in the SDP sector both directly and indirectly through its extensive development assistance program in the fields of humanitarianism, peacebuilding, and sport (for a history of SDP including an account of the 1980's Norwegian engagements, see Darnell, Field and Kidd 2019 and Darnell 2012).

At the UN, a pivotal moment in organizing the world body's organizations to integrate sport across the human rights, development, and peacebuilding agenda was the 2003 Task Force (UN Interagency Task Force on Sport, Development, and Peace 2003). The Task Force report sought to articulate the ways in which sport's power can be "harnessed" for the aims of attaining sustainable development, and began to catalog the activities of development partners, governments, and NGOs that were developing novel approaches to sport-based interventions through new programs and projects. While there were initial concerns about the "lack of evidence" for sport-based interventions, increasingly through improved development-project cycle innovations better approaches to assessment, identifying entry points, program and project design, and monitoring and evaluation have led to a now more-sophisticated approach to engagement.

In 2023, the UN unveiled a "New Agenda for Peace" (in a reference to the 1992 Agenda for Peace, which sought to address the turbulence of the post–Cold War era, and which introduced more broadly the notion of "peacebuilding" into the international community's lexicon (UN 2023b). The new agenda, reflected in the report Our Common Agenda, calls for new mechanisms to address conflicts, manage crises, and to build trust, and that these aims require "people-centered approaches" admonishes those in positions of power to forge a new social contract with their people through addressing the uncertainties and insecurities of the next generation.

The report commits the UN to address these directly through broadened efforts to address the global youth crisis.

> Some 267 million young people (15–24 years old) are not in education, employment or training, two thirds of whom are young women as a result of gendered expectations of unpaid family work and informal employment. The pandemic has only made this worse. . . .
>
> Efforts [by the UN] will be stepped up to increase youth participation in our support to electoral processes and in peacebuilding efforts, including by building the capacity of local youth networks and youth-led organizations.

And, as we explore further in this book, international organizations have increasingly sought to characterize sport as a "catalyst" for both development outcomes, and for tangible gains in delivering humanitarian assistance, peacebuilding, and social cohesion (UN 2022). Sport has become more mainstreamed in efforts to find more effective approaches to development engagement that is strategically targeted to improving education, enhancing food security, and for health (especially for girls) (Collison et al. 2019) in a manner that ensures local voices and priorities are at the center of interventions (Collison 2016).

Sport is a strategic key instrument for advancing human rights, furthering access to education and healthcare, building peace, and fostering inclusive national development. In practical terms, sport is a powerful instrument of liberal internationalism that sees the advancement of individual values of rights, gender equality, and for the authentic empowerment of often marginalized groups such as indigenous communities, war victims and those with disabilities. The liberal internationalist perspective equally puts the onus on governments to create the conditions for realizing such rights, for example in providing sport infrastructures and facilities to implement access to and participation in sport as a public good.

To find sport's true contribution to peace globally, we must look from the bottom up at how sport facilitates positive youth orientations of self-worth, engenders trust, empathy, and tolerance, and facilitates human development and human security through social cohesion and inclusive nation-building. Theories of change must be better informed by understandings from neuroscience, early childhood development, and social identity theory on the neuroscientific basis of knowledge on the acquisition of positive youth orientations and social identities (and potential harms associated with efforts to implement based on such knowledge), the origins of sport's association with key traits such as personal resilience, trust, empathy, and acceptance of diversity.

Further, knowledge is needed that further shows the now-established linkages between sport and development, primarily through direct and indirect effects of physical activity on early childhood development and lifelong resilience. The evidence is firm that play, physical activity, and sport contribute to lifelong benefits of physical and mental well-being and contributes to peace in society though the symbolic politics of representing peace and as a symbolic expression of shared or common destiny.

Sport-related events and interventions contribute to peacebuilding and social cohesion and community resilience by emphasizing community interdependence and inclusive national identity, and they form the basis for meaningful participation in sport at the international level. Perhaps in such circumstances, when sport is not seen as the tool of self-legitimizing political elites, it could be said that universal participation may contribute to peace.

QUESTIONS FOR CONSIDERATION

- How does the debate sanctioning Russian officially, but allowing Russian athletes to participate in the Paris 2024 Olympic Games as individuals or neutrals, reflect on the role of sport in international politics?
- How has political capture, both historically and in the present, limited sport's ability to contribute to international peace?
- How can sport-based interventions at individual, community, national, and global levels contribute more effectively to sustainable international peace in a deeply conflicted and violent world?

FOR FURTHER INFORMATION

In the last four years, the United Nations published reports of the Secretary General that give a landscape view of the world of international sport and the current concepts, orientations, and issues in sport-based policy and practice at the international level for contributing to UN aims as reflected in the organization's "pillars" of human rights, development, and necessary-condition aspects such as the empowerment of women and girls.

A good starting point for becoming more fluent is the UN state of knowledge on SDP and the frameworks, current action plans and perspectives of the UN specialized agencies (such as the World Health Organization, WHO). They report on issues in sport governance, sport-based advocacy, sport integrity, and the reporting of member states on their activities and initiatives:

- The 2018 Report of the Secretary-General, "Strengthening the Global Framework for Leveraging Sport for Development and Peace," A/73/325, August 14, 2018 (UN 2018).
- The 2020 Report of the Secretary-General, "Sport: A Global Accelerator of Peace and Sustainable Development for All," A/75/155, 13 July 2020 (UN 2020).
- The 2022 United Nations Alliance for Civilizations Thematic Paper for the Secretary-General's Report on Youth, and Security, "The Contribution of Sport to the Youth, Peace, and Security Agenda" (UNAOC 2022).
- The 2022 Report of the Secretary-General, "Sport: Catalyst for a Better, Stronger Recovery," A/77/161. July 15, 2022 (UN 2022).

PART II

Situating Sport in a Globalized World

Chapter 2

The Wide World of
Sports Globally

CHAPTER OVERVIEW

To understand both sports' relationships to international politics—importantly, why sports is so subject to political intrusions, the critical powerful of symbolism that links sports and politics, and the propensity for political capture—important definitions and concepts need clarification . . . not least of which is to carefully define "sport." The definition and study of sport is deeply tied to scholarly disciplines in anthropology, history, psychology, and sociology together with knowledge of medicine, human physiology, and kinetics (the science of movement).

Fluency in the issues and topics that arise in analysis of a very wide world of sport requires interdisciplinary knowledge from both natural and social sciences. Because physicality and physical recreation are seemingly salient across all cultures and social contexts, activity and play are enduring components of family, community, and national cultural life throughout human history.

Essential to an understanding of why sport is so attractive, and so emotive is the evaluation of how physical activity of the body affects the brain, and how these relationships in turn relate to key issues of psychological orientations and mindsets. The body-mind interaction, based in neurobiology, is what gives sport its proverbial "power."

CHAPTER HIGHLIGHTS

- Endless and sometimes heated debates can occur around the question of whether a physical activity, for example golf, is more of a "sport" than a game. So, what is a "sport" as such, and why does a definition of the term matter? The chapter presents a definition of sport and its association with physical and mental well-being, arguing that what is sport is a social construction . . . all sports are essentially rule systems continuously invented and reinvented.
- Sport as activity and culture is constantly evolving and changing in concert with human development, with the diffusion of sport globally enabled by new technologies and means of communication, near-universal universal broadcasting, and social media.
- The revival of indigenous sport underscores how sport is socially and individually important to so many people around the world reflecting how important it is to define and nurture sport in an inclusive manner, and to understand and respect the diversity of sport and its personal meaningfulness to those who participate.

WHAT IS "SPORT?" A SOCIAL CONSTRUCTION

The *Berkshire Encyclopedia of World Sport* (Levinson and Pfister eds., 2016) contains 300 entries and through sub-sport variation features more than 800 types of sports worldwide. The actual number of sports globally is unknown and perhaps unknowable; that is, there is no limit to human ingenuity in the development of new and different sports, or the revival of types of indigenous sports that had been disfavored or even outlawed (or unrecognized) by colonial authorities in many settings, and so to constant emergence and production of new sports. The scope of what constitutes a "sport" can be all very confusing, and many a conversation is had around the key issues of what is a "sport," what is "play," and what is a "game." While debates about whether some human physical activity constitutes a "sport" as such are typically jovial, and at times contentious, they are at best heuristic exercises; these are all somewhat arbitrarily defined types of physical recreation and play (WHO 2018: 14).

The *Berkshire Encyclopedia*'s introduction to these lays out these debates well, and, engagingly, highlights some of the world's most least familiar, or weird, sports:

> While there are many global sports, there are also vast numbers of regional and local sports. One might consider American football as an example that many

in the United States may think of as being "the" sport: certainly not a regional one. Indeed, the Super Bowl is a national holiday in all but name, and the annual Harvard–Yale football game, which dates to 1875, is simply called "The Game."

But despite its position as the most popular sport in the world's third most populous nation (a very similar version is also played in Canada), American-style football is played as an exotic minority pastime only in a few European nations, and it does not seem poised to become a major global sport. Others, like *capoeira*, the Brazilian martial art often called a cross between a dance and a fight, have been spread by Brazilian immigrants to many nations, and will continue to spread as Brazil stakes its claim to being one of the most modern, forward-looking, and rapidly developed nations in the world.

Less well-known traditional sports include bicycle polo, a good sport for those who can't afford to buy a pony; motorcycle polo, popular in the 1930s and enjoying a recent surge of popularity in East Africa; pedestrianism, or long-distance walking; *camogie*, an Irish women's game similar to field hockey; *buzkashi*, Afghan polo played with a headless goat; Finnish baseball; and curling, the Scottish/Canadian game described as "chess on ice" (but with brooms) that never fails to befuddle spectators of the Winter Olympics. (Levinson and Pfister, eds. 2016, Introduction)

The Australian Bureau of Statistics has sought to rationally and to precisely evaluate what constitutes a sport as such, come up with a *workable, operational definition*, and in doing so provide some key insights to the principal dimensions of sport. For the ABS, these definitions captured the widest possible range of formal and informal activities that can precisely or operationally be said to constitute sport across cultures and contexts (Pink, 8).

Sport. An activity involving physical exertion, skill and/or hand-eye coordination as the primary focus of the activity, with elements of competition where rules and patterns of behavior governing the activity exist formally through organizations.

Physical recreation. An activity or experience that involves varying levels of physical exertion, prowess and/or skill, which may not be the main focus of the activity and is voluntarily engaged in by an individual in leisure time for the purpose of mental and/or physical satisfaction.

Organized sport or physical recreation. Sport or physical recreation activities may be organized by a club or association or other organization, such as a sporting club, social club, church group, workplace, or gymnasium. An organized activity may vary from an organized one-off fun run or bush walk, through to an organized sporting competition.

In 2003, the UN Interagency Task Force for Sport Development and Peace offered a similarly broadly constructed definition of sport. Sport is "all forms of physical activity that contribute to physical fitness, mental well-being and social interaction. This includes play, recreation, organized, causal, or competitive sport, and indigenous sport or games" (UN Interagency Task Force 2003, v).

Figure 2.1 provides a framework of analysis, derived from the ABS and UN definitions, for analyzing sport and provides some examples of how various sports at specific levels may fit within what is a multidimensional approach to categorizing sport. It seeks to present a heuristic mapping of sport, with examples, along two important continuums.

- The first is that of along an *elite-wide participation continuum*, between highly organized, limited access, high-cost, or extremely high-risk sports, or those that involve complicated or expensive technology, extensive and/or extensive, resource-intensive sportscapes (such as a golf course), or those that require the acquisition and maintenance of costly or specialized animals (such as falconry).
- The second is that of a *recreational-competitive continuum*. Although most sports can be made competitive, and there are both recreational and competitive forms of most sports, key differentiators in these sports are fundamental characteristics such as the nature of winning-losing outcomes (if winning is in fact a characteristic of a sport), the extent to which it is organized and regulated by an authority, and the extent to which the sport itself is regulated . . . how specific are the rules, if there are any?

The ABS definition of sport and its relationship to recreation and play does much to create the foundation for a much understanding of what constitutes sport and the ways in which it might intersect with politics globally. With sport itself an elastic social construct, it is first and most important to emphasize that competition, common in most sports, is not an essential characteristic of sport. Due to the propensity of ingenious humans to invent new forms of physical exercise and play and to adapt and evolve existing sports and games—some sports involve winning and losing against others, and some do not. A good example: the tug-of-war seen in the 1900–1920 Olympic Games in Athens during which club-based national teams pulled on the two sides of a rope against each other to pull the other team across a middle line, thereby demonstrating who is the "strongest nation on earth." The tug-of-war doesn't seem likely to return to the Olympic Stadium, soon, even as some 72 countries are represented in the Tug of War International Federation.[1]

Indeed, highly competitive sports may exhibit and propagate orientations derived from hegemonic masculinity which emphasizes the origins of dominance and "winning and losing" in stereotypical constructions of masculine

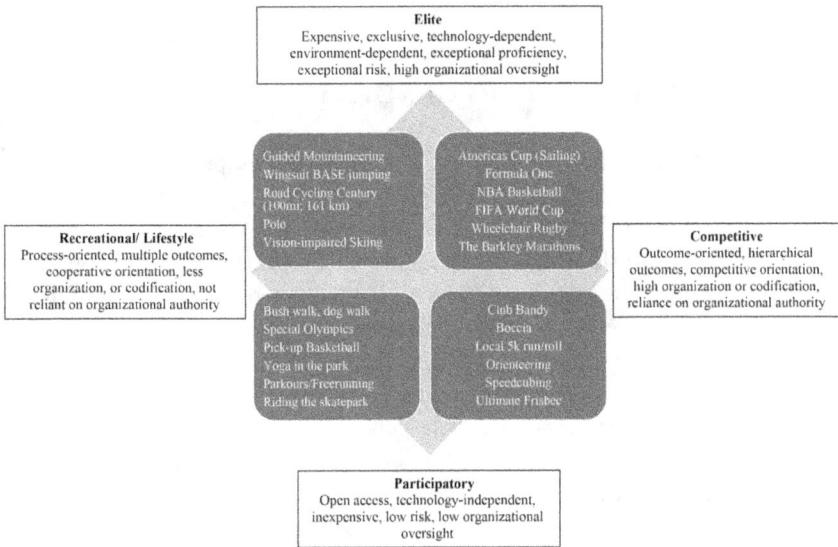

Figure 2.1.   The Sports Diamond: Mapping Sport by Purpose and Inclusion
Source: The author; loosely derived from Pink (2008)

traits. The problem of such approaches of simplifying sport into such categories of victors and vanquished and creating hierarchies of outcomes of sporting competitions often such simplifications fail to accurately reflect what occurs in a sporting event.

By emphasizing one outcome—fastest, highest, strongest, etc.—such winning-and-losing approaches may fail to relate to the drama of a sporting event, to the core human interest in exceptional performance, dedication and courage, and ethical behavior in sport (previously, "sportsmanship") that so ignite human emotions in both participating and gathering en masse to watch such dramas unfold (English 2017). Thus, the broad definition of sport from the ABS is right to emphasize "elements" of competition as a part of the definition, leaving space for a sport that is not directly competitive.[2] See Case Study 2.1.

Coalter (2002: 26) provides a useful typology of variation in sports that is helpful in understanding its diversity:

• Individual, partner, and team activities
• Cognitive, motor, and physical skills
• Contact and no-contact
• Competitive and recreation
• Outdoor or indoor.

CASE STUDY 2.1. SCIENCE AND
SPORT: DEBATING GENDER IN ATHLETICS

A look at sport in this multidimensional perspective provides insights into some of the critical knowledge bases about sport found in the natural and social sciences that, in turn, informs understanding and policies in the world of sport. For example, much of the issues around transgender athlete participation in sport involves research and knowledge of physical development by gender across a wide range of cultural contexts . . . very deep knowledge in comparative early-childhood development, medicine, nutrition, and cross-sex comparison of capacities in pre- and postpubescent adolescence.

Indeed, World Athletics cited the work of a technical task force on these issues in its decision in March 2023 on "protecting the female class" in world track and field. In March 2023, a World Athletics task force on gender development and athletic capabilities through childhood and adolescent into adult development considered these questions that inform its decision to revise prior guidelines on transgender athletes participating in the female category in sports.

Organization and codification. A critical differentiator between lifestyle sports which typically involve individual efforts and goals, but which can be made into forms of competition—including yoga, for example, which despites its inward oriented philosophical roots has evolved into a competitive sport.[3] Other sports defy much organization, and the extent to which a community walk is considered a "sport" event it may involve very little organization other than describing a beginning and endpoint, which no codification of organization of what constitutes "walking." On the other hand, the Paris 2024 Olympic Games will see the return of "race walking" in the Olympic arena, where the definition of what constitutes walking is highly regulated; so, too, are the subdisciplines of the event—including the Marathon Race Walk Mixed Relay in which a male and female participant will compete as a team, switching out with one another over a marathon-distance course of 26.2 miles (~42 km).[4]

Effort, intensity, strength, or endurance. A second recurring issue in the definition of sport revolves around the extent of effort, intensity, endurance, or strength required in a sport, from highly rapid events (such as bull riding, which unfolds in a few seconds for each athlete in a round) to multiday events such as the nearly three-week-long Tour de France cycling event.

Effort refers to the expense of energy in the event, intensity may involve a combination of effort and, for example, duration. Strength typically refers to physical properties or the ability to expend energy most efficiently to achieve an objective (such as distance in the hammer throw, an Athletics event). Endurance refers to persistence or the ability to perform over an extended period of time, for example in "ultra" marathon events that exceed the length of an Olympic marathon.

The 2023 Barkley Marathon, run since 1986 in Frozen Head State Park in the U.S. state of Tennessee, covers 100 miles and features 63,000 feet (19,202 meters) of elevation gain and loss . . . with a 60-hour time cap. Only 19 people have finished the full three-loop course of the Barkley marathon in what may be the world's most exhausting sport event; in 2023, British ultra-marathoner Jasmin Paris, an athlete in the sport of skyrunning (high-altitude mountain running) became the fourth woman ever to complete three full loops of the "fun run" at the Barkley events; she had started a fourth when time expired.[5]

Physical, kinetic, and mental proficiency. A third factor in evaluating sport is the extent of proficiency required, kinetic (movement) or in cognitive skills (for example, hand-eye coordination). Combinations of skills and physical capacities combine attributes of agility, flexibility, power, strength, ability, determination, and analytical aptitude. Many consider the sport of boxing to be one of the most skill-requiring sports, combining these attributes most extensively; perhaps it is also the cost of not being proficient across all these domains (getting assaulted with high potential for risk and injury) and the nature of fighting as interpersonal connectedness across two athletes, is what lends boxing to be often seen as the sport requiring exceptional proficiency; the implication is the need for very high levels of physical preparedness in amateur boxing (Finlay et al. 2021).

Reliance on facilities, technology or environmentally modified sportscapes. Finally, one may map sport according to the extent to which it may require or involve technology, facilities, or sportscapes. F1 racing, for example, involves extensive and ongoing technological dependency on the world's most top-end race cars, costing some $12–$14 billion dollars each; in 2023, teams can spend up to $135 million as a cap on expenses relating to car performance (Kanal 2022). The extent to which a sport is reliant on technologies, facilities such as dedicated racecourses, and environmentally modified sportscapes, varies widely and has important implications for access to sport (a topic in chapter 6). Some sports require no or little facilities, whereas others including adaptive sports such as wheelchair rugby may see costs for high-end, competition-level wheelchairs more than $7,000 each, raising questions about strategies employed by teams and players to compete in the sport through procuring funding and sponsorships (Cottingham et al. 2017).

Sportscape analysis becomes important later in this book, as in urban settings sportscape design may be a critical environmental determinant of youth sport participation in terms of the build infrastructure and its ability to enable or accommodate participation such as skateboard parks, swimming pools, or ice-rink facilities; key issues include not just the existence of such infrastructures, but also access, safety, and localized cultures at such facilities (O'Reilly et al. 2014).

As one looks toward the contribution of sport to social cohesion and to international peace and toward norms in the international arena related to "sport for all" (see chapter 3), it is critical to focus more importantly on widespread participation in sport, an inclusive definition of sport to include play, mainstreaming concern with gender, social inequality and exclusions, and the experience of those disabled. Inclusive definitions of sport, and inclusive participation in sport, are more important that the trivial rule books of highly codified, equipment-dependent, essentially "high-income" sports (or those that are highly costly financially or environmentally in creating "sportscapes"). And those that emphasize sport as displacing violence, not legitimizing or glorifying it, should be prioritized.

THE EVOLVING AND CHANGING NATURE OF SPORT

A further factor in contemporary sport is its continuously *evolving and changing nature*. One of the most innovative and fastest-growing sports globally started as a toy. In 1951, the Wham-O company introduced a novel new toy for kids: the "Pluto Platter," later renamed the "Frisbee," a highly durable piece of plastic that, due to its innovative aerodynamic qualities, would fly when thrown with remarkable precision and space-age artistic flight. Over time, "Frisbee" evolved into a team sport globally, Ultimate Frisbee. A spin-off sport features human/animal interface: born was the proverbial frisbee dog, or competitions in which handlers throw the disc in ways that artistically present the dog's speed, acrobatic skill, jumping skills, and, indeed, overall artistic expression (Bellinger 2015; Johnson, 2013).[6] See Case Study 2.2.

In ancient times through to the early modern period in the 19th century, sport and play were deeply connected to religious tradition and beliefs, with *secularization of sport* being a development associated with deep drivers of social change in industrialization, urbanization, the advent of mass communication (initially, the printing press, then radio and television; today, the internet and social media). Associated with these trends is also democratization and mass participation in broad social life, furthering the evolution of sport as something related to secular life and that should be rationally organized,

CASE STUDY 2.2. ULTIMATE
FRISBEE: GENDER DIVERSITY REQUIRED

Ultimate Frisbee is a modern, emerging sport: highly intense aerobically, with inclusivity-oriented rules that show sensitivity toward gender inclusion as a mixed-gender sport (Waters 2012), teams win with better communication and problem-solving, there is no contact or violence, and Ultimate may be the world's least expensive sport (and it can be played well barefooted, indoors, or out). The rules of Ultimate Frisbee involve no referee; teams are to work out disputes on their own. Today the Ultimate Frisbee Association (UFA) is global in nature, taps into grassroots organizations and it connects with global and local sports networks with corporate social-responsibility support from the Wham-O corporation.

For now, Ultimate Frisbee remains a club sport in the United States (not recognized by the NCAA), yet globally is now recognized as a partner of the IOC and is a candidate sport for future Olympic Games. The UFA and partners are developing a parasport in the sport through a small-grants program for development of Wheelchair Ultimate.

The "Pluto's Platter" (aka frisbee) example of the evolution of a simple toy into a global sport, adaptable, based on rules of gender inclusion, and emphasizing problem-solving and participation as core values, is reflective for four aspects of sport's constant evolution that characterize a rapidly changing world of sport. The organization Ultimate Peace (www.ultimatepeace.org) builds on the sport's value system in youth leadership training camps in the West Bank and Jordan in the Middle East and in the United States.

governed, and administered (for example, the increasing quantification of sports outcomes). Thus, over time, as sport became more organized, rationalized, and secular—primarily in the rise of organized sport in Northern Europe in the mid-19th century through "association football"—it also became the instrument of social control objectives and was, for example, disseminated through colonialism as a means to engage with, and exert authority over, colonial populations.

Most importantly, the processes of *urbanization, mass communication, and rising incomes* led to mass participation in sports for the proverbial middle class as forms of labor and leisure shifted. These processes are still unfolding today, for example, as we see exceptional development in erstwhile "Third

World" or developing countries, the growth of cities, and mass participation in sports. A case-in-point in the rapid expansion of the urban and peri-urban middle class in Africa since the 1980s, widespread advances in communication through mobile-phone adoption, and growing demand for sports in Africa and the concomitant development of sports such as the Basketball Africa League (BAL), a partnership between the global International Basketball Federation (FIBA) and the U.S.-based National Basketball Association (NBA). The BAL, with headquarters in Rwanda, features 12 club teams; Egypt's al-Alhy club won the 2023 BAL championship in May 2023.[7]

Sport, as social construct rather than precisely defined, has deep processes of historical production and wide variation in meaning, organization, and relationships to dominant meanings and beliefs: sport is intricately related to ideas within social situations about physicality and the body, organization, and relationship in society, around what constitutes achievement, conceptualizations of masculinity, feminine role expectations, and the significance of sports. Sport's *historical association with forms of toxic masculinity*—women's participation in sports remains constrained in many social contexts—and its sometimes association with either interpersonal human violence such as boxing or mixed-martial arts (MMA) is seen, for example, in its contemporary popularity in the former Soviet countries in the Caucasus and in Russia itself. In highly localized contexts, such as in Georgia and in the Russian province of Chechnya, MMA has emerged as a meaningful sport in a region where conflict is endemic and internationalized conflict feeds insecurity, militarism, and international rivalry.

The evolution and participation in sport is associated with the deep currents of *modernization*, that is advances in human settlement patterns such as urbanization, advances in technology from equipment to measurement and technologies that expand possibilities, such as the flying "wing suit," which evolved in the context of BASE jumping, which involves leaping from fixed objects such as bridges, cliffs, or buildings. BASE jumping is, of course, one of the most extremely risky sports and in the most extreme cases athletes livestreamed on social media their own death in the sport (Bisharat 2016). This example also illustrates the global expansion of lifestyle sports, or those that are primarily for individual recreation and personal achievement—or simply, thrill—rather than in collective competition and sports entertainment, often highly organized forms of interaction in sportscapes such as a "caged" MMA fighting ring.

The *advent and expansion of extreme lifestyle sports*, starting roughly in the 1980s—seems directly related to the drive by some for the inordinate release of brain-chemical secretions attracting those with exceptional drive, deep in their psyche, for a sport that produces an extreme thrill, a down-deep brain reward (Brymer and Schweitzer 2017, Musumeci 2021). As Musumeci describes (2021: 1): "The adrenaline rush increases the acceleration of blood flows to the muscles and brain, relaxes the muscles, and lastly helps with the conversion of glycogen into glucose in the liver. For every extreme sports athlete, this adrenaline rush is never enough since they are always seeking stronger emotions." As he further notes, extreme sport is also associated with self-destructive tendencies, given the risks.

A look at sports such as cage MMA raises questions about *risk and injury in sport*, and the related concerns about the role of violence in sports. With new research, for example, on the extent of concussive injuries in football, and reports of deaths of children in sports such as MMA, there is increasing and new focus on the nature and extent of violence in sports. One of the most controversial sports to emerge has been the sport of "slap fighting," which involves not much more than it sounds: participants exchange blows to the face repeatedly until a victor emerges or is declared. Fighters are at risk of chronic traumatic encephalopathy (CTE), a degenerative brain disease likely caused by repeated injury to the head and brain. "It's one of the stupidest things you can do," according to Chris Nowinski of the Concussive Legacy Foundation. "There's nothing fun, there's nothing interesting, and there's nothing sporting," he added (Anderson 2023). As neurologist and neuroscientist Lukascz Konokpa finds,

> Recent research has discovered that concussions frequently occur in head-jarring sports such as boxing, soccer, rugby, football, or lacrosse, and that following a concussion, significant neurophysiological changes occur in the brain. These often present as transient or lasting episodes of confusion, headache, irritability, inattention, changes in sleep patterns, and loss of working memory (Konopka 2015: 581).

Multisport events involve combinations of sports that work ostensibly in a complimentary way toward reflecting all-round athletic capabilities. While multisport events were found in the ancient Olympic Games in the form of the decathlon, the *scope and nature of multisport events* continues to change and evolve in the 21st century. Among those most common globally is the triathlon, now an Olympic event that appeared in the 2000 Sydney Games in men and women's endurance event that combines swimming, cycling, and running. The modern pentathlon, introduced into the Olympic Games by its proverbial founding father, Pierre de Coubertin, includes equestrian events to reflect cavalry skills of soldiers seeking to survive behind enemy lines. An Olympic event since 1904, the decathlon itself is rapidly changing: following an incident at the Tokyo 2021/22 Olympic Games in which a German coach punched an uncooperative horse, equestrian components were taken out of the decathlon to be replaced by cycling; the change has been controversial, with some decathletes opting to quit the sport as it evolves around them (Ingle 2021).

Historically, sport was deeply affected by colonialism and imperialism, and as described in chapter 4, sport evolved into a global phenomenon at the height of the age of nationalism when such exploitation was arguably at a historical peak. As described in the Introduction, the aligned processes of increasing universalism in sport and the independence and increased influence and role of postcolonial countries in global sports in the 20th century informs new trends on the *revival of "indigenous sport,"* or sport that was often discouraged or even outright banned under colonialism, but the practice of which has persisted or knowledge of the sport exists in oral, written, or archeological evidence. Colonialism had significant effects on contemporary sport cultures, and today organizations such as the Commonwealth, for example, bring together countries with a British colonial past together in sports more common to these countries such as cricket, rugby, and netball. The Commonwealth Games also includes para sports, including para lawn bowling and para triathlon.

First nations in Canada have been at the forefront of the movement to revive and further sports developed and practiced by indigenous peoples. In 1971, the first Native Summer Games were held in Enoch, Alberta, and featured 3,000 participants in 13 sports; in the games, sports are equally infused with other cultural events, ceremonies, and over time at indigenous-sport celebration events such as a "sacred ceremonial run."[8] Resurgence in indigenous sport is also about giving recognition to indigenous athletes who, in instances such as mountaineering, have been essential to the ostensible success of Westerners seeking to climb Everest for bragging rights as having reached (typically, with oxygen assistance) the world's tallest peak. In 2023, Nepali Sherpa guide Kamita Rita Sherpa, known as Topke, summitted Everest a record 28th time, twice in that year, at age 53. "This journey has taught me invaluable lessons about resilience, determination, and the power of human spirit," he posted to his Instagram feed, "it reminded me that anything is possible" (O'Kane 2023).

In Bolivia, indigenous girls and women ride the skatepark in Cochabama as a symbol of resistance. The skirt-and-flowery top attire is part of local identity and allows local young women skaters—known as *Imilla* in Aymara and Quecha, popular indigenous languages—such as Dani Santiváñez to express their indigenous roots (Dörr 2022). See Case Study 2.3.

CASE STUDY 2.3. REVIVAL OF THE ANCIENT MESO-AMERICAN BALL GAMES

At the ancient Mayan Chechen Itza in Mexico's Yucatán Peninsula is found the ballcourt of the pre-Columbian ball games of ancient Mesoamerica, a sport associated with various types of rituals with archeological evidence dating from at least 1650 BC. The ancient sport varied much in practice and, in essence, involved what was in some instances a rather heavy 4 lb, or 9 kg, ball of rubber that participants struck with their hips (or, otherwise, at times forearms or with handstones) to engage the ball back and forth with opponents. There is deep anthropological literature on the ancient sport and its practice among civilizations of the region among the Tlatilco culture and Olmec settlements and ruins have been found in various sites along the Oaxaca and Chiapas valley regions to the west of the Yucatán. Conquistadors, encouraged by their Catholic religious advisors, banned the sport as a heretical religious ritual following the Spanish conquest of the Americas in the 16th century.

The ancient Mesoamerican ball games might have been called today something like "netless volley-hip-ball," although the ancient sites also reveal goals that might have been subsequently added as the sport evolved. The sport is referred to today in different ways, colloquially as *juego de pelota* (ball games). There is some exceptionally engaging anthropological work on the ancient games, addressing the ever-present questions on the sport about when and how it was at time associated with sacrifice, reactions of the colonial Spanish, its association with civilization and society, and its deep relationships with political power (Scarborough and Wilcox 1991).

There remains a lot of uncertainty about this ancient sport, although much is known about Mayan rituals and the role of sport in them. Like today, there are the outfits: the ancient games are known through the archeological evidentiary record to have featured elaborate, feathered outfits, elaborately adorned hip guards, artful facial decorations, and protective girdles, and their depiction is found in a number of artifacts that provide glimpses into the highly complicated culture, ritual, and meeting of the Mayan ball games.

There are ongoing efforts to revive the game, and its revival provides deep meaning, esteem, and affirming performance of social identity in today's troubled Mexico, which is beset by high rates of criminal and interpersonal violence driven by the region's broader drug trade and poor governance. Participants in revived games have sought to re-create the iconography, ritual, and spirit of the ancient games. Moreover, they serve social development in Mexico. In the words of one of the young male participants,

> The game really changed my life, a lot. I was a different person. . . . I gave up drugs. I gave up alcohol, so I could focus. I'm a Mesoamerican ballgame player, with a lot of pride. I am Maya. I am a direct descendent. I want to be Maya. . . . I want to honor my ancestors. I want to speak my language and to show that I am me. (BBC 2020b)

The ball games are developed and overseen by the Mesoamerican Ballgame Association.

WHY SPORTS MATTER: WELL-BEING

The literature on sports and physical and emotional well-being is deep and bends much in the direction of the immediate and long-term effects of physical recreation for all ages and abilities when sport is safe, self-determined, and disassociated with social stress . . . particularly for young children (UNICEF 2019). This broad finding from the medical and related literatures on physiological sciences raises several important intersections that further develop conceptual framing for understanding the assumptions and approaches behind arguments related to the various issues around sports. And it helps to understand why one of the most common phrases used to justify sports-related work is that it is somehow a "universal human language." Much hyperbole in the world of its "transcendental power" is based on assumptions or arguments about the very nature of sport.

Sport, physiology, and health. There is widespread consensus in the field of public health on the positive immediate and long-term benefits to physical activity to health outcomes, at all ages, through direct effects such as improved circulation and immunity to indirect effect such as less alcohol consumption and better sleep (Malm, Jakobsson, and Isaksson 2019); not surprisingly, public health authorities in countries, together with the World Health Organization (WHO) provide data and guidance on the benefits. By avoiding direct potential harms, such as injury, and potential indirect harms such as eating disorders, obsession with body image, or overexercise and burnout, sports' contribution to health is unambiguous.

One of the most important findings in this area is the importance of sports throughout life and into older adulthood, with many stereotypes falling on continuance of sport life's later phases. An 83-year-old marathoner, Barbara

Humbert, a German-born French woman from Eaubonne, France, hopes to win an exception from not being chosen in a lottery to run the "Marathon for All," a non-elite race along the Paris 2024 marathon route in this inaugural public event to unfold alongside the elite runners in the Olympic Games (Olive and Libert 2023).

Sport and mental well-being. The UNICEF and Barça Foundation study reviewed the current literature on sports and mental well-being, and also found extensive consensus in the literature on effects of participation in sports and play on mental well-being. In children and youth, for example, review of the literature showed "a relationship between children's and young people's participation in sport and various types of personal and social development outcomes, including life skills (e.g., self-efficacy, confidence, self-esteem), social cohesion, education outcomes, psychosocial outcomes and physical health and well-being" (UNICEF 2019, 11).

Research in neuroscience confirms that sport is equally related to mental well-being in adults, and that sport and physical activity in older adults is directly involved in disease prevention through the direct mechanism of improved circulation in the brain, and indirect effects such as sleep and motivation, physical activity leads to neuronal regeneration in the brain, preventing dementia. Physical activity improves neuroplasticity, or the brain's ability to adapt and to form new neural networks and connections (Neuroscience News 2023).

These findings build on deep knowledge and scientific consensus on the positive benefits to individuals and societies universally to both individual outcomes such as mental well-being and resilience and the capacity to overcome shock and trauma, as well as social outcomes such as those articulated by UNICEF.

Neuroscience of sport and the brain. Exercise and physical activity are regularly prescribed for therapeutic benefits in treating adverse psychological conditions and psychiatric illnesses, brain injury recovery, post-traumatic stress syndrome, and neurodegenerative diseases. The mechanisms by which activity may help in treating these disorders is instructive for understanding, too, how activity affects the brain and, in turn, affects human emotions such as well-being, motivation, and, ultimately, empathy or positive orientations toward others. The mechanisms of exercise's contribution to the brain are increased circulation, oxidation, and energy adaptation. Is the "power" of sport reducible to chemical activity in the brain that occurs when participating—as simple as participating as a viewer where sport is entertainment—in sport? Exercise stimulates secretion of dopamine (DA), noradrenaline (NE), and serotonin (5-HT) . . . the principal neurotransmitters or chemical messengers that transport signals in the brain (Lin and Kuo 2013).

Engendering empathy, enabling society. Activity and play in early childhood contribute to life-skills acquisition and are critical in the early-childhood development of mindsets that facilitate later-life success and mental well-being. The literature further demonstrates the positive effects of activity and play, organized or not, on important life skills of self-efficacy (the ability of an individual to get things done), confidence and self-worth, personal esteem, and parity esteem of identity in social situations, education success and persistence, and attitudes toward others including nonconforming identities, physical characteristics (such as a disability), or ethnic or racial differences.

Chapter 8 returns to these issues with the articulation of how participation in physical activity as part of early childhood education is an essential component of "positive youth identity" and socialization processes of mindsets that enable later life development of personal capacities that in turn scales up to collective efficacy and public goods such as development and peace through collective mindsets or cultures based on empathy, inclusion, and trust . . . the core components of social cohesion.

Physical activity in older adults. Lifelong physical activity into older age—indeed, throughout life, countering many social myths that sports are principally for children and youth—contributes to longevity through physical well-being and immunity, mental well-being, lifelong emotional, cognitive, and social skills, reduced vulnerability to stress and depression, ability to learn over one's lifetime, and lower vulnerability to antisocial behaviors such as extremism or crime.

For example, recent evidence from the field of neuroscience shows that participation in sport in later life provides both indirect and direct weapons to stave off the potential for old-age dementia (Neuroscience News 2023a). The mechanisms are direct in that activity leads to increased blood circulation in the brain, facilitating new neuronal development (i.e., generating new neurons, the nerve cell railroad-switches of the brain that transmit information and directly link the body and the mind, or the muscles and the brain.

Indirectly, activity contributes to feelings of wellness, motivation for activity, self-esteem, and self-worth. As Portugal et al. describe in their review of research on the neurobiological relationships between exercise and mental disorders such as Parkinson's disease, "Physical exercise may improve both mood and adherence to an exercise program in healthy individuals and might modulate both the performance and mental health of athletes[;] exercise is associated with the increased synthesis and release of both neurogenesis, angiogenesis, and neuroplasticity" (2013, 1).[9]

These *fundamental neurobiological, cognitive, and physiological mechanisms*—together with the emotive factors in the next chapter that explore how social participation in sports also results in feelings of elation, mental well-being, and social connectedness—together begin to unpack the Utopian rhetoric in international sports and its potential (see chapter 6), setting the stage for its political manipulation and providing an underlying explanation for arguments about "why sportswashing works." In the meantime, there is consensus on the need to move . . . physical activity, when possible and when not introducing the potential for serious risk and injury, is unambiguously beneficial. See Case Study 2.4.

IMPLICATIONS: THE IMPERATIVE OF INCLUSIVITY IN SPORTS

The very properties that make physical recreation, play, and sports so reward-ing individually, and its power as an agent of social bonding for creating

CASE STUDY 2.4. THE WHO'S "GLOBAL ACTION PLAN ON PHYSICAL ACTIVITY, 2018–2030"

The WHO 2018–2030 action underscores these relationships and relates physical activity to the SDG attainment . . . the action plan motto— "Let's be active . . . everyone, everywhere, everyday"—summarizes the gist of the plan: regular physical activity mitigates the risk of especially noncommunicable diseases such as principal global causes of death from diabetes, stroke, heart disease, cancer, obesity, and hypertension.

The WHO action plan is motivated by concern that, according to its research, show that "1 in 4 adults and 3 in 4 adolescents do not currently meet the global recommendations for physical activity . . . globally, 23% of adults and 81% of adolescents (aged 11–17 years) do not meet the WHO guidelines on physical activity for health" (WHO 2018: 14). Factors that affect these rates are principally developmental, economic, culture, and social . . . a lack of access to safe sports and sporting spaces. The WHO data is clear:

Differences in levels of physical activity are . . . explained by significant inequities in the opportunities for physical activity by gender and social position, within as well as between countries. Girls, women, older adults, people with disabilities and chronic diseases, indigenous people and the inhabitants of rural communities often have less access to safe, acces-sible, affordable, and appropriate spaces in which to be physically active. (WHO 2018: 15) cultures of shared identities and values (as described in the next chapter), are the very properties that leave it so susceptible to being ensnared in international power politics. A look at the wide world of sports engages the underlying assumption seen through the world of sport is alleged transcendence of all forms of the human condition. This is at best a questionable claim, without any evident, global empirical evidence, and should be met with exceptional caution around the implications of the presumption of either universal understanding of sport, much less its putative acceptance as a universal set of values of some kind. Rather, a humble approach is required.

At least one step toward realization of remediating these deep inequities in access to the potential benefits of sport is to *expand common thinking about what constitutes sport and access to sport*, and to adopt a highly inclusive and expansive definition of sport . . . one that leaves open much space for the rapidly evolving nature of sport. Today, for example, the global sport federation that regulates cycling, the International Cycling Union (UCI) also regulates virtual cycling races on a platform known as Zwift, which involves internet-mediated racing among certified athletes on a proverbial stationary bike "ride to nowhere" racing a virtual racecourse from their homes, bedrooms, balconies, garages, or connected at the gym.[10]

Thus, sport's evolution in step with technological innovation may, too, be one way to address the core problem of access in realizing the physical and mental well-being benefits of exercise, physical recreation, or body and mind in movement through sport. As described in chapter 6, technological innovation has been critical in expanding access to sports for those with disabilities, where new medical prosthetic devices, ambulation aids, and biomechanical function have enabled expanding access.

For the argument presented in this book—namely, that sustainable peace begins from scaling up the capacity of individuals within a society to trust, or through social cohesion—any analysis of sport should start with a physiological understanding about how the body is related to the brain, and, in turn, how individual orientations toward empathy and collective mindsets that reflect a sense of shared or common destiny are the underlying building blocks of peace. If physical recreation and play are associated with the acquisition of orientations of well-being and empathy toward others, it may be possible to establish what is the essential neuroscientific linkages among activity, play, and sport and broader social outcomes of collective efficacy (willingness to work together cooperatively), shared and common destiny, and inclusive definitions of nation, society, and the collective destiny of humankind.

QUESTIONS FOR CONSIDERATION

- What is a "sport?" When is the definition of "sport" consequential for individuals, countries, and communities?
- How can the wide variety of sport globally be organized and evaluated according to some important dimensions such as their inclusivity, or access to participation, or the extent to which the outcomes are "winning and losing" versus sport for the sake of physical activity?
- Should indigenous sport be more fully integrated into the world of "organized" sport, or is it better for cultural protection to see indigenous sport as a somewhat separate sphere of international sport?

FOR FURTHER INFORMATION

A treasure trove of academic journals is devoted to the world of sport and to the intersections between sport and medicine and rehabilitation, biomechanics, sport psychology, and performance research. Among the most consulted of these journals are the *International Journal of Sports Medicine*, the *Journal of Sport and Exercise Psychology*, *Journal of Applied Physiology*, *Exercise and Sport Sciences Review*, and the *British Journal of Sports Medicine*.

The World Health Organization monitors the state of physical activity and related health effects around the world. The 2022 *Global Status Report on Physical Activity* provides an overview of current knowledge and trends, policy frameworks and enabling conditions for sport, measures of the health burden of physical inactivity, and data and analysis of the WHO's Global Action Plan.

Dedicated to the organized world of sport, the organization Sport Accord represents more than 125 sport federations and is comprised of four organizations that oversee many (but not nearly all) of the wide world of sports globally: The Association of Summer Olympic International Federations (ASOIF), the Association of International Winter Sports Federations (AIOWF), the Association of IOC Recognized International Sports Federations ARISF, and the Alliance of Independent Recognized Members of Sport (AIMS). The world's sports come together annually in the International Federation Forum. The IOC maintains a list of sport federations it recognizes at https://olympics .com/ioc/international-federations.

NOTES

1. See the TWIF online at: https://tugofwar-twif.org/.

2. If there is one sport that is, game-theoretically, oriented toward "pure cooperation"—i.e., there is no incentive not to be inclusive and enable others to succeed—it is the sport of footbag, sometimes known as "hacky sack." As players stand in a circle, the game can only be won with cooperation and inclusion of all members . . . and there is culturally to be no penalty for being "bad" at the sport (teammates are never to say "I'm sorry" in footbag . . . it's all for fun). It's a difficult sport from the outset, and there is understanding that beginners will be inherently bad in terms of initial proficiency. The official rules of footbag per the International Footbag Committee are found at http://www.footbag.org/rules/.

3. See the International Sport Yoga Federation (ISYF) at https://www.iysf.org/about/yoga-as-a-sport/; the ISYF is not yet recognized by the IOC.

4. The rules of race walking are promulgated by World Athletics. Race walking is defined as "a progression of steps so taken that the walker contacts the ground, so that no visible (to the human eye) loss of contact occurs. The advancing leg must be straightened (i.e., not bent at the knee) from the moment of first contact with the ground until the vertical upright position." See the rules at https://www.caf.com/media/4019608/c21-technical-rules.pdf.

5. See the International Skyrunning Federation at https://www.skyrunning.com/. On Jasmin Paris, see the profile in *Outside Magazine* (Huber 2022).

6. See "Ultimate Frisbee: A History," https://www.youtube.com/watch?v=sVRDfm1TShs and on disc dogs see https://www.topendsports.com/sport/list/disc-dog.htm.

7. See the BAL at https://bal.nba.com/ and on the FIBA website at https://www.fiba.basketball/africa

8. See the history of the North American Indigenous Games (NAIG) at http://www.naigcouncil.com/history.php.

9. For further articulation of these relationships and the extension of the causal mechanisms as they relate to athlete mental health, see Ghildiyal (2015).

10. For further description of the UCI-overseen of the platform and issues surround the UCI's embrace of esports, see Schwenker (2023).

Chapter 3

Mindsets of Devotion

The Social "Power" of Sports

Chapter Overview

Sports have historically been, and continue today, to represent social values, reflect underlying dynamics of nation, ethnicity, class, and ableism, to serve and reaffirm social inclusions and exclusions, to reinforce historical marginalization and unfairness, and highlight and demonstrate inequities in society. At the same time, it gives opportunity for social forces to advocate for, and claim, human rights.

There is a deep scholarly literature on the sociology of sports together with extensive literatures on sports and social issues across a wide range of considerations from disciplines such as anthropology, economics, political science, geography, and religious studies (Donnelly 2006). Sports are deeply intertwined with social dynamics, or the study of interactions among individuals, groups, and interactions among group-level behaviors. Today's trends of globalization and economic integration have reinforced such inequalities, such as in the localized environment externalities (or, side effects) from globalized adventure tourism such as guided mountaineering.

This chapter presents the argument that the very properties that make physical recreation, play, and sports so rewarding individually explain its power as an agent of social bonding for creating cultures of shared identities and values. These are the very properties that leave it so susceptible to being ensnared in international power politics.

CHAPTER HIGHLIGHTS

- The first section brings in *perspectives from social psychology* that explain further the emotive power of sport, taking forward from the effect of sport on the individual brain to what might be usefully considered the "collective brain."
- The second explores *the intersection between sport and social dynamics,* positing some of the important relationships between sport, social dynamics, and social bonding.
- The final section looks at when sport affects social dynamics in modernizing societies, at times in a way that does not conform to conventional cultural or social norms.

THE SOCIOLOGY OF SPORT: A PRIMER

Social psychological perspectives of bonding or within-group trust, linking or between-group trust, and the role of intermediaries in generating bridging or overarching trust in society are all powerful concepts for understanding the deeply sociological, economic, and justice implications of international sports, and it is these very concepts that can inform how international competition in sports may conceivably contribute to peace, rather than worsening it.

The sociology of sports is involved with both description, that is how sports is related to social forces and dynamics or relationships in society, and with implications for policy and practice for harnessing sports for social development purposes, such as expanding physical and mental well-being, development, and peace and strengthening social cohesion objectives. Essential to this undertaking is a critical look at the possibilities, and limits, of sports and its *contribution to public goods* such as health, education, livelihoods and meeting other critical human needs. Sociologists of sport are equally engaged in how sport contributes to addressing social ills such as racism, misogyny and gender inequality, poverty, marginalization, and stigmatization of groups, and meeting the needs of those with physical and intellectual disabilities.

Collective participation in sports, whether as a participant or as a fan, or devoted viewer, is shown to relate directly to feelings of well-being: the primary social psychological mechanism at play may well be the notion of solidarity, or a common feeling with others sharing a set of common subjective orientation and values. Recent research reaffirms this essential understanding; in the "Taking Part" survey of sport attendees in the sport-enthusiastic UK, researchers from Anglia Ruskin University found that attending live sport events resulted in improved well-being in two specific measures: that life is "worthwhile," and lower levels of loneliness (Keyes et al. 2023). This assertion, and research findings, have important policy implications: not only might sports be expanded for participants or athletes, but expansion of sport spectatorship may have knock-on social cohesion effects as well.

Concepts at the core of what is sport at individual, community, and national and global levels are drawn from psychology which studies behavior at the level of individuals, evaluating critical concerns such as motivation, self-esteem, cognitive processes, neuroscience (or the biochemical study of the brain), personality, resilience (capacity to absorb and recover from shocks), and perception. Scaled up beyond the individual, social psychology then explores processes of interpersonal and small-group dynamics, determinants of social bonding and attachment, and the adoption and performance of social identities.

At the core of the literature on the sociology of sport and its effects on social dynamics are theories and approaches to understanding the *nature of social bonding*; through collective efficacy (the need to work together for shared objectives), sport ostensibly contributes to especially in-group belonging among participants. In sport, such belonging also extends beyond participants into those in society who have attachment to the athlete, or, typically, team or sport and with whom they identify in complex ways of objectification, attachment, loyalty, devotion, and other expressions of "fandom." Recent research in this area of social psychology develops a highly insightful concept for this book, that of "performative social identity," which evaluates how social identity associated with bonding—devotion to a sport, and conformity within that sport (often driven by commercialism and branding)—is performed by individuals. One might conjure up Norwegian fans, who seek to relate and share an identity associated with Vikings, sometimes misappropriating symbols such as the horned helmet which, apparently, wasn't worn commonly historically by the Vikings in any event, (Buckhorn 2018).

Sport can *create microcultures of shared identities and symbolism* that reflect a value system related to the sport itself and to the broader social values it reflects and propagates. To unpack this complex claim, the elements can be disaggregated. First, is the concept of microcultures, which in the context of society—the word has biological meaning, too, of cell similarity—means shared subgroups with common orientation, beliefs, customs, behaviors together with shared reality constructs reflected in symbols, expression (chants), or outward social identities. That sport reflects a value system embedded in the ways in which the activity, symbols, or narrative around sport reflects and propagates values such as courage, resilience, strength, precision, or art in human activity. Importantly, however, the performative aspect of sport itself speaks to social values and relationships to shared histories, cultural orientations, and styles of appearance.

A strong example of such a microculture is that of Professional Bull Riding, PBR, a sport the evolved in the American West and which involves exceptionally risky efforts to ride a bucking, spinning, twisting, 1,500-pound bull (+700 kg) for as long as possible until time-out (typically, eight seconds for men). Bull riding is a highly conforming sport in terms of dress and appearance, with a notable feature of participants, commentators, spectators, and officials conforming around, for example, the ubiquitous "cowboy hat." Such symbols provide *systematic meaning making* and are highly interpretable within the sport and reflect to outsiders a common or shared set of meanings and orientations to include at times political values. Interpretative sociology which explores the relationships of social action and shared identities seeks to understand such behaviors and their meanings on social status, subjectivity, motives, and social change and resistance to change.

Participatory culture. Participatory culture approaches provide powerful insights into sport and is perhaps the most important conceptual orientation to explain fandom, or the relationship between those engaged in sport viewership for entertainment who form emotional bonds between themselves and sport athletic heroes, teams, or national representation. Some of the underlying psychological processes associated with participatory culture are concepts such as association (belonging and affinity), objectification (the idea that the club, team, or nation exists as such), and iconographic symbolism (connecting with the symbols and the meanings they convey). See Concept Box 3.1.

Sport-related participatory cultures foster deep ties of in-group belonging and they commonly strengthen community loyalty, and, often, pride-of-place and nationalist orientations. Participation may involve dress, colors, common music, gestures, tattoos, or costuming; taken to extremes, attachment and participatory culture can become extreme or toxic, fanatical, obsessive, or social aggressive expressed through concerns like racism in sport or in extreme we-they dichotomizations that further stigma and intolerance. See Case Study 3.1.

New orientations in the *social sciences of cultural studies* and critical race theory, media studies, gender studies, and human communication studies all contribute in various ways to both micro and macro aspects of sport, that is the role of sport in individual and small-setting analysis through to macro-level concerns such as the role of social media in diffusion of sports globally. Fields of law, religion, and medicine equally contribute to these analyses and debates on how sport and society are complexly related to make sense of the ways in which sport plays specific roles and functions, and contributes to meaning making, in different societies. In chapter 5, we explore in more depth how sport is an instrument of social control and power by elites, often working with deep corrupt interest in a sector of globalized life that is rife with billions in profit from multimedia and social media companies, retailers, tourism and travel interests, and often with deep-pocketed wealthy

CONCEPT BOX 3.1. THEORY INSIGHTS: BONDING VERSUS BRIDGING SOCIAL CAPITAL

Sport provides opportunity for the processes of bonding within and among social groups and the potential for development of social capital, or trust and willingness to cooperate toward shared goals or "collective efficacy." Team sports and other types of sports based on interpersonal interdependency or reliance are hard-wired toward bonding as cooperation, communication, and trust among participants. Moreover, experience together creates memories of trust, commonality—and uniforms—create feelings of cohesion and essential commonality in small-group contexts.

Yet *in-group bonding is but one form of social capital*, and such close inward connections easily fall prey to rivalry, out-group stigmatization, demonization . . . taken to higher levels such as social differences of race or ethnicity, or at levels of national rivalry in international politics, in-group cohesion can lead to out-group enmity, setting the stage for human rights violations and violent conflict.

Thus, a critical issue in sports is the question of when it may or could contribution to what is known as *"bridging social cohesion"* (or, related, "linking social cohesion," a set of concepts that appear in chapter 8 in the analysis of sports' potential contribution to peace in societies riven by ethnic, racial, or religious differentiations along group lines. In such divided societies, sport has been historically associated with sectarianism, and thus a critical concern going forward is how it might support inclusive multiculturalism in today's diverse and globalized societies.

elite who through their own fortune of financial independence are attracted to global sports.

SPORT IN GLOBALIZED SOCIETIES

Sport is deeply intertwined with social dynamics, and disciplines such as anthropology offer insights into aspects of ritual and meaning. History provides insights into the origins of sport and its evolution over time from the functional use of sport—such as military training, or for hunting and gathering—through to the historical institutionalism of modern sport institutions.

CASE STUDY 3.1. "RAISED ON BASKETBALL" IN THE PHILIPPINES

The hosting of the International Basketball Federation (FIBA) World Cup in the Philippines (together with Japan and Indonesia) was no accident: the country has a crazy love of the sport, which, poignantly was brought to the country in colonial conquest from the United States.

Associated Press journalist Tim Reynolds documented the street-level passion for the sport in his reporting from the FIBA 2023 World Cup; he quotes professional coach Tim Cone:

> People are raised on basketball from the age of 2 and 3 years old. . . . All they do is one sport and it's played throughout the year. We have three seasons: rainy season, wet season, and basketball season and we play basketball through it all. That's the passion. We always say we have three things in the Philippines: sport, basketball, and politics.

Reynolds reports that there are over 250,000 indoor basketball courts, and "countless" outdoor courts ("even rims fashioned out of barbed wire) in the Philippines (Reynolds 2023).

Economists explore the role of money in sports and the microeconomics of teams and clubs, bid cities for mega-events, incentives and mechanisms of corruption, and the ways in which sports contribute to personal capacities for generating livelihoods, to name a few (Zimbalist 2015).

The sociology of sport is a highly developed scholarly discipline, drawing on the deep conceptual foundations in theories of functionalism, Marxism, social systems theory, collective action theory, with laser-like focus on class, gender, race, sexuality, disability, and their interactions in work on intersectionality among these social categories. Marxist orientations, for example, may emphasize the role of athletes as labor, focus on the capitalist foundation of the international political economy of sport, and the hyper-commercialization of sport through corporate and sport-body marketing machines. Other critical orientations include the obsession and propagation of social norms on physicality in sport, and ways to reduce challenges of stigmatization around social conceptualizations of idealism in the human body, for example. See Case Study 3.2.

Further, sport sociologists also contend with how sport relates to social and cultural public policy needs such as provision of safe public spaces (for achieving social cohesion and reducing societal fear), addressing

CASE STUDY 3.2. FOOTBALL, THE
WORLD'S MOST POPULAR SPORT

Football—"soccer" in North America, or, more properly, "association football"—is indisputably the world's most popular sport: participants fall in love with the simple yet elegant game often from early childhood, football identities become part of family, community, class, and ethnic, racial, or national identities, and the sport has apparent universal appeal across cultures and contexts globally. Fandom for the top teams and players constitutes a set of global social movements, and male football stars garner the highest compensation packages in sport.

Football features some 240 million participants globally, and according to governing body FIFA (FIFA 2023), some 5 billion people reportedly "engaged' with 2022 FIFA World Cup, generating $7 billion in mostly rights-related viewership revenue to the global sports body (Library of Congress 2020). (More on FIFA's deep corruption scandal on bribery in host-city bidding in chapter 4.)

Football/soccer, with putative origins in 11th-century China (FIFA recognizes "kick ball, or cuju" in China as a predecessor sport to modern football; see https://www.fifamuseum.com/en/blog-stories/editorial/origins-cuju-in-china/). Football as is known today is more specific with modern roots in mid-19th-century England with the codification of "Cambridge Rules" in 1848, however, it is but one of hundreds, likely thousands when fully enumerated—of sports globally. Sport is an immensely widely varied set of individual and team-based behaviors around the world indistinguishable from broader categories of physical recreation and play. Moreover, sport is constantly evolving in concert with human creativity and new technologies.

With deep ties to history, religion, colonization, and the social dynamics of modernization (expanding education and incomes), sport globally is much more diverse, and in many ways more fascinating, than the proverbial beautiful game of football; sports such as athletics, basketball, cricket, cycling, field hockey, hockey, martial arts of various forms, or tennis also have participation in the millions. Whether football's spread is a result of it being a "beautiful game," or whether it is the consequence of the spread of sport through colonialism and imperialism, is an enduring question (Guttman 1993).

On the extent of participation in football, see FIFA 2023.

self-actualization or living a meaningful life, and addressing challenges of youth alienation and preventing violent extremism.

Much of the literature on sport and human rights (chapter 7) evaluates how sport has been a theater for breaking barriers of ableism, gender, race, class, race, ethnicity, indigeneity, and religious orientation. The sociology of sport does well to investigate the embeddedness of these barriers in sport, and how sport provides symbols and stories that animate these issues within rapidly dynamic modern societies and across borders in the diffusion and tension of global norms on issues such as gender and sexuality, equal rights, respect and representation for women and girls, and inclusive national narratives by which sport reflects contemporary diversities.

Gender and sexuality dynamics. The history of sport is the history of patriarchy, and perhaps of patriarchy's decline in the wake of modernization and globalization. Participation and stereotypes in sport have long been informed by patriarchal mindsets, hegemonic or toxic masculinity, male-driven ideations about the body, masculinity, and femininity, and resistance to social change to recognize the essential nonbinary nature of gender across all societies. Sport's clashing and transformation of gender norms historically is a leading issue today in sport, and deeply affects both the realization of access to safe play and sport by women and girls and to the ways in which societies and globally issues of transgender rights, intersex definitions and rights, and accommodations and design in sport account for gender differences.

Much focus in the consideration of gender in sports is the iconographic, bodily, and global beauty-making representation of female athletes and its effects on both commercialization of some "attractive" female athletes for blatant brand-making purposes and at the expense of equity and fairness in sports. Gender discriminations in sports lead to deep discussions about how to advance the rights, access, and involvement in international sports: Should women work through existing institutions and seek to level the playing field for equity in sports, or should there be concerted and more diligent efforts to protect women's sports and to ensure that there is equal treatment across traditional gender lines? Such discussions also inform ways in which cooperative approaches can be envisaged to engage men in evaluating the deep-seated causes of misogyny in sports and ways that together there can be greater efforts to ensure nontoxic approaches among men to gender relations.

Sports and social class. The long history of modernizing in industrial societies, featuring deep-drivers of history such as technological change and associated labor dynamics (i.e., the advent of wage labor), urbanization informs much of the history of the sociology of sports; since the late 20th century, this inquiry has expanded to analysis of global class dynamics with the expansion of a globalized, culturally integrated middle class, and, finally, a globalized, superrich elite. Historically, class dynamics, for example, in the evolution of modern association football, contained deep, localized symbolic meanings that often spoke socially about class and class dynamics in historical Britain; sports, in a way, served to contain these class dynamics within an overall capitalist system, in a manner that historians such as Eric Hobsbawn describes as generating bonds of loyalty across class, together with other deep drivers such as external threats (Hobsbawn 1983, 288–91).

Sports such as football, wrestling, and cycling opened up sports to the masses and created new forms of social organization—clubs, the basis of civil society—and established deep ties of loyalty. Athletes were miners, artisans, teamsters, and in "service" to the nobility and upper classes. Taking nationally, such as in the advent of the Tour de France in 1903, such sports served essential purposes of national citizen-making.

The *social division of labor in sports*, common across so many societies, was evident in the evolution of organized support from an upper-class preserve of "blood sport" by the royalty, elites sport for upper class in education (e.g., rugby at Eaton), is very much part and parcel of a vein of sociology that critically explores sport for the "leisure class." Such sport-for-the-elite orientations may well inform today some of the problems around globalized, elite, vacation-travel sport, and its environmental consequences for fragile ecosystems in both oceanic and mountainous contexts.

Today, one could also see global supply chain recruitment of athletes into major sport leagues—such as recruitment of Africans in the NBA, or Dominicans in U.S.-based Major League Baseball (MLB) are part of the international political economy of labor in sports.

Sports, race, ethnicity, and religious tradition. With competing philosophical doctrines in sport such as "social Darwinism" in historical times accounts for the deep association of sport with types of prejudice, racism, ethnic polarization and aggressive nationalism, and the expression of sectarian differences. While recent research affirms that such social constructed categories of race, ethnicity, or religious difference are learned and the product of early childhood socialization and experience (APA Taskforce 2020), the evolution of the nexus between sport and these identity dynamics has evolved considerably. See Case Study 3.3.

As is seen in the revival of *juego de pelota* in Mexico (chapter 2), there is an abiding association with many religious traditions globally, and this connection may offer insights into the social *dynamics of religious traditions and the role of physical activity within them.* Although modern international sport might be traced to a mid-19th-century trend of evangelical "Christian muscularity," the connections between sport and religion run much deeper and are part of understanding the role of sport any context globally. See Documentary Insights 3.1.

CASE STUDY 3.3. COMBATING DISCRIMINATION: THE OLYMPIC PROJECT FOR HUMAN RIGHTS

In some contexts, such as the United States, sport has been a vehicle for the expression of emancipatory advocacy against racial discrimination as African American athletes—such as boxer Muhammad Ali historically, or today's erstwhile NFL San Francisco 49ers star Colin Kaepernick and track star Sha'Carri Richardson have challenged racial discrimination in the United States and contended national narratives and public policy (in areas such as housing and policing) that perpetuate racial discrimination (Edwards 2017).

Advocacy by those such as sociologist Harry Edwards rippled beyond the U.S. context, forming the basis for the Olympic Project for Human Rights which was formed to lead the efforts to expel white-minority states Rhodesia and South Africa from the Olympic Games (Henderson 2013).

SPORT AND SOCIAL DYNAMICS

Debates that resonate in the sociology of sport grapple with these complex

DOCUMENTARY INSIGHTS 3.1. CHARISMA ON THE PITCH: *DIEGO MARADONA* (2019)

The legendary Argentinian footballer Diego Maradona is the subject of director Asif Kapadia's critically acclaimed documentary of the same name. This film explores the deep emotion in sport, from the athlete to the fans to vexatious decisions on citizenship, loyalty, honor, and heroism.

Born into conditions of depravity in an informal housing settlement in cacophonous Buenos Aires, the film traces his life from his early years as breadwinner for the family to his later years as a national icon. Strongly, it documents his amazing skills as a footballer, the speed, power, coordination, and spatial awareness that catapulted him from poverty to the pinnacles of football glory, https://www.imdb.com/title /tt5433114/.

issues between sport as reproducing social dynamics—such as notions that sport distracts and controls the masses; an "opiate," a bit like religion (Donnelly 2006, 208)—and changing social dynamics (ostensibly in the direction of equality and inclusion). Too, there remains deep analysis of sport as a venue for contesting social norms, both within countries and between them.

For example, in 2021 the Norwegian Women's Handball team challenged the rules of the International Handball Federation (IHF) that required players to wear bikinis in beach handball. Winning a fight with the IHF, the Norwegian women advocated and won to change the rule and have the ability to choose the inseam length of competition-attire shorts on their own. The Norwegian men's team advocated for the change side-by-side with the women in the protest that precipitated the rule change by the IHF (Radnofsky 2021).

Finally, today there is recognition of the role of *intersectionality across class, ethnic and racial identity, and gender* in identifying the nature and perpetuation of marginalization and inequalities along these lines socially. Indeed, in the history of sport, we find that intersectionality across lines of social differentiation is deeply linked to social dynamics. Hobsbawn notes that in the mid-19th century, as women's participation in sport expanded in its earlier years in tennis that sport provided a gateway from oppressive traditional roles: "Almost for the first time," he writes, "sport therefore provided respectable women of the upper and middle classes with a recognized public role as individual human beings, separate from their function as wives, daughters, mothers, marriage-partners or the other appendages of males inside and outside the family" (Hobsbawn 1983, 299).

What is evident in today's world is that many forms of sport that were previously exclusive or with origins as countercultural sport—such as climbing, flying disc, skateboarding, surfing, or breaking (or breakdancing)—have in recent years evolved in highly codified globally practiced sport with their legitimization through inclusion in the Olympic Games. See Case Study 3.4.

One of the enduring questions for the sociology of sport to raise at this juncture, however, is this: Can sport contribute to the diffusion of gender equality norms globally, which in turn may contribute to social movements to end autocracy, advance women's equality rights, and, ultimately, to democratize? See Case Study 3.5.

There is much more to Rekabi's story about sport such as competition climbing as a deeply sociological phenomenon. How does a sport like "competition climbing" evolve and spread globally? Climbing as a sport has deep historical origins and continued global significance, yet competition climbing—which is divided into three subdisciplines, lead, speed, bouldering—is a modern sport that has evolved from its early days of chivalrous pursuits by

CASE STUDY 3.4. TOTAL DISCIPLINE: *KUSHTI* WRESTLING IN INDIA

A sport in India that is struggling to persist through modernization and globalization in a rapidly changing world is Kushti wrestling. Wrestling, religious practice in Hinduism, and caste equality are found among the traditional wrestlers of Kolhapur, India. An ancient form of wrestling, the tradition requires celibacy, avoidance of tobacco and alcohol, and induction of young boys from age six.

Conducted in the soil, participants practice twelve hours a day—*Kushti*, or pehlwani, means "hallowed earth"—Davies (2020), in a poignantly artful photo essay by Australian photographer Mitchell Kanashkevich shows how the traditional sport dating from the fifth century BC that emphasizes "total discipline" and is practiced in schools inhibits recruitment of new athletes in a changing India. The reporting and photos were published in London's *Daily Mail* (Davies 2020).

Anthropologist Joseph's Alter's work explores the ways in which traditional competitive and lifestyle sports such as wresting and yoga relate to culture, religion, and meaning making in contemporary India (Alter 2018).

mostly men seeking to summit the world's highest peaks or scale the most sheer challenges of geologic structures on earth.

Competition climbing involves a created "sportscape," or artificial environment to facilitate the sport, in which athletes deftly move across walls adorned with features such as foot- and handholds in exceptionally challenging moves to complete a course. Competition climbing, like other sports, offers a common language, is adaptable across cultural environments, and speaks directly to the deep connections between physical exercise, mental rewarding ecstatic experiences, social norms, and social dynamics. Its introduction into the Olympic Games in Tokyo in 2020 has led to rapid growth of the sport following the first organized climbing competitions in 1985 and it has shaped cultural narratives in a myriad of national contexts (Taitague 2022).

Rekabi's statement was thus also about the progressive, globalized, youth culture of Iran which is so forcefully challenging the 40-year religious regime which has been so criticized in global institutions such as the UN for its repressive laws against women's rights. Thus, sport is deeply sociological in nature, tied to individual experiences and choice, microcultures of shared interests within a sport, local culture and communities, national social norms,

CASE STUDY 3.5. CLIMBING OVER GENDER OBSTACLES IN IRAN: ELNAZ REKABI

When Elnaz Rekabi, a 33-year-old Iranian woman and multiple medalist athlete in the new Olympic sport of competition climbing, overseen by the International Federation of Sport Climbing (IFSC), competed in the IFSC Asia–Continental Championships in South Korea in October, 2022, without the hijab, or head covering that is mandatory for women in her home country of Iran, she made history for her courageous global statement. Back home in Iran, the protests over the death of Mahsa Amini at the hands of the country's irregular "morality police," was in full swing. In a later statement, possibly coerced, she was apologetic and claimed competition was a mistake; when returning to her hometown of Tehran, she was greeted by a jubilant crowd of family and friends (Associated Press 2022a).

Competing without the head-cover requirement for women, which she had worn in prior competitions, became a deeply political issue. The brave defiance, intentional or not, of Iran's conservative morality laws on women's dress was a bold symbol of claiming equality of gender rights in a rapidly modernizing society.

Fearing for her safety, the IOC sought assurances that Rekabi would not be punished. Yet, a few short weeks later, her family's home was demolished in the middle of the night; Rekabi and her family paid a high price for her implicit political speech in international sport in defiance of an autocratic regime . . . her medals seen strewn among the debris in an unconfirmed video (BBC 2022a).

and at the international level in sport in transnational (across borders) and international (across regions) contexts. See Documentary Insights 3.2.

Finally, sport is culture, and cultural value is symbolic value. And, unlike other areas of international cultural cooperation, it has incredible economic power and globalized sport contributes to global social exclusions and inequities. Sport's undeniable, if not universal, popularity across societies and cultures explains why it is so deeply politicized, and why it is so economically lucrative, both domestically in contexts such as Iran and globally as outsiders in the West and in competition climbing lauded Rekabi's bravery against an illiberal government. The social "magnetism" of sport also helps to explain its effectiveness as a bottom-up approach to development and peace, a theme that will be returned to in chapter 8. Competition climbing-related programs

DOCUMENTARY INSIGHTS 3.2. INSIDE AN ATHLETE'S MIND: *CLIMBING THE DAWN WALL* (2018)

The "Dawn Wall" is a seemingly sheer, insurmountable, unimaginable rock face for a human (or another other animal, however deft) to attempt to ascend: the "Dawn Wall" (which sees morning sun) soars nearly 1,000 meters (3,000 feet) in Yosemite National Park in the U.S. state of California. *Climbing the Dawn Wall* is a documentary about American climbers Tommy Caldwell and Kevin Jorgensen, the first pair to free climb—that is, without fixed protection—the imposing rock face.

Tommy Caldwell, the son of a mountain-guide father, had been captured earlier in life, in 2000, by armed rebels in Kyrgyzstan, and he escaped. *Climbing the Dawn Wall* is a riveting documentary film about sport, resilience, and the athlete's mind caught between obsessive devotion to a sport and its physical and well-being consequences, https://www.imdb.com/title/tt7286916/.

can be an effective tool of intervention to reach disadvantaged or nonconforming youth for personal growth and development.

IMPLICATIONS: HARNESSING SPORT'S POWER

Many early-childhood participants in sport form deep psychosocial attachment to sport and bonding within microcultures and global communities. Sport is so deeply related to small group bonding initially, which over time scales up to international engagement through national channels along the so-called lines of the "norm of national recognition." This book argues that this is actually the source of much harm in global sport and is one of the ways in which the global sport regime should be reimagined.

At the end of the day, with football as the world's most popular sport, it is natural that the lion's share of sport-related programs for youth involve football, or at least some type of team sport. However, understanding the wide world of variety in sport offers up new possibilities and innovations to meet these aims, from ensuring that sport is more safe, accessible, and reinforcing for all participants, to reducing the cost, to taking "winning and losing" as the principal objective out of the outcome set. Sport today, as a deeply psychological, highly emotive, and highly fluid, component of a healthy society, needs considerable broadening as a social construction to realize its full potential for contribution to international public goods of human rights, development, and peace.

QUESTIONS FOR CONSIDERATION

- In what ways does the physiology and neuroscience of sport help explain the putative power of sport, and in what ways is physical activity related to the development of empathy and trust in society?
- Why are people so fundamentally animated, motivated, enthused by, and mobilized in relation to sport, and what are the origins and functions of such bonding and attachment?
- What are the implications of globalization and modernization of sport in rapidly changing societies, and how does engagement in "new sports" often contend with and challenge social norms, hierarchies, and biases?

FOR FURTHER INFORMATION

The 2015 *Routledge Handbook of the Sociology of Sport* provides an in-depth resource into core theories of sociology and deep thinkers in the historical discipline such as Bourdieu, contributions from leading scholars on intersections of sociology with related scholarly disciplines, analysis of race, class, sexuality, gender, and disability divisions in society in relation to sport, and seminar contributions on the sociology of sport on issues of the body, risk, doping, fandoms, violence, traditional and new media, corporations, and globalization (including several other topics) (Guilianotti, ed. 2016).

Scholars in International Sociology of Sport Association (ISSA), founded in 1965, in the North American Society for the Sociology of Sport, and others have generated a remarkable body of knowledge about the individual aspects of choosing to and participating in sport, on sport and socialization, and on the critical issues of race, ethnicity, gender, and ability in sport. Important recent trends in the sociology of sport are its expansion of work beyond North America and Europe and engagement of Global South orientations and voices, the emergence of "physical cultural studies," new frontiers of urban sociology, and the effects of new technologies such as mass surveillance systems within sporting arenas (Giulianotti 2015, xxi).

PART III

Politics in Sports

Comparative and International Perspectives

Chapter 4

Power

Sports in the National Interest

CHAPTER OVERVIEW

From 1936 in Berlin to Beijing 2008 and 2022, global sports have been used by autocratic regimes to reflect, and advance, national identities and to legitimize ruling systems. So, too, examples such as London 1948 and Salt Lake 2002 (post-9/11) reflect the association of sports with nationalism in democracies, and the pursuit of "triumphalism" in conflict. Regional powers such as Brazil embrace sports to reflect their regional leadership, hosting back-to-back FIFA World Cup and Olympic Games mega-events. Newer powers such as Rwanda have adopted sport-based policies to advance development, tourism, and national prestige on the African and world stages.

Sports nationalism, as such, is deeply intertwined with notions of organic nationalism or what has been called "primordial orientations" (a belief in shared kinship and myths of consanguinity), in economic nationalism and market dominance (to include, for example, imperialism and colonialism), in territorial nationalism or the statement of claims in disputed regions, and associating sports and national identity in religious terms when sports and religious tradition interact. Sports are employed as part of cultural policies of political regimes, autocratic and democratic alike, to form and to build coherent national identities, "make" national heroes, symbolize, personify enemies, and to advance preferred national narratives and reflect the superiority of ideology and social systems.

This chapter grapples with the ways in which sport on the global stage has been an instrument of nationalism and in foreign policy as sport diplomacy, arguing that it is the emotive power of sport for social control that lends this domain of national and global culture subject to politicization by governments globally for internal public-policy and international foreign policy alike.

CHAPTER HIGHLIGHTS

- Powerful symbolism makes sport attractive for the purposes of further-ing political aim. The politicization of sport is attractive to autocratic and nationalistic political elites to serve efforts to invent, shape, and perpetuate a particular historical narrative within a country, and to use sport to generate legitimacy within political regimes and to project pres-tige. Thus, sport is politicized for domestic image-making purposes and reflecting a regime's ideology to the world.
- Ensnared and politicized, sport is part of a realpolitik or realist orienta-tion in which sport is a project of foreign policy and key component of cultural diplomacy, or soft power: efforts by states to influence global opinion and to engage in direct diplomacy and national brand-building. In this exploration, the chapter presents some of the most significant international rivalries in sports.
- Countries around the world today have integrated sport into their foreign policies and regularly report on these activities through the UN (UN 2022). The use of sport for "soft power" projection in the international area has evolved from quaint exchanges of athletes to significant finan-cial and human resource investments in sport-based relationship build-ing, often across deeply entrenched international rivalries.

SYMBOLIC POLITICS AND THE POLITICIZATION OF SPORTS

To approach the manipulative capture of sports for political power, two important conceptual approaches from political science help explain how the power of sport is attractive to political regimes and elites in pursuit of political power domestically and in projecting identity and power in an inse-cure world.

- The first, found in the literature on comparative politics, is the *quest for legitimacy by states and by ruling regimes*: sport provides a theater of opportunity for performative nationalism and reinforcement of an offi-cial or regime-determined historical narrative.
- The power of the states allows for sport to serve the purposes of invent-ing traditions (and symbols) and thereby affirming the legitimacy of the state. Sport is the perfect arena for advancing politics through national symbolism, serving as a vehicle for political socialization and the solidi-fication of political loyalty.

- From the literature on international relations, the chapter explains how sport is an extension of realpolitik (or "realist") projection of "soft power" by regimes and ruling elites, destined to further international prestige and perform such power in the international arena (Houlihan 1994: 29–53).
- The hosting of the 1978 FIFA World Cup in concert with the military elite's prosecution of a "dirty war" against its domestic enemies by, among other ways including disappearance and dropping political prisoners from airplanes; football had been used by the fascist junta as an instrument of social control and they were subsequently accused of match-fixing (Arbena 1990). Violent clashes erupted in the game with Argentina's rival, Brazil, who asserted that they were cheated by the referee in the contentious match.

Sport at the national level is designed and conducted in a manner to reflect on the historical narrative, and political culture, of a country and relates directly to its pursuit of national identity, power in the international system, and global prestige toward national "self-actualization." Sport is an essential, sometimes *the* essential, element of cultural policies of political regimes to form and to build coherent national identities, to advance the regime's domestic and international legitimacy, and to demonstrate superiority of social systems. Historically, the association of sport broadly, and football specifically, with the rise and mobilization efforts of fascists in Germany, Italy, and Spain underscored how prowess in sport was associated with a social Darwinist view of the world and the mythmaking around restoring historical greatness in the face of social stress (Bolz 2016).

Much of the history of sport and its relationship to national identity formation focuses on the effects of colonialism and imperialism on the diffusion of culture, and particularly sports. Sport was diffused in colonial settings in ways that reflected the unjust social hierarchies of race, citizenship, and social status and engaged in the portrayal of colonial subjects in starkly dominant terms of the spread of cultural ideas. Too, sport then sparked resistance and engagement of sport figures and disadvantaged communities in some areas: sport was about the spread of identity and the formation of communities of colonialism and of resistance to exploitation and oppression. Sport historian Francois Cleophas writes that the diffusion of sports such as cricket, netball, rugby, and mountaineering in South Africa, for example, had deep social implications and enduring legacies (Cleophas 2021, 212):

The imperial legacy remains strong today. Contemporary ideas that true sport is morally pure, that it is based on "fair play" or that it offers a "level playing field" that can overcome divisions in society or even still—the Nelson Mandela mantra that sport "unites like nothing else"—are derived directly from the moral evangelism of Victorian sporting missionaries. . . .

Yet these attempts to use physical culture to discipline the minds and bodies of working-class and colonial peoples could not be successful. . . . Sometimes resistance was imposed on athletes simply to survive in the face of racial or social exclusion.

Indeed, the literature on the history of sport in the British imperial era, such as the British Empire Games held from 1930 to 1950 (the predecessor to the Commonwealth Games), articulates how soldiers and agents of the empire used sports to build common ties of loyalty to the imperial throne in London (Houlihan 1994: 132–51). See Concept Box 4.1.

CONCEPT BOX 4.1. WHY IS SPORT SO SUSCEPTIBLE TO POLITICAL CAPTURE AND INTERFERENCE?

Conceptually and historically, sport events, athletes, and teams have been subject to politicization in domestic and international contexts for three enduring reasons.

- First, athletes—whether they intend to, or not—are exploited for purposes of *political representation*, typically to reflect and reinforce authority-driven values, norms, and belief systems . . . as patriotic physical manifestation of national ideas.

  For example, when Liu Xiang, a 21-year-old high hurdler, won a gold medal at the 2004 Athens Olympic Games, he extended his own representation to China as an ostensibly patriotic athlete, commenting after his victory that "It is kind of a miracle," he told a post-event news conference. "It is unbelievable—a Chinese, and Asian, has won this event" (Yardley 2004). To him and to the close watchers in the Communist Party of China (CCP), the victory in Athens showed that China's athletes were not limited to well-tried tropes about table tennis, gymnastics, or, contemporarily, in diving where China is the unambiguously dominant country.

- Second, the very rituals and feeling of bonding and belonging that are at the heart of the sociology of sport are those that serve the often officially sanctioned or project dominant view of national belonging. Sport is symbolically organized and presented to further symbolic *representations and performance of a national-identity oriented and privileged form of social identity*.

Perhaps the most important process in sport for achieving these ends is the playing of national anthems in award ceremonies in international sports, which serve the purposes of reinforcing, reifying, and performing national belonging. Anthem-playing in Olympic competition is limited to 80 seconds, even though some full national anthems are more than eight minutes long (Marshall 2016).

- Third, sport institutions and organizations within a country are *targets of opportunity for state interference* and capture. In many countries and contexts, athletes can be said to be a politically vulnerable class.

Among the worst instances in history of state capture and abuse of sport organizations, athletes, and the Olympic ideals is the horrific human rights abuses of torture that emanated from the Iraq National Olympic Committee under Saddam Hussein. Following a five-month investigation, the IOC annulled the Iraq committee, finding that "all allegations" of torture and abuse were "absolutely credible" (Shipley 2003). The torture had been documented by the London-based organization Indict (McKay 2003), and was led and perpetrated by Hussein's son, Uday.

PERFORMING SOCIAL IDENTITY: NATIONALISM IN SPORTS

When taken to the level of sport, the national ideal is directly associated with the social psychological processes of in-group bonding, identity definition, and ritualized performance—generating both more positive notions of heroic patriotism and more negative connotations of hateful nationalism—as is seen in the social psychology of sport described in chapter 3. Sport becomes an instrument for national prestige, "soft power" in the international system, extension of a realist perspective of the world (Grix 2016). Thus, athletes themselves are patriots, wielding the symbols of the state in pursuit of athletic prowess and expressive of loyalty to the nation and the state.

Historian Earnest Gellner gets at the constructed nature of modern states, which serves as the bedrock of the international state system—giving priority to national identity and power to state sovereigns—and so, too, the historical evolution of international sport. He opined:

Nationalism provides the sole legitimation of states the world over. For most people, nations—especially their own nations—seem perennial and immemorial. We cannot easily imagine a world without nations, nor are we happy with the idea that our nation is a recent creation, or a construct of elites.

The portrayal, and, in many instances such as 1978 in Argentina, internal contestations over sport highlight some of the key linkages between its use for national identity-making purposes and its role as a theater of contestation over such narratives. As an instrument of nation-making, sport serves as platform or stage for extension of national identities, symbols, collective traumas, and narratives of origin, struggle, and core values. For example, sport was used in Communist China to advance "ideological purity," and in contexts such as South Africa during the apartheid period, sport such as Springbok rugby was a form of social expression of white national tenacity and identity as related to, and part of, a broader Christian civilizing movement. That is, sport is deeply involved in creating "imagined communities" (Anderson 1983) of nation in both symbolic and tangible ways.

From international survey research data, Seippel contends that *sport can create "a nationwide romance"* (Seippel 2017): individual, community, national and global processes interact to provide meaning and order in a chaotic world; national identity serves the purposes of constituting and precipitating boundaries and defining identity in a way consistent with the international system of sovereign-state politics that has evolved, mostly unintentionally, over time. The Seippel study tested a number of relationships between sport and nationalism, such as whether higher GDP is associated with lower prevalence of nationalist sentiments (confirmed), and whether sport activity and watching sports supports nationalism (also confirmed). Most important, though, he finds that "sports activate ideas and memories of who we are as citizens of a country" (Seippel 2017, 56).

There are three principal ways in which sport feeds into exclusive conceptualization of nationalism that are offered: using youth-based sport for socialization into ideologies and nationalist mythmaking; performance of the national narrative in the context of sport; and the politics of "organic" nationalism based on exclusive identity-based citizenship. See Concept Box 4.2.

Sport is a tool for early-childhood socialization into regime-oriented worldviews and mindsets consistent with the mission of the ruling political regime and, at times, ideologically driven elites. Sport-based efforts for youth socialization, so widely seen in 1936 Germany were the National Socialist regime that used local sport-oriented youth clubs, or "Turnen," for ideological socialization into the Nazi myth, and was designed to propagate ideological orientations in an effort to ensure the next generation of loyal cadres for the regime; after coming to power, the Nazis banned alternative sport organizations associated with socialists or in church settings to concentrate all youth sport (Krüger 2003).

CONCEPT BOX 4.2. ORGANIC NATIONALISM, CIVIC NATIONALISM, AND NATION-BUILDING

One of the core distinctions in the literature on nationalism is between that of what is described as "organic nationalism" versus "civic nationalism. The first concept of organicism refers to the coincidence of the ethnic idea and some notion of exclusive identity based in common past and kinship ties, or "ethnic nationalism."

In turn, civic nationalism refers to a broader notion and definition of nationalism based on acceptance and adherence to citizenship values. Such differences play out in debates today about populist nationalism versus multicultural nationalism, with quite different implications for what constitutes "social cohesion" and the role of sport in promoting such cohesion (see chapter 12).

Some see the modern Olympic Games, with its history-grounded norms of national recognition, as the basis for perpetuating the former, illiberal, variant of nationalism over the more liberal—rights-based and inclusive—definition of nationalism reflected in the concept of civic nationalism . . . the Olympics is about stimulating "communal passions" (Large 2016).

On the other hand, in many instances in Africa, such as Cameroon, Kenya, Senegal, South Africa, and Zambia, it can be said that sport nationalism has helped the cause of inclusive nation-building in these diverse societies where in each of them there have been key moments of sporting success internationally that have in turn contributed to strong feelings of commonality and social cohesion within. How sport nationalism can contribute to social cohesion is the subject of chapter 8.

Yet such manipulative use of sport for early-childhood socialization into ideologies appears particularly strong, historically, in fascist and communist systems with very clear ideological aims of associating sport with the "purity" of the nation (in the case of fascism) or toward a particular worldview of the messianic role of the state in transforming society to create "socialist man" (and woman) as seen in contexts such as North Korea and Cuba (Lee and Bairner 2016).

Many similar dynamics are found in Russia today, with a clear orientation of the regime to use sport to extend the nationalist mythmaking of empire and historical destiny over Eurasia that is at the heart of nationalist fervor in the post-Communist era (Arnold 2018; Grix and Kamareva 2019). See Case Study 4.1.

CASE STUDY 4.1. SPORT IN THE PUTINESQUE RUSSIAN NATIONAL IMAGINATION (AND A UKRAINIAN RETORT)

As Russian president Vladimir Putin has clearly articulated, sport in Russia features no pretense of being autonomous from the project of the state, or politically neutral. Putin said to the Sochi athletes after the Games:

> You have accomplished the mission assigned to you. . . . The results scored by our national team show that we have left the difficult period in the history of national sports behind us. . . . Any competition where athletes defend the honor of their nation are important and crucial. But the highest responsibility that rested on the shoulders of our national team was that of the highest level: The Games in Sochi were destined to present the new and multi-faceted Russia to the world. (Anishchuck 2014)

By some accounts, domestically, this effort has been successful. Celebrating the victory of OAR Vitalina Basarashkina, who won the first gold medal by a Russian participant at Tokyo 2020 in the women's 25m pistol (she later won another gold and a silver in the 10m pistol, a team event), the Russian military sports-based unit where she trained called the success in Tokyo "the highest form of patriotism" (Shevchencko 2022).

Russian newspaper *Vedemosti* opined that sport is an instrument of the regime to inculcate patriotism, "We need victories as a way of doping patriotism," it wrote, "victories are a part of state policy" (Shevchencko 2022). Ian Garner argues that in the context of the war in Ukraine,

> Thousands of [young] Russians today are participating in [a] public display of hatred and warmongering on the Runet—the Russian-language internet. . . . Ukrainians are attacked as subhuman; the latest government narrative about Western evil is repeated ad nauseum; Putin and Goad are praised for leading Russian into Ukraine to destroy the fascist threat; and dead Russians are lauded as saintly martyrs. (2023b; Garner 2023a)

When rallying Western allies to prevent Russian athletes from appearing in international sport competitions in the run-up to the Paris 2024 Summer Olympic Games, Ukrainian President Zelensky made it clear that even if supporters of political neutrality in sport win the debate and Russians—mostly like, if they appear at all, tennis players—could never be seen within Russia, or beyond the country, as anything other than national icons, patriotic athletes.

"If, God forbid, the Olympic principles are destroyed and Russian athletes are allowed to participate in any competitions or the Olympic Games, it's just a matter of time before the terrorist state forces them to play along with the war propaganda" (AP 2023).

So, too, in China, the patriotic education campaign of the Xi Jinping era has led to a new generation of youthful nationalists in China (Lu 2016)—many of them only-child young men, a product of sex-selection preferences in the context of the erstwhile "one child per family policies"—the most nationalistic of which are known as the "little pinks" (Zhao 2023). The latest generation of nationalists is the product of the *close association between sport nationalism in China and its pursuit of "supremacy" in international relations*. As Lu and Fan observe, the top-to-bottom campaign of the ruling Chinese Communist Party (CCP) through the Chinese sports ministry since 1966 has been a deliberate, strategic approach to creating "sports heroes" to further political ends (Lu and Fan 2019).

China's state operates a series of training camps designed to create a pipeline of nationalistic future gold medalists in international sports, with a specific target on specific sports such as trampoline where Chinese athletes are expected by the regime to be particularly competitive (*Economist* 2016). Among the various Chinese athletes who have displayed deep nationalistic sentiments, the Chinese female national volleyball team stands out; patriotic press in China lionizes the "Chinese Female Volleyball Spirit" which is also linked in the public's mind to Confucian values of social virtue (Chen and Zhang 2023).

Sport is intricately associated with national identity and the performing of national identity narratives, symbols, and imagined-community mythmaking. The role of sport in nation-building and overarching loyalties to the state and creating and extending national identity. As Carlos Less observes, the Brazilian experience is one in which culture and sport are intricately related to the national narrative and national ideals: "The passion for football, the sport that socializes Brazilian childhood, creates national heroes," he writes, "the star player reaps unlimited warmth and admiration beyond that reserved for even the founding fathers of the nation" (Lessa 2008: 251). See Case Study 4.2.

The politics of citizenship. The row between Noah and Araud described in Case Study 4.3 underscores, like in the ancient Olympic Games, national

CASE STUDY 4.2. WHOSE SYMBOL, WHOSE BRAZIL? THE YELLOW-AND-GREEN *CANARINHO*

In Brazil, the ubiquity of the country's national football jersey is both a symbol of sport nationalism, begun in 1958 and led by subsequent national icon Pelé in leading the country to its first World Cup win over host country, Sweden 3–1. Yet in Brazil the national jersey, and the myth and meaning it implies, has become a politicized symbol as representing populist nationalism in the country; in the nationalistic protests following the defeat of the populist president Jair Bolsonaro in 2022, the outfit of choice was the ubiquitous yellow-and-green shirt and attire, the shirt of the *canarinho* (nickname for the Brazilian national football team, which is also used to refer to the jersey).

Following the postelection protests, the Brazilian Football Federation (CBF) condemned the use of the *canarinho* symbols in the far-right protests. "The Brazilian national team shirt is a symbol of the joy of our people," the CBF admonished, "We encourage that shirt to be used to unite and not divide Brazilians" (Firstpost 2023).

identity is contested in sport through the politics of citizenship . . . a seemingly enduring issue at the nexus between sport and nationalism. As in the case of the French 2018 World Cup team, global migration has undermined traditional notions of nation-states; today, like France, most countries are multiethnic and citizens such as Paul Pogba may well have multiple identities. Research by the Migration Policy Institute, presented in Figure 4.1, documents that, in fact, foreign-born athletes are common in World Cup competition, relatively steady historically, and the notion that national teams represent ethnic or racial identities has always been a myth. See Case Study 4.3.

What is less documented, but nonetheless significant, is the extent to which *political elites have social-network or patronage influence* in national sport organizations. One study showed that one in seven, or some 25 percent, of NOCs are linked directly to governments and their ruling elites, including one in three in Asia (Around the Rings 2021). In countries such as Azerbaijan and Belarus, the head of state is also the president of the NOC. As Bainer, Kelly, and Lee argue, "The myth of sport's autonomy has been so widely and successfully promoted as to effectively block attempts by all but the most tenacious to set it within a broader socio-political context" (2016, 2).

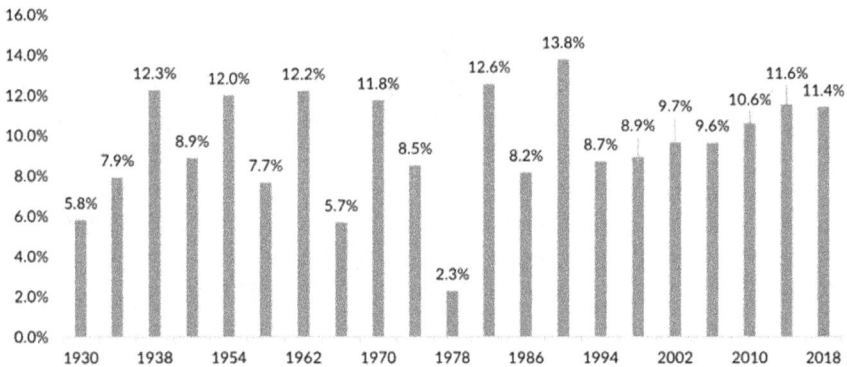

Figure 4.1. Foreign-Born Athletes in the World Cup. Credit: Originally published by the Migration Policy Institute in Gijsbert Oonk, "Who Represents the Country? A Short History of Foreign-Born Athletes in the World Cup," Migration Information. November 17, 2022, https://www.migrationpolicy.org/article/international-athletesworld-cup -nationality. Reprinted with permission.

CASE STUDY 4.3. WHO REPRESENTS WHOM? CITIZENSHIP AND IDENTITY AT THE 2018 WORLD CUP

When France won the 2018 World Cup in Moscow, comedian and television personality Trevor Noah, a South African, joked in a monologue on his program, *The Daily Show*: "Africa won the World Cup! Africa won the World Cup!," pointing out that the lion's share of athletes on the tournament-winning French squad (some 80 percent) had origins in Africa.

Paul Pogba, who scored the final goal for France sealing the World Cup victory, is a first-generation Frenchman whose parents are from Guinea (BBC 2018).

Yet the French Ambassador to Washington, Gérard Araud, rebuked Noah, arguing "They were educated in France, they learned to play soccer in France, and they are French citizens. They are proud of their country, France" (BBC 2018).

In 1984, sprinter Zola Budd competed for the UK, but she had been raised and trained in South Africa and was able to evade—with the participation of conservative Prime Minister Margaret Thatcher's government—the sport and cultural boycott over apartheid in the country to compete at the Los Angeles Summer Olympic Games (Llewellyn and Rider 2018). Her appearance ended traumatically, however, as she and US sprinter Mary Decker tripped or tangled (the incident was controversial), and both fell with three laps left in the 3,000 m final in Los Angeles in one of the modern Olympics' most iconic moments involving athlete citizenship.

Yet such toxic views of nationalism as essentially ethnic in nature persist, and persist strongly, in international sport. Nationalism in China, pursued vigorously by the CCP regime, unleased a new controversy in sport over an athlete's citizenship. See Case Study 4.4.

CASE STUDY 4.4. NATIONALISTIC NETIZENS: TOXIC FANS AT THE BEIJING WINTER 2022 GAMES

During the Beijing 2022 Winter Olympic Games, the political scientist Suisheng Zhao, an eminent scholar of Chinese politics and society, commented on the nexus between toxic nationalism and misbehaving Chinese netizens during the glorified events. He observes,

For the Chinese domestic audience, one of the exciting focuses of the Games was the unprecedented number of foreign-born athletes who were competing for China. For decades, China's best and brightest had flocked to the US to pursue the American dream. Now the Chinese public was pleased to see some American-born athletes choosing to represent China in the Games, a resounding affirmation of China's rising power.

Freestyle skier Eileen Gu, who was born and raised in California, won two golds and one silver for China, and she was instantly embraced as a national darling and the pride of China. This reveals China's power to attract foreign talent and is emblematic of a perceived victory over America.

In contrast to the Eileen Gu craze, figure skater Zhu Yi, another American-born athlete who opted to compete on behalf of China but faltered on the ice during two consecutive competitions, was criticized for not being "Chinese" enough, a disgrace and embarrassment who brought shame upon the country. The hashtag "Zhu Yi has fallen" gained 200 million views by Chinese netizens in just a few hours. The authorities had to censor these comments to present a more hospitable face as the Olympic host.

Chinese netizens also expressed hatred and scorn of figure skater Nathan Chen who won a gold for Team USA. Chen was called a "traitor" and accused of "insulting China" due to an interview several months earlier in which he appeared to have backed American ice dancer Evan Bates' criticism of China's human rights record. . . . In this context, one commentator found that "There's a tight connection between sports and nationalism in many countries, but in China, it has reached very high levels. . . . Their success is the nation's success, their failure is the nation's failure." (Zhao 2023, 4)

Figure 4.2 is but one of the iconic moments of the setting of the freestyle competition in a former industrial area of Beijing on a sportscape of wholly artificial slopes and snow.

In Turkey, the consolidation of power by the regime of President Tayyip Erdoğan has been aided by the creation and capture of a parallel system of football clubs, ones that can be reliable in extending the aims and purposes of the ruling regime throughout the country to the community level; when some Turkish football clubs participated in protests against the regime, the

Figure 4.2. Grabbing for Gold: Freestyle Skier Eileen Gu, Representing China, at Beijing 2022. Freestyle Skier Eileen Gu, who chose to represent China, wins the Gold Medal in freestyle skiing with impressive mid-flight grabs at the Beijing Winter 2022 Olympic Games. Credit: © David G. McIntyre/ZUMA Press Wire (Cal Sport Media via AP Images)

government moved to supress the discontent by football through various measures (such as controlling ticketing, and heavy policing) and backed two pro-regime teams (Irak 2020).

SPORT DIPLOMACY: "SOFT POWER" IN A HARD WORLD

Sport diplomacy is used by global, regional, and "humanitarian" powers in asserting influence within other countries, sometimes with a purposeful focus on *furthering cultural ties amid economic interdependencies* or in *the diffusion of norms or values*. In international relations terminology, sport is a form of "soft power" tools by states, or cultural diplomacy. In theory, soft power can be either benign—genuine efforts to share and disseminate wholesome cultural values across national differences—or malignant, i.e., used in a "traditional realist" foreign policy where the sport is part of the projection of state-based power for security in a dangerous, anarchic world. Hosting global mega-events as a means of attraction for public diplomacy—reaching the hearts and minds of publics around the world—is perhaps today's most common form of such soft-power project in international sports (Grix 2015; Grix, Brannagan, and Less 2019).

Scholars Håvard Nygård and Scott Gates have developed a framework of sport as sport-power diplomacy as a tool of states in the international system, homing in on the mechanisms by which such activities are linked to core national-interest outcome of states and in light of the wide range of forms that sport diplomacy can take (exchanges, mega-event hosting, tournament sponsorship). They argue that sport diplomacy is used to these ends.

- *Image-building,* or "investing in political capital" as a form of enhancing prestige in the international community (Nygård and Gates 2013: 239). They cite examples such as the BRICS hosting of mega-events as a means of reflecting rising-power status. Moreover, they note that such image-building approaches can backfire if international attention is brought to issues of human rights abuses or the autocratic nature of regimes.
- *Trust-building* efforts are those where sport is used to reach across boundaries in contexts where countries may be former enemies, for example the role of that baseball exchanges played in post–World II relations between the United States and Japan, or between the United States and Cuba during the Cold War. Like image-building efforts, these can also go wrong as scholars Caruso and di Domizio (2013: 262–73) find in their analysis of European Championships and World Cup football

that hostility between countries can be as easily reflected in the sporting arena and undermine the aims of sport exchanges.

• *Reconciliation, integration, and anti-racism* goals are those where sport diplomacy is used explicitly to address prior conflict dynamics and to further goals of sport's contribution to human rights and nondiscrimination. For example, while South Africa was sanctioned by global sport bodies for its racist policies during apartheid, following the transition to democracy in the 1990s the country was chosen to host the 2010 FIFA World Cup to celebrate the transition's success.

Many find the origins of contemporary practices of cultural diplomacy to the exchanges in sport following the "opening" to China by the United States in the early 1970s, a well-analyzed series of events in international relations known as "Ping-Pong diplomacy." The moniker is well-earned, as the sport exchanges were conceived by then-Chinese premier Mao Zedong who was himself fond of the sport. The exchanges between China and the United States were highly symbolic of the resetting of relations between the Communist regime and the United States in the Cold War and presaged the now much deeper economic and cultural ties between the countries even as geopolitical rivalry between them persists. The China-U.S. case is one of the best known overall positive examples of sport diplomacy in international relations scholarship (Kobierecki 2016), although many of the athletes involved faced cruel consequences and the Ping-Pong diplomacy effort was deeply related to the regime's propaganda messaging (Xu 2008). See Case Study 4.5.

Sport diplomacy has been used in a myriad of contexts as a confidence-building measure in enduring international rivalries. Scholars of international relations have long focused on dyadic disputes in the international system, often driven by deep histories, prior wars and conflicts of origin and territory, and often in contexts such as North and South Korea (or, historically, East and West Germany) where the protagonists are very intimate enemies which have or may in future share a common country together.

Enduring international rivalries are associated with intractable conflicts: militarized territorial disputes, such as between India and Pakistan over Jammu and Kashmir; arms races, as was common in the Cold War and is still a feature of US-Russia rivalry today; long-term dynamics, where stability and equilibrium mean that rivalries run deep historically, and memories of the past conflicts set up the next; and intensely nationalistic publics who put pressure on political elites to further rivalry and inhibit space for dialogue. International rivalries can be deadly, as in the infamous "soccer war" between El Salvador and Honduras in which rioting erupted during a FIFA World Cup qualifier match in 1970. The match and riot was the precipitating event for what is also known as the "Hundred Hours War" between the international

CASE STUDY 4.5 MILITARY-TO-MILITARY
SPORT, THE CISM: WAR WITHOUT WEAPONS?

The close association of sport with military training, as well as with the associated values of discipline, bravery, and risk-taking, is found in deepest history. Ancient Rome featured more wrestling, boxing, and javelin in contrast to the ancient Greek preferences for footraces and discus (Christesen and Stocking 2022). In modern times, in World War I the bicycle played a pivotal role as a new technology of warfare, and two-wheelers were used to provide rapid-reaction troops, tow small artillery, and in field communications (see the online exhibit on bicycles at the World War I history museum, https://www.theworldwar .org/learn/about-wwi/spotlight-bicycle-battalions).

Today, military sport diplomacy is widespread, and many events are organized through the International Military Sports Council (CISM). The organization's "green paper" sets out the goals of sport diplomacy among the militaries of the world, principally to foster "mutual respect, solidarity and Promoting [sic] peace" (See the CISM site at https:// www.milsport.one/cism/what-is-cism.)

Founded in the wake of World War II, the organization today hosts the CISM military summer and winter games, cadet games, and a football cup and features a parasport division. In 2023, for example, it organized an event that brought military participants to Damavand Mountain in Iran for games involving mountaineering members of the military from Armenia, Iran, Iraq, Russia, Oman, and Pakistan together for a "Climbing for Peace" event (CISM 2023). Among the partners of the CISM is the IOC.

foes with much deeper economic and citizenship disputes that went well beyond football and was based in local dynamics of resource scarcity and the pursuit of collective survival (Durham 1979). See Case Study 4.6.

As the sole bidder and likely host for the 2034 FIFA World Cup, the controversial soft-power projection by Saudi Arabia in sport is clear foreign-policy calculus: "Saudi Crown Prince Mohammed bin Salman said in response to human-rights based criticism of his regime, 'If sportswashing (is) going to increase my GDP by 1%, then we'll continue doing sportswashing'" (Reuters 2023).

Among the other most engaging instances of soft-power diplomacy in sport, these examples show that the use of soft-power diplomacy is a seemingly

CASE STUDY 4.6. A STRATEGIC VISION: SPORT IN SAUDI ARABIA'S DOMESTIC AND FOREIGN POLICY

Saudi Arabia has an annual GDP of $1.1 trillion (https://data.worldbank .org/country/SA). So, the investment of the country-supported SRJ Investments of $100 million from the Professional Fighter's League (PFL) MMA organization was a modest one, given the country's extensive dedication to sport-based diplomacy globally through financial ownership of major sport organizations.

While the PFL is small in comparison to the principal MMA organization, the Ultimate Fighting Championship (UFC), the 2023 purchase by the Saudi-backed organization is yet another example of the extent to which the wealthy Gulf State country has incorporated sport into its foreign and domestic policies (Anderson 2023). It recruited football icon Cristiano Ronaldo for $200 million a year to play in its soccer league and bought an 80 percent stake in the UK football club Newcastle United. It invested an initial $2.5 billion in LIV Tour, a rival to the long-standing Professional Golfers Association (PGA), a move which subsequently garnered investigation by U.S. authorities with concerns over foreign financial influences.

Saudi Arabia's "Vision 2030," however, is a broad social vision for sport in efforts to diversify the country from the source of its vast wealth: oil. Among the elements of this wide-ranging program to transform the country's external image, and modernize its society inwardly, is a comprehensive policy on sport (Leveille 2023). Among the other features of the program: a goal to host the Olympic Games (Brennan 2022).

Saudi Arabia has been widely criticized for human rights abuses and for its role abetting the war in Yemen by Human Rights Watch in its 2023 World Report (Human Rights Watch 2023).

common feature of enduring international rivalries. Three examples reflect contemporary sport-related, soft-power efforts in global geopolitical rivalries.

- Sport diplomacy between *the two Koreas—North and South*, divided in the wake of war in the 1950s—was best exemplified in the joint women's hockey team fielded for the 2018 Pyeongchang Winter Olympic Games, which was rationalized and related to the Olympic Truce for that event. Following extensive negotiation, the two sides marched together under a unified Korean flag in the opening ceremonies, and the two countries contended in the women's hockey tournament as a single team (with a Danish coach). Despite a long history of sport diplomacy across the divided peninsula, the two Koreas—except for the potentially effective use of the 2018 truce for bilateral peacebuilding—remain stuck in a frozen conflict with ongoing risks of escalation and continued pursuit by North Korea to develop intercontinental nuclear missile capabilities (Park, Koo, and Kim 2021).

- Having fought three wars and with continued conflict along their disputed border, *India-Pakistan* sport diplomacy, too, reflects that despite a myriad of efforts—notably, in cricket, field hockey, and tennis—sport-based efforts at peacebuilding have not been able to address the underlying geopolitical tensions between the South Asia rivals. Since 1952, the countries have turned to sport diplomacy to ease tensions following their very violent partition in 1948, having met more than 200 times in various efforts over the years. In 2010 tennis Pakistani Aisam-Ul-Huq Qureshi and Rohan Bopanna of India teamed up as a doubles pair—nicknamed the "Indo-Pak Express." They did well, reaching the finals of the Grand Slam U.S. Open. Qureshi remarked after the finals (which they lost to American twins Mike and Bob Bryan), "It was great to see all the India supporters, most of them wearing Pakistani flags on their faces and cheering for the same team . . . that's a moment I will never forget in my life, so many Indians supporting us" (Hurst 2010).

In 2023, a row between the rivals erupted over Pakistan's hosting of the 2023 Asia World Cup when India threatened not to participate unless the venue was moved from Pakistan, citing "political tensions" (Hussein 2023). Following negotiations that placed events in India, Pakistan, and Sri Lanka, the games proceeded and in September India bested Pakistan by 228 runs in Colombo (Al Jazeera 2023b).

- *Australia and China* vie for influence in the Asia-Pacific, with the rivalry playing in countries such as Papua New Guinea (PNG) where the countries vie for economic and security cooperation. In 2018, Chinese President Xi Jinping traveled to the country together with top table-tennis stars to a Chinese-funded new sport facility for the sport in Port Moresby; PNG is the largest creditor to China in the South Pacific with a nearly $590 million debt at the time stemming largely from infrastructure projects including stadiums (Reuters 2018).

Australia has used rugby-, cricket-, and netball- centered sport diplomacy in PNG though the PacificAus Sports program, a broader sports diplomacy initiative of Australia. Australian indigenous cricket teams toured PNG (and Vanuatu) in 2022 with the explicit secondary outcome of promoting empowerment of women and girls (Reuters 2022). Australia has also developed extensive rugby ties in PNG through the program Get Into Rugby PLUS, an initiative that includes a focus on participant life skills, gender equality, and gender-based violence prevention (Mills 2023).

Sport diplomacy is today a common and oft preferred tool of national branding and global cultural imaging making, typically to reflect them as

DOCUMENTARY INSIGHTS 4.1. BITTERNESS BEYOND THE BORDER: *GRINGOS AT THE GATE* (2012) AND *GOOD RIVALS* (2022)

The United States and Mexico share a 3,145-km (1,954-mile) border, are each other's top trading partners, and have one of the deepest and longest soccer rivalries in sports. While the United States has been historically more powerful, wresting territory from Mexico in wars of the mid-19th century, Mexico has historically been dominant in soccer. Over more than 70 years the soccer rivalry has played out, with the overall theme of pursuit by the United States of respect in soccer in contrast to the more capable Mexican squads (with soccer having been much more popular in Mexico than the United States). Between 1935 and 1980, the United States beat Mexico once.

The U.S.–Mexican rivalry is compounded by the potential for dual loyalties of the nearly 20 percent of U.S. citizens who are of Mexican heritage, dual nationalities, and adjacent cities along the border such as San Diego and Tijuana. Many of the most enduring themes in international sport, nationalism, citizenship, representation, family and identity, women's and LGBTQ representation and rights, and fandom are found in the fascinating history of the rivalry (Kassing and Meân 2017).

Does the U.S.-Mexico rivalry contribute to, or make worse, relations between Mexico and the United States?

The 2012 documentary *Gringos at the Gate* (https://www.imdb.com /title/tt2057954/) and the 2022 docuseries *Good Rivals: The Game is Only Half the Story* (https://www.imdb.com/title/tt23271056/) explore the history, meaning, and implications for social cohesion between borders of this iconic football rivalry.

modern, dynamic, youthful, attractive destinations for tourism, foreign direct investment, and diplomatic capital for participating in global regimes related to these economic interests (Dichter 2022, Kobierecki 2017). The case of the FIFA World Cup in Qatar is returned to in the next chapter. Most poignantly, though, with events such as Russia's 2018 World Cup to dual football and Olympic and Paralympic events in Rio (2014 and 2016), the South Africa 2010 World Cup, the dual winter and summer Olympics in Beijing (2008 and 2014), the use of sport-hosting for prestige-signaling and power projection has been a systematic tool of the "rising-power" BRICS configuration of countries (Brazil, Russia, India, China, and South Africa). See Documentary Insights 4.1.

In Western Europe, countries such as Germany, Norway, and Switzerland have positioned their foreign policies strongly toward sport as a central element in cultural diplomacy; sport is a well-integrated dimension of foreign policy for each of these three liberal internationalist countries. Germany's sport diplomacy includes, for example, long-standing and substantial support for the International Paralympic Committee and development assistance for sport and peacebuilding through its aid agency GiZ and funding for sport-based programs for social inclusion and development within Germany.[1] Norway's detailed, articulated sports diplomacy strategy is directly linked to supporting the global SDP community of practice and in using sports instrumentally for peacebuilding; its strategy document features 32 references to peace or peacebuilding (Norwegian Ministry of Foreign Affairs 2005).

We'll return to donor-funded initiatives for purposes such as peacebuilding in chapter 8.

IMPLICATIONS: SPORT, A POLITICAL INSTRUMENT

Into the 21st century, the international regime of sport is caught between its own aspirational philosophy and the stark reality of the manipulation of sport by ruling regimes for both domestic and foreign policy purposes. Within countries, sport is wrapped up in symbolism and mythmaking and associated with national identity; internationally, the authoritative institutions of global sports are vested in the hands of a wholly nongovernmental regime whose legitimacy and practice is widely popular, yet deeply contradictory. Thus, the Olympic Games may seek to reflect a global universality of sport, the reality is one of a confused and contradictory global regime, the very history and structure of which inhibits its ability to contribute significantly to international peace, as is once again apparent in the Ukraine crisis of 2022–2023.

The goal of "running sport and politics separately," as the passionate IPC and its president, Andrew Parsons, aspired to do after Beijing 2022 (see chapter 1), is elusive. Power is not just confined to states, but athletes, and outsiders—seeking to advance their own narratives about national recognition and human rights, such as the terror attack on the 1972 Munich Olympic Games—have shown an ability to wield nationalistic political power in sport.

What we learn from the politicization of sport is what for many years autocrats, nationalists, and policymakers around the world have realized; there is inherent power of mass human emotions through sport. The question going forward is not just how to tame the harmful manipulation of sport by power-wielding elites, but how to flip the power narrative toward reimagining and reforming how such power is put to social development aims, those of advancing human rights, extending inclusivity in development, eradicating extreme poverty, and purposefully orienting sport more directly toward the cause of peace.

QUESTIONS FOR CONSIDERATION

- What is the role of nationalism in contemporary sport, for example the controversial Beijing 2008 Olympic summer and 2022 Winter games, and the debate it has generated on China's human rights record, the environment, engagement with the Chinese Communist Party regime, and the integrity of host city bid process?
- How do emerging powers in the international system (such as Brazil, India, and South Africa) use sport to reflect their regional and growing global clout in the international system?

FOR FURTHER INFORMATION

Among the top scholarly journals on the topics of power and national identity in sport is *The International Journal of the History of Sport*, *International Journal of Sport Policy and Policies*, and the *Journal of Sport and Social Issues.*

Readers, practitioners, and participants in sport diplomacy will find comprehensive coverage of the field in Murray (2018) which examines the origins of traditional sport diplomacy and points to new approaches and practices by governments and by nongovernmental organizations to sports-related exchanges.

The Center on Public Diplomacy, University of Southern California, offers a news hub on a wide range of sports-diplomacy initiatives at https:// uscpublicdiplomacy.org/story/sports-diplomacy-z.

NOTE

1. The internal funding is provided though the Federal Ministry of the Interior and Community; see https://www.bmi.bund.de/EN/topics/sport/sport-funding/sport-funding-node.html.

Chapter 5

The Olympic Games

Swimming in the Currents of History

CHAPTER OVERVIEW

The Olympic Games are held under the aegis of the arguably most powerful sport organization globally: the International Olympic Committee (IOC) and the associated "Olympic Movement"—all who aspire to the belief systems articulated in the Olympic Charter—has evolved to become unique, and uniquely powerful event, brand, and symbol in international sport.

The evolution of the Olympic Games from a late-19th-century spectacle and association with fleeting modernist cultural trends of the day to the present-day biggest-brand set of global institutions and practices is a unique story in modern history. The Olympics evolved from a committee of a few "humanist-oriented" bourgeois European men into a transnational entity of an unparalleled brand of cultural legitimacy, access, and participation in the international arena. With that, the Olympics has also become a unique tool of political elites and of corporate interests, and a powerful interest-broker in international politics.

The chapter explores these themes through the lens of "secular religion." It evaluates the Cold War period, the post–Cold War period (early 2000s), and the present, looking beyond the most-recent Games in Beijing toward Paris 2024, Milan-Cortina 2026, and Los Angeles 2028.

In what ways have the Olympics evolved commensurate with fundamental changes in the international system through world wars, the Cold War, and into the turbulent 21st century?

CHAPTER HIGHLIGHTS

- The Olympic Games and Movement are guided by an ideology: *Olympism*, derived from humanism. The value orientation of Olympism informs the perspective that international sport is replete with symbolism of this philosophy, with the expressed intent of being a "secular religion."
- The early Olympic Games might have reflected as much of a circus as what might be thought of as today's highly quantified, organized, and choreographed sport event. What they share in common is the notion of a *spectacle*: such symbol-mongering and public spectacle nature of the Olympics was harnessed for ill in the never-far-from-sport-history-memory of the Berlin 1936 Olympic Games.
- As the world recovered from the horrors of the World War II, so, too, the Olympics in the 20th century were reborn and further evolved into wider participation, not least of which was the entry of the Soviet Union and its allies and the reflection of the bipolar Cold War between the USSR and the United States . . . played out poignantly in the Olympic arenas for some 40 years.
- These hopes for an Olympics-coming-of-age in the 21st century, too, have been dashed on the rocks with continued geopolitical trends such as the rise of illiberal China as a global sport power, the "war on terrorism" in the wake of the September 11, 2001 jihadist attacks on the United States, and—more than any other factor—the blatant capture and manipulation of sport by autocratic Russia in its state-sponsored doping and Olympic Truce–breaking 2022 attack on Ukraine.

OLYMPISM: PEACE, MOSTLY SYMBOLIC

To understand contemporary international sport, especially in the Olympic Games, which purports to be the supreme authority of organized sports globally, this chapter explains the value system that underlies global sports. This value system repeatedly crashes upon the realities of global power politics and political capture for nationalist purposes. A good starting point is a look at the origins and evolution of the contemporary Olympic movement, the Olympic Games, and the beginning of the IOC. The revival of the ancient Olympic Games occured during a height of nationalist fervor in Europe in the late 18th century as a modern, nation-state-centered phenomenon. What are the rights-based ideology of Olympism that tends to get sacrificed on the altar of power politics, capture, and corruption?

Olympism is the secular religion of international sport: an ideology that stems from the philosophical tradition of "humanism"—which presupposes humanity's essential potential—and which is institutionalized in the value codification, symbols, rituals, and performative aspects of international sports. As articulated by the IOC, the official dogma of Olympism:

> Olympism is a philosophy of life, exalting and combining in a balanced whole the qualities of body, will and mind. Blending sport with culture and education, Olympism seeks to create a way of life based on the joy found in effort, the educational value of good example and respect for universal fundamental ethical principles.
>
> The goal of the Olympic Movement is to contribute to building a peaceful and better world by educating youth through sport practiced without discrimination of any kind and in the Olympic spirit, which requires mutual understanding with a spirit of friendship, solidarity, and fair play.[1]

Olympism is a potentially all-encompassing ideology or worldview, consistent with and interacting with global religious traditions. Like other religions, and the concept of sport itself, the ideology of sport is a social construction of symbols, narratives, and rituals all working toward the advancement of a value structure grounded in the Great Sport Myth that associates sport with purity and goodness (Coakley 2015).

In a philosophically oriented book released in the run-up to the Sydney 2000 Olympic Games, historian William J. Baker asks the question: What if a sentient, pious, and ultimately moral individual—say, Jesus Christ—were to appear at a modern Olympiad on earth? The book, *If Christ Came to the Olympics* is such an exercise in imagination into the fundamental philosophical underpinnings of the Olympic ideas and the unfolding of ritualized celebrations of the "springtime of humanity" that the Games seek to metaphorically represent. In weaving this metaphor, Baker presents an important insight that informs the mythmaking and meaning making of the Olympic Games. Through ritual, symbols, and icons the Olympic Games presents itself as a secular religion; what would a "cosmic" Christ (or an idealized image, not the historical man) make of the rituals, performances, and emotions that surround Olympic sports?

It's a good question, as answering this question is critical to understanding theories of political symbolism, which further articulate this perspective of the foundation of international sports as situated within an ideological context that is at once progressive—directly liking sport to dignity and human rights, and thus to development and peace—while at the same time inhibiting those values to be realized. The Olympics has historically struggled, unsuccessfully, to free itself from international politics and rest solely on its ostensibly overarching, apolitical ideology of Olympism. See Concept Box 5.1.

As is described more fully in chapter 6, women's participation in sport expanded commensurate with the suffrage movement for women's rights in the interwar period and only expanded fully in the post–World War II era driven in part by the widespread appearance of women athletes from the Soviet Union and allies such as East Germany. The first openly transgender athlete appeared in the Olympic Games at Tokyo 2020, 43-year-old Laurel Hubbard, a trans woman weight lifter in the 87-kg class from New Zealand; her participation was enabled following an IOC rule change in 2015 if medical tests showed testosterone—which builds muscle mass—was below a defined maximum (BBC 2021a).

Avery Brundage, former IOC president (1952–1972), articulated Olympism clearly in secular religious terms. [The Olympic Games] are "a religion, with universal appeal which incorporates the values of other basic religions." Yet Brundage himself has been seen as antisemitic, racist, and sexist, having earned the nickname "Slavery Avery" in the late 1960s given his stance on issues such as the revocation of Muhammad's Ali's boxing medal from 1960 and his unwillingness to back bans on participation by white-minority

CONCEPT BOX 5.1. HUMANISM: THE PHILOSOPHY OF INTERNATIONAL SPORTS

Humanism, on which Olympism is based, is a philosophical orientation that is fundamentally about human agency, or ability and potential, and which in romantic elements sees an inspiration ideal in the human condition. Typically, humanist movements are secular and have a nonreligious orientation—science, reason, ingenuity replace God-centered values—and are ostensibly thus focused on a universality in human nature. Through progressive thinking, humanism forms the basis for human rights, and it is accurate to describe humanism as applied to Olympism as the philosophical foundation of the belief system.

One of the logical extensions of humanist thinking is toward gender equality and the rights of LGBTQ persons, and it is through organized sports that many gender, and more recently historically, gay and transgender rights have been expressed.

states Rhodesia and South Africa. In 2020, Brundage's bust was removed from display at the Museum of Asian Art in San Francisco (Zirin and Boykoff 2020).

Baker argues artfully that the origins of the Olympic games are deeply, inexorably grounded in notions of religion, and that this religiously inspired ethos presents sport as associated with higher-order values, including that of reifying—making something concrete and actual that is notional or ethereal—Olympism norms, rituals, and practices. And the history of the Olympic Games is replete with symbolism, meaning making, and ideological orientations that undermine the aspirations to advance human rights.

Table 5.1 presents an overview of some of the principal norms, rituals, and symbols of the Olympic Games, the Paralympic Games, and those that are in form or in essence. The function of the symbol is presented—that is, what purpose for the propagation of the Olympic faith it may serve—together with how the symbol contributes to representation and meaning making in these leading international sport symbols. These symbols and ritual designs, for the most part, were designed initially by Coubertin in the early days of the IOC to woo the young men of France and Europe to the games—to instill devotion—and to give the games a spectacle that would animate their overall purpose as cultural events beyond sport-as-such.

At the outset, Coubertin designed the Olympic Games to be competitive and elitist, in pursuit of the energetic physical and mental limits of the human condition, and understood that through mass participation in sport those most capable would emerge and those with the most exceptional capabilities— today, we might call it "talent"—emerge to wear the ceremonial wreaths of laurel placed on the victors in the ancient games (Krüger1995, 5). As Cara and Mauritzen (2015) have observed in their analysis of the semiotics of Rio 2016 symbols and logos, which sought to reflect "collectiveness, harmony and participation, without gender, social status, or hierarchy," Olympic symbols, rituals, and nonverbal representations "are iconic nonverbal cues that carry a strong relationship with the Games and their meaning-making processes."

Commensurate with the role of ritual in many religious traditions, steeped in metaphors, meaning, and grounded in myth are the spectacle-like ceremonies that are part and parcel of the Olympic Games. The opening ceremonies are carefully scripted to reflect the historical mythmaking and value orientation—typically, as chapter 4 described, according to the dominant narrative of ruling social systems and political regime—and reaffirm both the origin myth and the norm of national recognition in the parade of nationally designated, costumed athletes, flags and pomp and circumstances.

Table 5.1. Norms, Rituals, and Symbols of the Olympic and Paralympic Games

Symbol	Function	Meaning Making
Olympic Games		
The Olympic Charter	The Olympic Charter, original norm of the Games frames preambular values and defines authority and role relationships in the Olympic Movement.	Provides a putative constitutional foundation for the Olympic Games as the "supreme authority" in international sports. Authority does not derive directly from international law, treaty, or delegated authority.
The Motto, *Citius, Altius, Fortius*	Motivating ideology to frame the fixation on unending pursuit of the human-condition frontier.	Related to humanistic views of progression capacities of the human condition; doesn't relate to risk in sport.
The Rings	The master symbol of the Olympic Games is one of the most guarded copyrights in the world. The rings seek to represent unity—five rings, five continents—amid global diversity; the colors were those found in the flags of the 14 countries at the inaugural games in Athens, 1896.	The rings are the most powerful symbol of bonding and identity-making in the Olympic movement. From flags to marketing to athlete hairstyles and tattoos, the current form of the logo dates to 2010, with seven approved versions. The rings first appeared at the 1920 Antwerp Games.
Paralympic Games		
The Agitos	Derived from the Latin word for movement (think, "agitation"), the Agitos is the symbol of the International Paralympic Movement. With three elements in red, blue, and green in cyclical flow around a center point, the symbol represents "spirit in motion."	The Agitos of the paralympic movement is a powerful symbol of claiming the right to participate, to "move," despite challenges of disability, and the related values of resilience, persistence, and overcoming adversity. As Flindall observes, the Agitos represents a distinct philosophy of "Paralympism," related to Olympism although not specifically named as such in the IPC's Vision, Mission, and Values (Flindall 2020, 79).

Shared Rituals and Symbols

The Olympic Flame and Torch Relay	To attempt to create a direct relationship between mythology by using the sun to light the Olympic torch in the ancient-games site; efforts to provide divine legitimacy to sport and to imply the purity of fire and ritual of lighting transfers to the purity of sport.	The flame first appeared in Amsterdam in 1928. The torch relay, with its invention and design for the Nazi-captured Berlin Games of 1936, has proven a remarkably useful and resilient symbol and process for the Olympic movement. It offers a channel of direct participation in Olympic mythmaking. More than 10,000 participants are expected in the 2024 Paris torch relay process.

As Baker describes in his Christ-at-the-Olympics metaphor and articulation of the "secular religion" perspective on the Olympics:

Christ would recognize ceremonies that are vaguely reminiscent of His own experience, not to mention the preoccupation of His followers through the ages. Olympic humans, processions, liturgies, mythologies, and proclamations resonate with traditional assertions of faith and hope. (2000, 10)

How have the Olympic Games varied with the global *zeitgeist*—or "spirit of the times"—in the roughly 130-year history of the Olympics? While there is a strong literature on the overall evolution of the Olympic Games (Guttman 1992, Tomlinson 2017), and strong historical record and scholarship on each of the various events or Olympiads, in this inquiry there is focus on the evolution and implicit symbolism in the games.

This analysis, too, begins a more concerted look at interactions between global conditions and the evolving Olympic Games over time and to provide a broad overview of how sport has functioned in international politics, and how global political currents, relationships, and issues have affected the Games. The Olympics have evolved into more than a regular celebration and incarnation of Olympism; they have become a recurrent, global-stage cultural event. As Pop argues:

In the information age, sport takes place on the Internet, which liberalizes cultural, artistic, and sporting events, making them instantly accessible worldwide. Such exposure makes the Olympic phenomenon an ideal target for marketing and economic gain. In addition, globalization makes athletic talent cross borders and unite in multinational teams whose performance exceeds the potential of many national ones. (2013: 733)

Onset, stagnation, and spectacle: Early Games, 1896–1916. The *1896 Athens Games* begins the Olympics of the modern era, and, other than some remarkable and notable historical events—such as the victory in the marathon by Spyridon Louis, a Greek, when medals in running went to Americans affiliated with the Boston Athletics Association (BAA); Louis, entering the marbled Olympic stadium in Athens, was joined on the track by hat-waving Crown Prince Constantine. In these games, a British athlete scaled a flagpole and replaced the British Union Jack with the Irish colors in an expression of Irish national identity.

The *1900 Paris Games*, held in conjunction with the Paris World's Fair (Exposition Universelle), symbolized the association of sport with the concept of progress and futurism, together with spectacle and exoticism. While the host country France won the most medals, athletes from 26 countries participated even though at the time athletes did not represent national teams as such; for the first time, athletes from countries such as Colombia, India, and Iran participated.

Similarly, the *1904 Olympic Games* in St. Louis took place in the context of a World's Fair, and the sport events were very much part of a spectacle with a circus-like quality to the events to include "human zoos" and feature exhibitions of indigenous sport in the context of the exhibition's "anthropology days" that reflect notions of colonialist thinking and the "civilizing mission" of Western civilization. The *1908 Summer Games* in London, which also unfolded over many months, saw the first-time teams paraded in opening ceremonies with national flags, which then as now was associated with sovereignty disputes and political prestige gestures: some Finnish athletes refused to march under the Russian flag (Finland was part of Russia then), and the U.S. flag-bearer Martin Sheridan refused to "dip" his country's flag to King Edward, the British monarch.

Stockholm 1912 was the last Olympic Games that allowed for individuals to participate outside of national teams, a practice still in place (with the exception of the Olympic Refugee Team and occasional use by the IOC of neutral-athlete status; see chapter 1). The 1916 Olympic Games were canceled in light of the onset of World War I in 1914; social Darwinistic nationalistic fervor seen in Stockholm boded the Great War that would follow. "If the Olympic Games showed in a social Darwinist way which was the strongest nation that had the least to worry about in the survival of the fittest, the Great War soon took over and replaced mere games by deadline reality," Krüger observes (1999, 11).

The devastation wrought by World War I, together with the influenza pandemic that helped bring it to an end, resulted in a highly constrained set of Games in Antwerp in 1920. And countries such as Germany and its erstwhile Austro-Hungarian and Ottoman allies were banned from competing. In a world of geopolitical flux, with many new countries emerging in the wake of these collapsing empires, the Antwerp Games served to represent peace, saw some of the first global sports heroes emerge such as Finish runner Paavo Nurmi, and a 72-year old Swede, Oscar Schwan, won a gold medal in the "running deer two-shot" shooting event (a record that still stands). In 1924, the Olympic retuned to Paris, France, with expanding participation and new countries such as Ireland participating, and the first games to feature an athletes' village; like earlier Olympiads such as Stockholm, the *1924 Paris Games* also featured art competitions; symbols such as the Olympic motto first were used in the Paris Olympics. The first Winter Games were held in Chamonix, France, in 1924.

In a turbulent world reeling from the effects of the Great Depression, the *1932 Games in Los Angeles* and Winter games in Lake Placid saw declining participation in the Games, and a lack of attention by political elites; then U.S. President Herbert Hoover declined to open the games and did not attend, and there was a decline in the number of countries at the Summer Games over 1928. Sports like field hockey debuted at the games, and sprinter Stanislawa Walasiewicz, who won the 100m event, was later discovered to have been intersex and not eligible under later gender rules of the IOC; women's team gymnastics began as a demonstration event. See Case Study 5.1.

CASE STUDY 5.1. A PINNACLE OF POLITICIZATION: THE 1936 BERLIN GAMES

No Olympiad in modern history is as engrained for its capture of Olympic symbolism for the purposes of nationalism than the *1936 Olympic Games* in Berlin. In 1933, with the National Socialist takeover of Germany—the Games had been awarded to Germany in 1931—there had already been some efforts within the IOC to relocate the Games given the anti-Semitic and racist policies of the Nazi regime, and the Games were allowed to occur in Berlin only after assurances were provided by the German officials that Jewish athletes would be allowed to participate on the German team.

The 1936 Games were staged to symbolically link the purity-of-sport themes to the nefarious ideological orientations of fascism, racism, and the cult of personality surrounding the German Chancellor Adolf Hitler. The dripping symbolism of the fusion between Nazi symbols and propaganda and Olympic symbols is poignantly portrayed in the film *Olympia* by German director Leni Riefenstahl; in the two-part film, the first part is captioned "Festival of the Nation." The virulent nationalism of the 1936 Olympic Games in Berlin accelerated the National Socialist ideology and racist mythmaking, paving the way for the most egregious violation of human rights in history: The Holocaust.

While there are many moments from the 1936 Olympic Games, none are more important than the four gold medals in athletics won by the son of an Alabama sharecropper, African American Jesse Owns, shattering in both a material and symbolic victory the racial-superiority myths of the fascist Nazi regime (Hitler refused to shake his hand).

An ethnic Korean, Sohn Kee-chung, won the Olympic Marathon but since Korea was occupied at the time, he participated for Japan. Betty Robinson, a U.S. sprinter on the gold-medal-winning women's 4x100 m relay event, was once taken to an undertaker, believed dead from a car accident; she wasn't dead, recovered from a coma, spent months in a wheelchair, and took two years relearning to walk. See Tables 5.2 and 5.3.

The IOC allowed the *1938 Winter Games* to be held in Garmisch Partenkirchen even though Germany had invaded Czechoslovakia and was thus a country at war. So, too, the nationalist hysteria at Berlin presaged World War II, and the Olympics were canceled in 1940 and 1944 amid a world at war.

Table 5.2. Summer Olympiads: A Historical Overview

Global Era	Year	Summer Olympiad	Host City and Country	Country Teams Represented	Athletes	Women's Participation
Early Games	1896	I	Athens, Greece	14	311	0
	1900	II	Paris, France	24	1,331	22
	1904	III	St. Louis, United States	26	1,226	6
	1908	IV	London, England	22	2,008	37
	1912	V	Stockholm, Sweden	28	2,406	48
	~1916	VI	Berlin, Germany	CANCELED		
Interwar Games (1918–1945)	1920	VII	Antwerp, Belgium	29	2,626	63
	1924	VIII	Paris, France	44	3,089	135

Global Era	Year	Summer Olympiad	Host City and Country	Country Teams Represented	Athletes	Women's Participation
	1928	IX	Amsterdam, Netherlands	37	1,332	277
	1932	X	Los Angeles, United States	37	1,332	126
	1936	XI	Berlin, Germany	49	3,632	331
	~1940	XII	Tokyo, Japan	CANCELED		
	~1944	XIII	London, England	CANCELED		
Post–World War II, Cold War Games, 1948–1990	1948	XIV	London, England	59	4,104	390
	1952	XV	Helsinki, Finland	69	4,932	519
	1956	XVI	Melbourne, Australia	72	3,314	376
	1960	XVII	Rome, Italy	93	5,338	611
	1964	XVIII	Tokyo, Japan	93	5,151	678
	1968	XIX	Mexico City, Mexico	112	5,516	781
	1972	XX	Munich, Germany	121	7,134	1,059
	1976	XXI	Montreal, Canada	92	6,073	1,260
	1980	XXII	Moscow, Soviet Union	80	5,256	1,115
	1984	XXIII	Los Angeles, United States	140	6,800	1,566
	1988	XXIV	Seoul, South Korea	159	8,453	2,194
Post–Cold War Games, 1990–2000	1992	XXV	Barcelona, Spain	169	9,386	2,704
	1996	XXVI	Atlanta, United States	197	10,339	3,512

Global Era	Year	Summer Olympiad	Host City and Country	Country Teams Represented	Athletes	Women's Participation
21st-Century Olympic Games, 2000–	2000	XXVII	Sydney, Australia	199	10,647	4,096
	2004	XXVII	Athens, Greece	201	10,625	4,329
	2008	XXIX	Beijing, China	204	10,942	4,637
	2012	XXX	London, Great Britain	204*	10,768	4,676
	2016	XXXI	Rio de Janeiro, Brazil	207**	11,238	5,059
	2020	XXXII	Tokyo, Japan	206***	11,420	5,457

*Including an independent Olympic athletes (IOA) team of four participants from the Netherlands Antilles and newly independent South Sudan.

**Including an independent Olympic athlete team of nine drawn from Kuwait as the Kuwaiti NOC had been suspended by the IOC due to government interference. This figure also includes the Olympic Refugee Team (EOR).

***Including the EOR and Russia competing as the ROC following suspension for state-sponsored doping (see chapter 4).

Source: For NOC country teams participating, https://olympics.com/en/olympic-games. For the gender distribution of athletes in Olympiads, see the 2023 IOC Factsheet "Women in the Olympic Movement" (IOC 2023b).

THROUGH WARS HOT AND COLD: THE OLYMPICS IN THE 20TH CENTURY

With the onset of the "post–Cold War" period, the Olympics fully evolved with nearly universal participation of sovereign states globally, and games such as Barcelona 1992 and Atlanta 1996 reflected the optimism of a new world order beyond the stifling geopolitical conflict of the Cold War.

The Olympic Games in the Cold War Era. When the war ended and the Olympics resumed, they were convened in traumatized, rubble-strewn London in 1948. Opened by the wartime monarch and hero, King George, the symbolism of the 1948 games was undeniable: victorious in war, the Olympics would survive the 1936 debacle as an oracle of the new liberal international order. The United Nations had been founded with 50 member states in 1945 in San Francisco, and UNGA adopted the Universal Declaration of Human Rights in 1948.

Table 5.3. Winter Olympiads: A Historical Overview

Global Era	Year	Winter Olympiad	Host City and Country	Countries Represented	Athletes	Women Participants
Interwar Games (1918–1945)	1924	I	Chamonix, France	16	260	11
	1928	II	St. Moritz, Switzerland	25	464	26
	1932	III	Lake Placid, United States	17	252	21
	1936	IV	Garmisch Partenkirchen, Germany	28	646	80
Post–World War II, Cold War Games, 1948–1990	1948	V	St. Moritz, Switzerland	28	669	77
	1952	VI	Oslo, Norway	30	694	109
	1956	VII	Cortina d'Ampezzo, Italy	32	821	134
	1960	VIII	Palisades, Tahoe* California, United States	30	665	144
	1964	IX	Innsbruck, Austria	36	1,091	199
	1968	X	Grenoble, France	37	1,158	211
	1972	XI	Sapporo, Japan	35	1,006	205
	1976	XII	Innsbruck, Austria	37	1,123	231
	1980	XIII	Lake Placid, United States	37	1,072	232
	1984	XIV	Sarajevo, Yugoslavia	49	1,272	274
	1988	XV	Calgary, Canada	57	1,423	301
Post–Cold War Games, 1990–2000	1992	XVI	Albertville, France	64	1,801	488
	1994	XVII	Lillehammer, Norway	67	1,737	522

Global Era	Year	Winter Olympiad	Host City and Country	Countries Represented	Athletes	Women Participants
21st-Century Olympic Games, 2000–	1998	XVIII	Nagano, Japan	72	2,176	787
	2002	XIX	Salt Lake City, United States	77	2,399	866
	2006	XX	Turin, Italy	80	2,508	960
	2010	XXI	Vancouver, Canada.	82	2,566	1,044
	2014	XXII	Sochi, Russia	88	2,780	1,121
	2018	XXIII	Pyeongchang, South Korea	92	2,883	1,169
	2022		Beijing, China	91	2,834	1,267

*This host city in California was renamed Palisades, Tahoe, in 2021 to acknowledge the racist past of the prior name, which is not replicated in this table due to its derogatory nature. The prior name continues to appear on the IOC database.

The 1948 Games were held in a postwar country and city still devastated economically and in collective trauma after the devastating war. Germany and Japan were not invited, and the Soviet Union deferred on participating in the world of bourgeois (upper-class) international sports. Awarded to London in 1939, the *1948 London Olympic Games* were an exercise in triumphalism by the victorious allies. UN Secretary General Trygve Lie of Norway attended the opening ceremonies, as did the then Shah of Iran, Mohammed Reza Pahlavi. The London Games were the first to be broadcast live on television by the BBC.

Reflecting significantly on the evolution of the Olympic Games, and the global spread of Olympism as such, were the *Helsinki Games* in 1952. China's entry into the Games at Helsinki was historically significant as it later evolved to be the second country for which cities have served as the host of both Summer (Beijing 2008) and Winter events (Beijing 2022).[2] The Helsinki Games equally introduced the post–World War II, Cold War era that drove evolution of the Olympics to be the real, not just nominal, pinnacle of international sports, but that also showed how subject they are to politization in the international arena. At Helsinki, the Soviet Union also appeared and won a gold medal in the women's discus, and Germany—war perpetrator now split into two states, West Germany (BRD) and East Germany (DDR)—participated as a unified team. We'll return to sport in the DDR in the following chapter.

In terms of the evolution of the Olympic Games, however, perhaps no period of the 20th century is more important than the Cold War period, when the Games were subject to enduring intrusion of politics into sport and a tool of foreign policy toward those ends. At the same time, the Olympic Games were one of the very few places of interaction—and about the only form of any extensive people-to-people interaction, across the proverbial Iron Curtain that divided East and West.

Although, at the Helsinki Games, Soviet athletes were housed separately from the others. Decisions within the Soviet Union on fielding an Olympic squad at Helsinki are an intrigue of their own, and the decision to participate in the first more inclusive post–World War II games sets the stage for the mass development of sports within the Soviet Union to generate patriot athletes to fight the Cold War.[3]

The Cold War accelerated, as did its spillover into the Olympic Games, in 1956 at the Melbourne Cricket Grounds, the site of the Games. With the Soviet crackdown on the Budapest uprising in the run-up to the Games, conflict among the Eastern bloc athletes turned violent, with the infamous "blood-in-the-water" incident when fighting erupted between angered Hungarian athletes (who were not aware of the crackdown until reaching the Olympics) and Soviet swimmers.[4] Overall, though, the Soviet Union won the lion's share of medals and the Cold War could not have been on more display.

While the *1956 Melbourne Games* offered so many more international political intrigues, including some of the first major boycotts, the Cold War overlay was infused in the competition. Arab states together with allies (Egypt, Iraq, Cambodia, and Lebanon) boycotted the Games over the 1956 Suez Crisis in which the UK and allied forces turned back the seizure of the Suez Canal by Egypt, and the Chinese boycotted over Olympic recognition of Taiwan (Chinese-Taipei).[5] It was at Melbourne that the practice began that Olympiads begin with athletes marching into the stadium by nation, whereas in the closing ceremonies all athletes march into the Olympic stadium together.

The Games of the 1960s, particularly *1960 in Rome* and *1964 in Tokyo*, saw the Games go to bid cities in countries that had perpetrated, and lost, World War II. In this era, issues of Cold War politics continued, including a fifth-straight gold medal win for a collegiate U.S. basketball team that later became stars in the NBA, the remarkable marathon performance by Abebe Bikila, and the first gold medal of newly independent Pakistan in men's field hockey against its arch-rival, India. In Rome, South Africa appeared for the last time in Olympic competition, banned afterward for the pernicious policies of apartheid, only to reenter the Olympic stadium in 1992 after its white-minority government had launched on a process of scrapping discriminatory racial laws, democratization, and the broadening of the franchise to include all persons regardless of race, and the release of political prisoners such as Nelson Mandela, who was later elected president in 1994. See Case Study 5.2.

Bikila's momentous and highly symbolic victory in Rome in 1960 is the historical turning point toward universalization, or full global inclusion, in international sports, with equal rights, recognition, and esteem of all recognized countries and athletes . . . with profound implication for international politics. The first Olympic gold for an African gave meaning to sport's long aspirational association with advancing international peace and securing human rights as a universalist ideology grounded in humanism and romantic aspirations for the human condition. See Figure 5.1.

CASE STUDY 5.2. ABEBE BIKILA: AN ATHLETE AND A SYMBOL

When Shambel (Captain) Abebe Bikila of Ethiopia, running barefoot, leaned into the finish line to win the gold medal in the marathon at the 1960 Rome Olympic Games, his courageous feat forever changed international sports. The son of a humble shepherd, member of the Emperor's guard, and a virtually unknown athlete prior to the Rome marathon, Bikila artfully glided over the cobblestoned streets of Rome's Appian Way to set a World and Olympic record at the time (2:25:16.2), besting the prior record set by the legendary Czech athlete, Emile Zátopek of then Czechoslovakia (now Czechia) who had won three gold medals in the 5,000-meter, 10,000-meter, and marathon at the 1952 Helsinki games.

In the last 1,000 meters of the Rome course, Bikila dug deep to out-sprint then-favorite Moroccan and Soviet athletes to become the first African person to win a gold medal in the Olympic Games, doing so poignantly in the Game's most historically symbolic event: the marathon. Bikila started his kick, or sprint, in the last kilometer of the course as it passed the Obelisk of Axum, a monument plundered from his native Ethiopia by Italy during its occupation by Italy in 1937. Rome, in 1960, hosted the Games as an Italian city, and the world, still reeling from the collective trauma of World War II . . . the Olympic Games were deeply politically symbolic to begin with as a symbol of global reconciliation in the 20th-century world twice shattered by two world wars and the horrific crimes of the Holocaust.

Abebe Bikila was a remarkable individual. As a member of the security detail for the Ethiopian emperor Haile Selassie II, he began running at age 24 with the coaching guidance of Onnie Niskanen, a Swedish trainer of the imperial guard. From these simple rural and military roots, Bikila went on to win Olympic gold in Rome and months later won the "Peace Marathon" behind the Iron Curtain in the then–Eastern Bloc country of Czechoslovakia in 1961. Bikila won again in Tokyo in 1964 (where he competed only 40 days after an appendectomy), setting another record—this time wearing white Puma trainers and socks. Bikila entered the 1968 marathon in Mexico City but injured his leg less than halfway into the race.

Tragically, he was paralyzed following an automobile crash in 1969; the car he was driving had been given to him as a gift by Emperor Selassie for his athletic achievements on the ultimate global stage. Turning tragedy into opportunity, Bikila rehabilitated to become one of the first paralympic athletes with his newfound personal challenges, participating in some of the first organized sporting events for those with disabilities, the 1970 Stoke Mandeville games, where he competed in archery and table tennis. He died in 1973, at the early age of 46, and was given a state funeral in Addis Ababa (Brockman 2006, 75; Judah 2008; *New York Times* 1973).

Bikila's remarkable performance forever changed international sports because it was both a material and symbolic victory. In that moment, Bikila represented much more than himself or his country, Ethiopia; he symbolized an emerging Africa and its long-oppressed colonial peoples; he was an agent of globalization, a "witness to his times." (Violette 2020)

Bikila's symbolic victory and personal resilience accelerated international sport's evolution into a truly universal dimension of global culture beyond its principally Western origins and then mostly European character. In December 1960, just months after the Rome celebrations, the United Nations General Assembly adopted resolution 1514 (XV), the "Declaration on the Granting of Independence to Colonial Peoples": the "rights-based" document that paved the way for an end to colonialism and expansion of rights of participation in the UN and global governance to the newly independent country and citizens.[6] In 1961, Bikila paced to win the "Peace Marathon" in Prague (wearing shoes).

Freed from colonial trappings and on the path toward universal inclusion of all "nations" in the world, could universalism in sport finally contribute to universal peace?

Figure 5.1. Abebe Bikila: Pacing the Czechoslovakia "Peace Marathon," 1961. Abebe Bikila paces the pack into the "Locomotive Stadium" to win the International Peace Marathon in Kosice, Czechoslovakia, October 11, 1961. *Credit: Zuma Press, Inc./Alamy Stock Photo*

The *Tokyo Games of 1964* were equally symbolic in the restoration of the Japanese role in international affairs, following its occupation after World War II and the consolidation of democracy under the MacArthur Constitution (Gajek 2016). The games reflected the Cold War era of bipolarization, but also marked the first games beamed globally (to the United States in this instance) by satellite, and thus could be said to be the first modern Games in terms of globally televised reach. The Soviets continued to demonstrate sporting dominance across a number of disciplines, increasingly in women's gymnastics, and Soviet gymnast Larisa Latynina's 18 medals in a sport stood as an Olympic record until broken by U.S. swimmer Michael Phelps at the Beijing 2008 Olympic Games.

So, too, the *1968 Mexico City Games* saw the rapid evolution of international sport into a modern institution, with a myriad of globally significant political events, some etched forever into Olympic history. Among the globally significant events were the first time that East and West Germany competed separately, the exposure of the deeply authoritarian nature of the Mexican ruling regime under the Institutional Revolutionary Party, or PRI, and an ill-fated effort by the IOC to try and return South Africa to international sport (a move that African, Soviet-allied, and anti-apartheid activists fought to reverse).

The "etched-in-memory forever" moment from 1968, the Black Power salute of U.S. Olympians Tommie Smith and John Carlos, protesting racism in the United States, is returned to in the next chapter. Kip Keino of Kenya won the 10,000m and 1,500m in Mexico City, furthering the era of East African runners as leading in these disciplines. Mexico City's closing ceremonies were the first to be broadcast globally, in color.

The *1972 Munich Games* are forever known for the criminal tragedy that occurred there—when the Israeli wrestling team and coaches were taken hostage, and 11 killed, by the Black September militia championing Palestinian statehood. The very return of the Olympics to Germany in 1972 was a poignant moment: Germany sought to portray itself as a modern, secular, rights-promoting upright citizen in the international order . . . such that security itself was relaxed at the Games. The 1972 Games sought to reflect the détente or relaxation of tensions between the United States and Soviets, even as a controversial incident in the men's basketball gold-medal game featuring the two superpowers will be marked as a moment in which sport made the Cold War worse: the Soviet team won by one point after the referees added time back to the clock (due to a foul on the play), allowing the Soviets to score the winning bucket during the final seconds of the heated game. See Documentary Insights 5.1.

The Games moved to *Montreal in 1976*, remembered mostly as being a case study in how the Games could produce significant losses for the host city, and those in which East German swimmers—who had been coercively doped with anabolic steroids—swept women's swimming, winning gold medals in all but two events; the DDR—at best, a middle-sized country demographically and economically—won the second number of gold medals after the Soviet Union . . . both besting the sports-powerful United States, who came in third.

The Soviet invasion of Afghanistan in 1979 brought a pause in the Olympic Games' evolution, as the United States and Soviet Union engaged in mutual boycotts, together with some allies, such that neither the *Moscow 1980 nor 1984 Los Angeles Games* could fulfill the claims of universalism at the heart of the Olympic Movement. Some 59 allies joined the United States to boycott Moscow, and 13 countries joined the Soviets and did not participate in Los Angeles; in 1984, the United States won an Olympic record of 83 gold medals as the only proverbial superpower at the time present in the Olympic arena. The Lake Placid Winter Olympic Games in 1980 did little other than to further the Cold War, when the United States won the gold medal in hockey; the event, dubbed "Miracle on Ice," has become a moment of triumphalism in a

DOCUMENTARY INSIGHTS 5.1. *ONE DAY IN SEPTEMBER* (1999): LOWEST POINT IN OLYMPIC HISTORY?

One Day in September takes the viewer through one of the most politicized, and historically significant, events in Olympic history: the hostage-taking terrorist attack on the Israelis in the Olympic Village by Palestinian terrorists/freedom fighters.

The intense documentary directed by Kevin MacDonald features original footage of the events, includes interviews with attackers, describes the ineptitude of German political and Olympic sport officials during the event (Olympic officials continued with the sport event after the hostage siege was underway in the Village), and through this low point in Olympic history reveal the complex relationships between the Olympic Games and violent armed conflicts around the world. The attackers chose the Olympic Games for their symbolic value as the "religion" of the West, in the words of one of the terrorists interviewed in the film (https://www.imdb.com/title/tt0230591/).

In 2023, Germany announced an independent panel to probe the 1972 events and to revisit issues of the government's response and culpability in the handling of the crisis, the role of the IOC, and the aftermath by which some of the terrorists were released in a subsequent hostage exchange (AFP 2023). See Case Study 5.3.

Andre Spitzer was one of the Israelis killed in the attack, and a Canadian Broadcasting Corporation docuseries follows his wife's 40-year effort to keep the memory of the Munich attack alive in the docuseries *After Munich* (https://www.cbc.ca/documentarychannel/docs/after-munich).

jingoistic interpretation of the U.S. historical narrative, with some members of the squad later associated with Trumpist populist nationalism.[7]

This period also saw the only Winter games held within the Eastern bloc, the *1984 Winter Games in Sarajevo*; the Olympic facilities from the 1984 Games became infrastructure for armies in the Bosnian civil war (1992–1995) and the bombed-out remains of the erstwhile Olympic celebration are an ongoing monument to both the Olympics in that era and to the civil war in Bosnia-Herzegovina that followed.[8]

The *Seoul 1988 Olympic Games* were the last of the Cold War era, and there the Soviets again topped the medal table. The holding of the Games in

CASE STUDY 5.3. OLGA KORBUT, HUMANIZING THE SOVIETS

One of the most important moments of representation by athletes in the Olympic arena, a hero-making and lionization of transcendent global importance, was the unforgettable performances of Soviet athlete Olga Korbut, particularly in the tension-filled, Cold War context of the 1972 Olympic Games and the associated rivalries between East and West. The infectious performances of Korbut, a talented gymnast, charmed global audiences, especially in the West and the United States, with the direct effect of "humanizing" the Soviet Union with her playful smiles, tearful recoveries from simple mistakes, artful gestures, and energetic balance-beam and floor routines.

The "sparrow from Minsk," as she became affectionately known, won three gold medals at Munich (and another one at Montreal 1976). Asked later about how she felt being later personified by the state's public relations efforts as reflecting a new, young, vibrant (and humanized) Soviet Union (Meyers 2012, said in an interview with PBS [Public Broadcasting System, U.S.]),

"I must do, because this is like rules. Politics. To show the world [the] former Soviet Union is the best. I think this is politics. More than competition. Exhibition to show United States how strong even in sports Russia is." (PBS 1999)

South Korea was equally symbolic given the country's emergence from Cold War–induced war in the 1950s, its process of democratization, and its emergence as a global economic power.

With the fall of the Berlin Wall and the end of the Cold War in 1989, the world of sport witnessed another leap forward toward universalism in sport, leaving behind (presumably) the bipolar world of U.S.-Soviet rivalry in the history books and opening the way for a new era of potential for sport's contribution to peace.[9]

Games of the post–Cold War era. After the fall of the Berlin Wall, and the end of the Cold War with the dissolution of the Soviet Union, the *Olympic Games of 1992 in Barcelona*—the last under the long-standing presidency of the IOC by Juan Antonio Samaranch, a legendary and controversial figure in the Olympic movement over the commercialization of the Games—the Olympics finally emerged into the institution of mostly universal participation that is seen today. At the *Albertville 1992 Winter Olympic Games*, the

Soviet Union and 11 former East bloc countries marched together with poignant images of Russian and Ukrainian athletes entering the Olympic stadium and waving their respective national flags in the bland, nonnational uniform of the "Unified Team" cobbled together to allow the erstwhile Soviets to compete even before the countries had all formed recognized NOCs.

In 1994, the first Winter Olympics not held in the same year as the summer event was staged in Lillehammer, Norway; the move was important for the evolution of the Olympics, for now the events, brands, and emotional roller coaster of the Olympic Games—and associated broadcast revenues—would occur every two years rather than four. *Lillehammer 1994* was the first organization by the International Paralympic Committee (IPC) of the Paralympic games, which had been created in 1989.

The *1996 Summer Games in Atlanta* affirmed the Olympics in the post–Cold War era as a modern manifestation of the Olympic Games. New sports such as mountain biking and whitewater slalom appeared, nearly all the then-recognized countries in the world participated, greater than member states of the UN,[10] the Olympics were used to revitalize a neglected part of the city, and the event generated a profit for the organizing committee. More than 10,000 athletes participated, roughly what one saw in the Tokyo 2022 Games. A century after the first 1896 event with 14 countries and no women, Atlanta saw some 3,422 female athletes; the US Women's National Soccer Team (USWNT) won the first women's football tournament, overcoming China 2–1 in the gold-medal match.

BACK TO THE FUTURE: THE OLYMPIC GAMES INTO THE 21ST CENTURY

The attraction of the Olympic ideal continues to grow globally with the expansion of the Olympic Games into the 21st century in which the evangelical forces of Olympism continue to spread with the holding of the Games in Global South countries such as Brazil, the return of the Olympics to Russia, the "COVID-19 pandemic games in Tokyo 2020" (postponed until 2021, but still captioned "Tokyo 2020" and initial post-pandemic triumphalist hosting of the 2022 Winter Olympic Games in the 21st-century rising superpower, China. This period marked the moment, as the post–Cold War era consolidated around a more "unipolar" world led by the United States, when international liberal institutions such as the UN were further empowered to undertake peace and security peace operation missions around the globe, when progress had been made creating the International Criminal Court (ICC) in 1998, former autocracies were democratizing and plans were afoot for a 2005 World Summit that would further the efforts to consolidate a universalistic world order centered around global human rights.

Yet, the rise of China, the furthering of the kleptocratic Putin regime in Russia, and the 9/11 al-Qaeda attacks on the United States put the trajectory of the Olympic Games back to the past of geopolitics, sportswashing, boycotts, sanctions and suspensions, leading to the impasse in global sports that would fester through the 2010s and would lead to complete rupture with the Russia's Truce-breaking incursion in Ukraine in 2022.

If there were a zenith of modern Olympic history, it may well be *2000 Sydney Summer Olympic Games*. The torch was lit by Cathy Freeman, an Aboriginal (indigenous) Australian who had delighted her country and the world with dramatic performances in the 400m at the 1996 Atlanta Games, winning gold, as she also did through the 1990s in World Junior Championships and Commonwealth competitions. Freeman's lighting of the torch in Sydney was deeply symbolic for Australia, a country which had come a long way in race relations since the 1956 Melbourne Games, when discrimination against indigenous persons was institutionalized and rife. Freeman sealed the symbolism, winning the 400m event in Sydney in a full green-white-yellow body suit (the Australian flag colors), celebrating afterward with both an indigenous flag and an Australian flag, running into the stands to give her mother a bouquet of flowers (Carter 2020). The Sydney Games were well-managed, saw a record-breaking 300 sports on the program, and led to athletes from countries such as Kyrgyzstan, Macedonia, and Saudi Arabia winning first-ever gold medals for their countries.

Sydney 2000 may also represent the moment with the Paralympic Games came of age, with some 120 countries represented by nearly 4,000 paralympic athletes, although the games were marred by the scandalous cheating—one of the most egregious cases of in all of sport history—of the Spanish para basketball team in which 10 of the 12 members on the team were determined not to have a disability (Tremblett 2004). See Case Study 5.4.

The return of the Olympics to *Athens 2004* served to reinvoke the mythological origins of the Olympics with an official flag evoking the historic champion's laurel wreath, with the opening ceremonies reinforcing the overall narrative of Olympism. Prior to the Games, for the first time, the torch relay encompassed all five continents, passing through the UN headquarters in New York. Occupied Afghanistan sent five athletes to Athens, including two women who were the first-ever female Afghan athletes to compete in the Olympic arena. In the closing ceremonies, the Olympic Flag was handed over to the next host city for the summer games, Beijing, and that handoff gift of the world's most prestigious sporting event to rising power, China.

China used the 2008 Beijing Summer Olympic Games to its best interests. Pouring incredible resources into the Games—the most to date ever spent

CASE STUDY 5.4. REVENGE MODE: THE
2002 SALT LAKE CITY WINTER GAMES

After the 9/11 attacks, the Olympic Games became quickly re-politicized, and militant jingoism entered the Olympic arena along with the athletes. *The 2002 Salt Lake City Winter Olympic Games* in the United States, held months after the terrorist attacks, were held in a country at war: the United States had invaded Afghanistan to chase the organizer of the attack, Osama bin Laden, and the host country under President George W. Bush refused entreaties to pause the war during the Games.

In a deep display of nationalism, as the tattered flag from the World Trade Center was paraded into the Opening Ceremonies, "God Bless America" was sung by a New York City firefighter, and Bush deviated from common opening scripts by a head of state opening the Games; sitting among the U.S. athletes, Bush declared the Games open on behalf of a "proud, determined, and grateful nation," a thinly veiled political reference to prosecuting the war in Afghanistan (Bush 2022).

Nationalistic press in the United States, NBC (National Broadcasting Corporation), which had rights to air the games in the United States, cut away from the opening ceremonies to flag-waving U.S. troops on the ground in Afghanistan, poised for what would be an ultimately twenty-year occupation of the country that despite occupation and international state-building efforts, the mission failed to create a government able to protect itself from a return to power by the Islamist Taliban (NBC 2002).

by a host city or country, with the construction of major new facilities and stadiums ($6.8 billion, including $423 million for the iconic "Bird's Nest" stadium)—the investments paid off. Not only did China host the world, but its athletes also topped the list of gold medals won at the Games (the United States led the "medals table" overall). China called the Beijing Olympic Games the "fulfillment of a 100-year dream"; according to China sport analyst Xu Haifeng, Chinese political elites and the Chinese people saw Beijing 2008 as righting historical wrongs of marginalization and subjugation of China. With the Olympic Games, Xu contends, "they wanted to demonstrate to the world that China is [sic] strong country now. 'But they are not so confident that the outsiders accept China's new status and therefore want the Games to prove it'" (Mulvenney 2008).

The *2012 London Summer Olympic Games* returned to a much different country than 1948, one still fully engaged as a member of the European Union prior to the Brexit withdrawal in 2020. Much has been written on London 2012 in terms of its success in comparison to other Olympiads, both from a public policy perspective in terms of sustainability and urban renewal but also in terms of successful evolution of the Olympic Games.

Countries such as Serbia participated independently for the first time, and Nepal participated as a republic for the first time—emerging from a civil war toward an inclusive democracy—and newly independent countries such as Tajikistan won nation-building, first-ever gold medals. Taekwondo athlete Rohulla Nikpah of Afghanistan, who had won the country's first gold medal in Beijing, once again medaled with bronze in the 68-kg weight class, reflecting as well that this war-torn country combat sports are popular for both young men and young women, as well (Ferris-Rotman and Hassib 2012). Saudi Arabia fielded two female athletes at London, portending its further engagement in the world of sport (including the IOC, which hailed the decision) in response to global criticism of its repressive gender policies (BBC 2012).

The *Sochi 2014* Olympics are related to the back-to-the-future capture of the Olympic Games by an autocrat engaged in the most transparent and sophomoric efforts to cleanse and legitimize a regime with human rights abuses at home and nefarious interference and militarization abroad. Combined with the state-sponsored doping scandal that helped produce a result of Russia atop an Olympic medal table, Sochi 2014 goes alongside Berlin 1936 in the annals of corruption and oligarchic patronage, power politics, and sportswashing under the bright light of the Olympic flame.

Former Soviet chess champion and grandmaster in the sport Garry Kasparov wryly observed:

> Moscow (1980) and Beijing (2008) were games that authoritarian systems established to generate propaganda for their country and for themselves, the ruling party. Sochi, as Berlin, stands under a different sign: these games . . . revolve entirely around a single man. In Sochi, it was Putin. It's about a personality cult. (Reitschuler 2014)

If the *Rio 2016 Summer Olympic Games*, coming on the heels of the 2014 hosting of the World Cup and the 2010 World Cup in South Africa were to further consolidate the narrative of a realignment of world politics in the direction of the BRICS (Brazil, Russia, India, China, and South Africa), the Rio Olympics seemingly failed to meet that overarching symbolic perspective. From the foul open-water swimming venues to the "pacification" campaign against criminal capture of the city's streets, the Rio Games appeared destined for difficulty from the beginning.

The Rio Games were replete with both epic sport performances, important symbolic moments (such as the Olympic Laurel award to Kenya's Kip Keino), and close ties to both Brazil's internal political turbulence in the wake of the "Car Wash" scandal and the resignation of President Dilma Rousseff, an outbreak of mosquito-borne Zika virus, the fallout of the Russian doping scandal (which broke in 2014), and the breakup of an Islamist terrorist plot casts a pall, historically, over Rio 2016.

The *2018 Pyeongchang Winter Olympic Games* in South Korea, the first in which the Russians participated under the post–doping sanctions regime of appearing as Olympic Athletes from Russia (OAR), is but one of the notable events from these games (see chapter 6); these games were a watershed for the Winter events, however, with countries such as Ecuador and Malaysia fielding teams for the first time.

The Pandemic and Post-Pandemic Games. The outbreak of the COVID-19 pandemic catapulted the world, and the Olympic Games, into a new uncertain future. Amid global shutdown, the

> 2020 Tokyo Games were postponed to 2021, and even then, it was highly uncertain whether, and how, the Games could be held while much of the world was suffering from the effects of the public health, economic, and social effects of the pandemic and whether, symbolically, it even made sense to stage a global event such as the Olympics amidst such world war–like global turbulence. Nonetheless, given the rapid development of vaccines, containment measures such as the absence of fans, some 206 countries participated in the Olympic Games in Tokyo, with countries such as Burkina Faso, and Turkmenistan winning first-ever medals for an athlete from their countries: Burkina Faso's Hughes Fabrice Zongo won bronze in the men's triple jump, and Turkmenistan's Polina Guryeva won silver in weightlifting (59-kg class). (Africanews 2021; RFE/RL 2021)

The *2022 Winter Beijing Games* brought with it a close scrutiny of China's internal policies and international interactions, and the event was ushered in with a now-infamous summit between Chinese premier Xi Jinping and Russian president Vladimir Putin. With UN-verified claims of atrocities of "ethnocide" (efforts to eradicate in whole or in part an ethnic group) in the western, Muslim-majority Xinjiang province, international human rights groups sought to once again identify the Games as the "genocide games."[11] As China implemented a "Covid-zero" policy, the Games were challenging to organize and weather conditions undermined some of the hoped-for symbolism that the Games would reflect a strong China in winter sport as well. An athlete of Uyghur ethnicity, 22-year-old cross-country skier

Dilnigar Ilhamjan, who—taught Nordic skiing by her father—was the first skier, male or female, for China to ever win a medal at an International Ski Federation (FIS)-sanctioned event (Euronews 2022). See Case Study 5.5.

IMPLICATIONS: THE OLYMPIC GAMES, STILL SWIMMING

From a small committee of seven bourgeois European men, meeting in the late 19th century, to the globalized, modern Games of Atlanta 1996—the last of the turbulent, violent 20th century in which the Olympics has unfolded—the modern games are highly universal in participation across states in the international system, extensively evolved in terms of the range of sport seen in the Games, much more inclusive along lines of gender, race, ethnicity, and sexuality, and in recent years have seen small erosive cracks in the norm of national recognition. Borne of a deliberate effort to create a secular religion,

CASE STUDY 5.5. A PROFILE IN COURAGE: OKSANA MASTERS AT THE BEIJING 2022 WINTER OLYMPIC GAMES

If there was a moment of symbolic representation of sport's contribution to peace at the Beijing Winter games, it wasn't in the controversial Winter (ablest) Olympics, but in the Ukraine war-shaken 2022 Winter Paralympic Games. There, an erstwhile Ukrainian orphan, disabled from birth with tibial hemimelia (likely from radiation poisoning from the Chernobyl nuclear disaster of 1986), Oksana Masters double-poled her way to para-Nordic gold in cross-country skiing, winning three gold medals in the 1.5-km sprint, 5-km sitting, and team disciplines of para cross-country skiing, racing for the United States. She had previously medaled in adaptive sculling (rowing) at the 2012 Paralympic Games.

Masters was adopted from the Ukraine orphanage at age seven by her mother Gay, a professor of speech pathology (Adams 2020). If there were to ever to be considerations by the Norwegian Nobel Committee for a sport-related prize, perhaps it should be awarded to Oksana Masters and her mother Gay for representing how sport contributes to personal resilience, which can in turn lead to some form of demonstrable representation of what constitutes "peace" on the world's biggest cultural stage.

the philosophical orientation of humanistic Olympism and the principal institutional and charter-based structure of the Olympic movement have proven remarkably persistent.

As a secular religion, however soaring the rhetoric, anthems, and flights of doves, as an articulation of a human condition far removed from today's reality of deep deprivation and inequality (see chapter 7) or persistent armed conflict and interpersonal violence (see chapter 8), the Olympism is bound to disappoint. With all religious traditions comes potential for harmful interpretations, for deviation from the dogma, and departure from the core tenets by even the most deeply devoted. This is and has been the case with Olympism. Manipulation of sports for political power and political intrusions into sports corrupt its ideals and reveal its use in the national interests—or, typically, the interests of a narrow ruling elite—rather than as a global public good.

Despite its origin of myth in humanism and human rights, its glorification of the ancients in aestheticism and glory in patriotic sports, and its overall commitment to social development as a rights-based philosophy, Olympism continues to disappoint. Nationalism, power pursuits, and a world in which a state can at once participate in a celebration of mankind, and at the next attack civilians in a neighboring state shows a world in sharp contrast with the putative values of Olympism. As historian Baker observes,

> Nationalism is like the Hydra of old. You lop off one of its heads and another sprouts immediately. The question for future Olympics is not so much whether or not nationalism will be present, but what form it takes. Christ would surely recognize it for what it is: a false god that wraps patriotic symbols, rituals, and mythologies around athletic events, forever seeking true believers who will be both ideologically committed to the nation state. (2000, 52)

At the same time, Baker contends that the world is better off with the secular religion of Olympism than without it. "For all their petty flaw and garish excesses," he concludes, "the Olympic Games embody a buoyant faith, a hopeful optimism, and a charitable ethic . . . sport as well as religion depends on faith from start to finish."

QUESTIONS FOR CONSIDERATION

- Does the concept of *Olympism* have much relevance in such a turbulent, uncertain world, or are the symbols and quaint philosophy a relic of a bygone era with little relevance to modern issues such as LGBTQ rights?
- How was sport waged in the Cold War and U.S.-Soviet rivalry and did the rivalry contribute to, or possibly help manage, the long period of

geo-political polarization that characterized most of the post–World War II 20th century?

- How does nationalism get expressed in contemporary sports, for example, the controversial Beijing 2008 Olympic Summer and 2022 Winter games where such nationalism and the regime's human rights record were subject to international scrutiny and calls for boycott?

FOR FURTHER INFORMATION

There is a wealth of resources on the Olympic Games of ancient Greece, on which the modern Games are loosely based, the revival period in which the humanist framers conceived the new festivals, and many high and low points of the Games across the 20th century and into the 21st. Among some of the most notable books are *The Naked Olympics* on the Greek festivals with their javelin throws and chariot races (Perrottet 2004), Jules Boykoff's *Power Games: A Political History of the Olympics* (Boykoff 2016), and the book *Fire on the Track: Betty Robinson and the Triumph of Early Olympic Women* by Roseanne Montillo on women in the early Olympic Games (Montillo 2017).

For an insider's perspective on the Olympics, see Richard Pound's authoritative volume *Inside the Olympic Games: A Behind-the-Scenes Look at the Politics, the Scandals, and the Glory of the Games* (Pound 2004). A carefully researched, archives-informed account of the Olympics during the Cold War is Toby C. Rider's *Cold War Games: Propaganda, The Olympics, and U.S. Foreign Policy* (Rider 2016), which explores how the United States and the Soviet Union equally sought to manipulate the Olympic institutions and events for propaganda purposes.

Scholarly journals such as the *Journal of Olympic Studies*, *Diagoras: International Academic Journal on Olympic Studies*, and *The Sport Journal* regularly publish peer-reviewed research on the Games. See, too, *The Journal of Sport Philosophy* and *The Journal of Sport History and Social Issues*.

The Library of Congress in the United States provides a guide to reference sources on the Olympic Games at its website: https://www.loc.gov/rr/main/olympics/.

"Around the Rings" is a news site devoted to all things related to the Olympics and Paralympic Games and including content in Spanish; it is found at https://www.infobae.com/aroundtherings/. The newswire *Reuters* is a good resource for daily news related to the Olympics: https://www.reuters.com/news/archive/olympicsNews.

NOTES

1. See the IOC definition of Olympism at https://olympics.com/ioc/olympic-values#:~:text=Olympic%20values.%20The%20three%20values%20of%20Olympism%20are,%E2%80%9Cencourage%20effort%E2%80%9D%2C%20%E2%80%9Cpreserve%20human%20dignity%E2%80%9D%20and%20%E2%80%9Cdevelop%20harmony%E2%80%9D.

2. Russia and the United States have also held both Winter and Summer Olympic Games, albeit not in the same bid city.

3. On the role of the 1952 Helsinki Games in the evolution of the Cold War between the United States and the Soviet Union, see the dossier and documents at Woodrow Wilson Center Cold War International History Project (Edelman and Prozumenshikov 2018).

4. See the 2006 documentary *Freedom's Fury* (Gray 2006).

5. For an overview of boycotts in Olympic history, see Boycotts in Olympic History https://www.youtube.com/watch?v=U82crBtlTtA.

6. United Nations Resolution 1514 (XV), 14 December 1960.

7. See the video of the 1980 U.S. Cold War sport patriots with former President Donald Trump on the public network C-SPAN at a rally just after he was allegedly involved in inciting the insurrection at the U.S. Capitol on January 6, 2020, at https://www.youtube.com/watch?v=fZRYzy4k-ck.

8. See the photo essay of the Sarajevo ruins at Garfield (2018).

9. For more on the history of sport in the Cold War, listen to the 40-part podcasts on the most memorable events and issues at the Cold War International History Project of the Woodrow Wilson Center for Scholars, at https://www.wilsoncenter.org/podcasts/sport-cold-war.

10. The variance in the number of countries is due to "Olympic geography" or the recognition of non–sovereign state Olympic committees such as a Palestinian team which debuted in 1996 (the Palestine Olympic Committee had been recognized by the IOC in 1986).

11. The same moniker by these global human-rights advocacy groups was used to describe the 1936 Olympic Games in Berlin and the 2008 Beijing Summer Games; apropos of the latter, the label was applied to describe alleged Chinese support for the Janjaweed militia in Darfur, Sudan, which had committed genocidal acts with the alleged backing of China with arms and possible other material aid.

PART IV

The Basis of Peace

Human Rights and Sustainable Development

Chapter 6

Sport for Human Rights

A Long Association

CHAPTER OVERVIEW

In response to the myriad challenges of human rights abuses in sports, new organizations have been created to both evaluate the nature and extent of human-rights violations that occur in sports, and to explore and advocate for advancement of human rights within and by international sport. Mary Robinson, former president of Ireland and former UN High Commissioner for Human Rights, founded and served as the initial president of the Centre for Sport and Human Rights, which in essence fills a major global-governance gap in the monitoring and advancement of human rights through sport. The center was launched in 2022, with the World Academy of Sport, a new Global Sport and Human Rights academy to share knowledge and build capacity for integrating human rights more fully into the "sport ecosystem."

Human rights are related to sport in two fundamental ways; there are issues of human rights *within* sport—such as the cases of abuse of athletes within a sport, by gangs, or national authorities—and there are violations of human rights *related* to sport, as in suppression that may occur before major sport events. The first section presents a map of relationships between sport and human rights to include civil and political rights, so-called "second-generation rights" (of which right to sport could be located), and transnational solidarity in relation to human rights.

Sport provides a theater of opportunity for claiming human rights, and through sport those within and beyond the arena have sought to use the publicity and spectacle of sport to advance ethnic and racial, marginalized minority, sexuality, and gender rights.

CHAPTER HIGHLIGHTS

- This chapter explores the ways in which sport contributes to, and ways it is hampered from, direct contributions to the expansion of human rights.
- Sport and the right to physical education are enshrined in numerous international covenants, treaties, and agreements, and sport as a right is related to empowerment of communities whose rights are at eminent risk (such as refugees and displaced persons). Discrimination by gender or ability, neglect, or other prioritization often limits this right in reality.
- In the final section, this chapter explores how human rights are contended in sport, sport's relationship with advancing human rights, the global diffusion of human rights norms through sport, and the integration of human rights into national human rights institutions, mechanisms, and related civil society.

ADVANCING HUMAN RIGHTS
IN AND BEYOND SPORT

Sport is a fundamental human right—the right to play, physical recreation, and thus participation in "sport"—has been claimed, as such, by the International Olympic Committee. The IOCs 2022 human rights strategic framework, the IOC Strategic Framework on Human Rights, defines the organization's view that access to sport is a human right (IOC 2022): it asserts that sport is a codified, universal human right, that it is in the IOC's very existential being to support, and advance sport-related human rights, and it outlines a strategic framework much as would any other international organization (to explicitly relate its role and function to human-rights attainment). Normatively, at least, the IOC is a rights-based organization with a clear commitment to and mission of furthering human rights.

While the IOC strategic framework on human rights outlines a number of important ways to improve human rights in and beyond sport, such as strengthening athletes' access to reporting harm in sport, the framework does not deeply analyze why its 28 recommendations for improving human rights are needed. Poignantly it notes that future hosts of Olympic events will be asked to fill out questionnaires that contain human rights questions "to identify and address adverse human rights impacts" (IOC 2022, 30). In terms of global governance, the IOC places its mission in the context of a private, autonomous entity vis-à-vis the UN; the IOC seeks to align its normative framework with the UN Guiding Principles on Business and Human Rights: meaning, although participation in sport is a human right, the human-rights aspects of governing sport are private, not global public, business.

With sport's long association with human rights, some enduring questions arise. What are the ways in which sport can lead to human-rights violations? When can sport activism and protest lead to greater realization of human rights? How can sport promote or lead to greater civil and political rights? What is the relationship between sport and social and economic rights?

Sport contributes to human rights by providing an arena of opportunity for rights claiming. To their credit, especially since the end of World War II, most global sport organizations have a relatively good record of advocating for advancing human rights, including advancing ethnic, racial, gender, sexuality, and labor rights. At the same time, advances in rights through sport have come from the ability of those claiming rights to do so through sport: in seeking and claiming gender equality and rights on nonbinary gender identities and expressions, in promotion of ethnic minority, indigenous, and racial equality rights, and in the codification and expansion of rights for those disabled. This struggle continues, however, and the promise of sport contributing to human rights remains limited by the lack of institutional avenues for those engaged in rights-claiming through sport.

From Jesse Owens's four gold medals at the Berlin Games in 1936, a feat which in some ways shattered the National Socialist myth about racial superiority and sport, to the present focus on advancement of sport for women and girls, sport has been seen by many as a way to advance international human rights. From the expulsion of South Africa from the Olympic Games (beginning as early as 1956, but more extensively in the 1960–1992 Games), to the 1968 "Black Power Salute" in Mexico City, to the label of "Genocide Olympics" in Beijing in 2008 that helped change Chinese policy on its support for the Sudanese government's prosecution of war in Darfur, human rights advocates have used sport as a grand global stage for putting a spotlight on global rights violations by participating countries. See Case Study 6.1.

Organizations such as Human Rights Watch have created dedicated teams to monitor and call out human rights violations in sport, such as its report on toxic physical and verbal abuse in the gymnastics program in Japan released prior to the Tokyo 2020–2021 Games (Human Rights Watch 2020a).

These normative questions require a step back to evaluate evolution of human rights, and rights-claiming, in international sport. Mapping the relationship between human rights in sport, Kidd and Donnelly (2000) through in-depth analysis of the deep historical and institutional relationships outline a helpful typology that highlights how international norms, notably the Convention on the Rights of the Child, create a right to "play" that rolls up in interpretation and practice to the right to participate in sport and physical recreation. They assert that human rights are advanced through sport through interaction between the existence of norms and the ways in which sport provides an arena for them to be claimed. Further, they investigate sport's

CASE STUDY 6.1. "HEY, KIDS: GO OUT AND PLAY!" IT'S YOUR HUMAN RIGHT

The *1989 Convention on the Rights of the Child* provides a normative grounding for the "right to play" which is in turn more broadly interpreted as the right to engage in sport.

Article 30

In those States in which ethnic, religious or linguistic minorities or persons of indigenous origin exist, a child belonging to such a minority or who is indigenous shall not be denied the right, in community with other members of his or her group, to enjoy his or her own culture, to profess and practise his or her own religion, or to use his or her own language.

Article 31

1. States Parties recognize the right of the child to rest and leisure, to engage in play and recreational activities appropriate to the age of the child and to participate freely in cultural life and the arts.
2. States Parties shall respect and promote the right of the child to participate fully in cultural and artistic life and shall encourage the provision of appropriate and equal opportunities for cultural, artistic, recreational and leisure activity.

The text of Articles 30 and 31 of the Convention is found at https://www.ohchr.org/en/instruments-mechanisms/instruments/convention-rights-child.

contribution to realizing the rights of those facing historical discrimination and marginalization, such as those with disabilities, and the complementary gains from using sport to eradicate multiple intersectional marginalization.

Human rights norms in sport are overlapping, well-developed, and involve core global governance treaties and covenants and globally accepted "soft law" norms such as the SDGs. In human rights law, participation and cultural life, recreation, leisure, and sport are variously defined in a number of declarations and covenants. Among them as most important are the 1948 Universal Declaration on Human Rights, the International Covenant on Civil and Political Rights, and the 1988 Convention on the Elimination of All forms of Discrimination against Women.

Significant human rights violations occur in the context of sport—especially labor, environmental, and security-force abuses—so that sportswashing and/or soft-diplomacy aims can be successful. In the interests of presenting a country or city host as a peaceful, prosperous place, sport can be misused in certain situations, as when "mega-sport projects" displace local inhabitants, or when sport teams mobilize along identity-based cleavages and reflect or exacerbate local community conflict dynamics, to instances in which competition between national clubs leads to street clashes among jingoistic fans. As Amnesty International notes, human rights violations often increase in the run-up to mega-events.

> It often occurs that in countries that organize major international sporting events, human rights violations increase. Freedom of expression is suppressed, people are forcibly evicted from their houses without compensation, or construction workers building stadiums are exploited. There is an urge to whitewash the country's reputation, stifle critical voices and hide all wrongs.

There are serious gaps in the system of preventing, reporting, investigating, and adjudication abrogation of the human rights of athletes in international sport, including their civil and political rights, physical and sexual rights, labor rights, and freedom to travel freely globally without political interference. In 2020, the OHCHR reported on the intersection of race in gender in sport, and it pointed to globally low participation of women in sport as a result of a lack of access to safe sport, discrimination in sport, barriers to persistence and the specialization needed to become elite athletes, a lack of access to resources, and xenophobia and racism in women's sport (UN HRC 2020; see also UN Women 2023). The in-depth OHCHR analysis pointed to the myriad abuses within sport against athletes, particularly lack of access to sport—especially those from marginalized and minority groups, such as migrant women. The OHCHR report further cited abuses in sport to women through mandatory sex testing through harmful procedures in female-eligibility regulations and unequal pay.

So, too, *athletes face limits on their civil and political rights*; while the old-style ban on political speech in sport has eroded as athletes have directly or indirectly violated the bans, athlete civil and political rights are (as the case of Elnaz Rekabi in chapter 3 attests), highly limited. While there may increasingly be athletes' free speech outside of sport, such speech directly inside of sport—in the middle of the stage—is closely policed. When globally ranked #2 Belarussian tennis player Aryana Sabalenka told a press conference at the 2023 French Open that although she is not "an expert in politics . . . I don't support the war, meaning I don't support [Belarusian President] Alexander Lukashenko right now." It was a bold statement from the 25-year-old athlete in a challenging press-conference moment: she had just won her quarterfinal match against Ukraine's Elina Svitolina (6–4, 6–4), but Svitolina refused to shake her hand at the net at the end of the match (Al Jazeera 2023).

Despite rules against political speech, athletes are increasingly turning to tattoos, nail polish, hairstyles, and other clever nonverbal ways to communicate patriotism while staying just inside the non–political appearance rules of the IOC and the sport federations (i.e., IOC Rule 50). Symbols are amorphous and consistently changing, so the IOC wages a Sisyphean struggle to contain political speech within the Olympic arena. In the run-up to Tokyo 2020, following the recommendations of the IOC's Athletes Commission, the Executive Board reformulated its Rule 50.2 code on athlete political speech to allow more personal political speech outside its venues (IOC 2021), ostensibly to prevent future "Black Power"-type salutes from the podium as courageously seen in the 1968 Mexico City games.

The 2020 OHCHR report on race and gender discrimination in sport goes beyond the identification of challenges to human rights that exist in the context of sport, especially for women and girls, with factors such as discriminatory social norms, obstacles related to burden of care for family, imperatives of work and livelihoods, harassment and violence in sport including sexual exploitation and abuse (UN HRC 2020, 2).

Moreover, when athletes have been harmed—for example, in the case of Caster Semenya, a South Africa middle-distance track-and field athlete who battled with international sport organizations over sex testing for athletes with differences of sexual development (DSD) is perhaps the most common (Mohamed and Dhai 2019)—there are significant barriers in access to justice to remedy harms in sport. Among these are the following:

- Regulatory control in the global governance regime of sport is controlled by private, nonprofit sports bodies where authority is vested through contractual relationships, regulations, and local laws and policies such that the "autonomy of sport" creates confusion on law and regulations.
- National courts may provide domestic remedies, but these courts have no authority over discriminatory rules in international competitions; international sport bodies have avoided jurisdiction of national courts, requiring, for example, mandatory arbitration.
- Routes to appeals are limited, with most appeals going to the CAS, which rules in reference to international sport regulations and does not have a mandate to consider human rights as "binding sources of law for adjudication" (UN HRC 2020, 12).
- Decisions of the CAS can be appealed only to the Swiss high court, the Swiss Federal Tribunal, with further appeal through the European Court for Human Rights . . . each of which is a highly lengthy process.

The CBC documentary *Category: Woman* exposes the nefarious harm done in sex-testing in athletics in tracing the humiliations imposed upon four women in the global South: https://www.cbc.ca/playersvoice/entry/category-woman.

In the case of Caster Semenya, her career was in its twilight when World Athletics changed its sex-testing regulations and procedures in March 2023, in part in response to the injustices wrought in the Semenya case. Finally, the OHCHR notes that addressing these gaps in athlete access to justice requires fundamental reform, and the report mentions calls for an overarching global agency to monitor human rights and good governance in sport to include an antidiscrimination entity in such body.

BREAKING BARRIERS: ADVANCING HUMAN RIGHTS THROUGH SPORT

Sport-based efforts have led to the expansion of human rights in racial and ethnic social justice, toward gender equality and the rights of gender-nonconforming identities, disability rights, and historical marginalized groups such as indigenous persons and those suffering from discrimination and stigmatization (such as caste-based discrimination).

Specific incidents of claiming rights in and beyond sport have a long tradition, both now recognized events of furthering demands for ethnic and racial justice as in the 1968 Black Power salute or claims for national recognition rights to include the terrorist attack on the 1972 Munich Games. More recently, grounds dissenting against autocratic regimes have used sport events in efforts to draw attention to rights abuses and injustices: at the Sochi 2014 Winter Olympic Games, members of the anti-regime pop group Pussy Riot were teargassed and beaten while attempting to sing (they were later arrested), and in the run-up to Rio 2014 FIFA World Cup protesters were teargassed while contending against corruption. See Case Study 6.2.

Protest and social activism in sport has deep roots in contexts such as the United States, where sport-related protest has been integral to claiming civil rights and countering racism, social inequities, and discrimination (Totten 2016), underscores that sport is not automatically associated with social cohesion and for the sport to contribute to such cohesion, it must be consistent with social values and changing social norms related to human rights and its concerns with fairness, inclusion, and freedom of expression. Today, sport activists contend against autocratic regimes and corruption in sport, commercialism in sport, social injustices within and beyond sport by athletes, fan groups, and sport clubs (Lee and Cunningham 2019).

The literature on sport and rights-claiming runs deep, drawing on historical cases such as the famous breaking of racial and ethnic discrimination barriers

CASE STUDY 6.2. CLAIMING DISABILITY
RIGHTS IN THE RUN-UP TO PARIS 2024

In the feverishly intensifying anticipation of the Paris 2024 Olympic Games in Paris, disability-rights activists in France seized an opportunity to protest against lack of accessibility for those with disabilities in the Olympic host city. Disability-rights activists invited the media to accompany them as Babou Sene, a disabled person in a wheelchair, struggled to use Paris's public transportation infrastructure.

President Emmanuel Macron, hosting an international conference he organized by several local disability-rights organizations and organizations of persons with disabilities, conceded to the protesters' demands and he pledged to spend 1.5 billion Euros on improving disability access, helping small businesses make access improvements, and vastly improving transportation infrastructure . . . all in the run-up to the Olympic Games (*Euronews* 2023).

in sport, to claiming gender and sexuality rights, to advocating for the right to participate in and to elite competition for those with disabilities. In this literature, there is a deep concern with how athletes, fans, and clubs engage in rights-claiming, to what effects, and the ways in which international sport organizations have responded in efforts to keep politics out of sport while at the same time being responsive to such rights-claiming, as Totten (2016, 4) suggests, primarily as a result of pressure from corporate sponsors to protect sport-organization brand images.

In sum, rights-claiming in sport has a deep and long tradition of activism from across the range of civil disobedience tools that civil rights activists have developed and continue to develop principally across three domains: claiming identity rights, gender and sexuality rights, labor rights, and disability rights.

Sport-related organizations and processes, to include mega-events and celebrations, and in the mundane, everyday work of organizing sport internationally, is a constant process of contending and advancing human rights. As societies rapidly evolve around the world, and global and local norms interact and collide, sport serves as a venue for contending rights and for advancing human rights through progressive evolution of norms, mechanisms for monitoring, and traditional methods of human-rights enforcement through, for example, naming and shaming.

Among all the rights that have been claimed in sport, among the most recurrent and consistent are *efforts to claim identity rights: national, ethnic, and racial* recognition rights in relation to contexts where such rights have been abrogated. As with disability rights and Paris 2024, sport provides an arena—a public stage—for claiming human rights. This section explores such rights-claiming through sport in ethnic and racial identity, gender and sexuality, disability rights, and labor rights. See Case Study 6.3.

CASE STUDY 6.3. A CLEAN-AND-JERK FOR MINORITY RIGHTS: NAIM SULEYMANOGLU, "POCKET HERCULES"

One of the most engaging cases historically is that of "Pocket Hercules," the affectionate nickname for the phenomenal Bulgarian-born, ethnically Turkish weight lifter in the 59–64 kg featherweight class who—while standing only 147 cm, or 4'10"—could lift three times his body weight in the clean-and-jerk subdiscipline.

Suleymanoglu set his first record at age 15 and went on to win gold medals in 1988 at Seoul, in 1992 in Barcelona, and in 1996 in Atlanta, among a slew of gold medals in this period at world championships, European championships, and weight lifting world cups.

The Suleymanoglu story is one of human rights as well as remarkable athletic performance: born in Bulgaria as a member of the country's Turkish-speaking minority, he and his family were subject to the discriminatory "Bulgarianization" campaign, or, as the regime called it, "Revival Process," by which ethnic Turks as a Muslim minority were required to change their names and other measures to enforce "Slavicization" and forced assimilation.

Naim was forced to change his birth name to "Naum Shalamanov." After international outcry over his and other ethnic Turks' oppression, in a series of events with deep international intrigue, Suleymanoglu defected to Turkey—with the personal involvement of Turkish president Turgat Ozal. Turkey paid $1 million for his weight lifting "license," and he became a Turkish citizen . . . and national hero. Bulgaria was shamed into abandoning its discriminatory "Bulgarianization" policies, the border was opened to allow hundreds of thousands of ethnic Turks to leave Bulgaria, and Suleymanoglu became a sports icon in Turkey.

While Suleymanoglu's later life was marred by illness, possible but unconfirmed steroid use (he died at age 50 following a liver transplant), he later served as vice president of the International Weightlifting Federation (IWF) (Keles 2021).

Among the myriad other instances of ethnic and racial justice rights-claiming in sport are the well-studied instances of U.S. boxer Muhammad Ali resisting discrimination and forced conscription in the United States and Cathy Freeman's claiming of indigenous rights at the 2000 Sydney Olympic Games. Beyond these are many more, such as marathoner Feyisa Lilesa of Ethiopia who, crossing the finish line in the Rio 2016 marathon, made a locally recognizable crossed-arms gesture in support of the Oromo in his home country—the country's largest ethnic group—who have suffered marginalization and discrimination including forced displacement in the run-up to Rio; he later sought asylum for his bold rights-claiming gesture in the Olympic arena (Burke 2016).

The human-rights-based "naming and shaming" of China with regard to human rights abuses against the Muslim-minority Uyghurs by the regime toward "ethnocide" was a major international relations issue in the run-up to the 2022 Beijing Winter Olympic Games. The organization Human Rights Watch sent a letter to the IOC calling for the postponement of the games and published commentary and reports on the Uyghur and other human rights issues in China (such as censorship) contending that more than 1 million members of the minority have been detained and abused in detention camps (Human Rights Watch 2020b).

That sport provides an arena for *confronting racial discrimination, breaking barriers of social discrimination through sport, and highlighting the intersectionality of race, gender, and other forms of marginalization* (such as sexual orientation) highlights that historically and into the present, sport and race are inexorably linked (Long and Spracklen 2011). African American athletes in the United States have consistently used both the legal frameworks of nondiscrimination in sport—in the United States, known as Title IX (of the 1972 Education Amendments to the 1964 Elementary and Secondary Education Act)—to advocate for and to advance civil rights in sport despite social pressures that they should "shut up and play" or be politically neutral despite facing widespread discrimination (Towler, Crawford, and Bennet 2011), as have women, indigenous minorities, and transgender athletes. See Documentary Insights 6.1.

Such barrier-breaking and contention of rights against racial discrimination continue into the present such that any effort to suggest that international sport is an arena in which race doesn't matter—so called "post-raciality" in sport—is a farcical claim even as athletes of color have broken barriers in most major professional sports. The very discourse on race in sport is driven by categories and state-based ideologies in a manner that actually perpetuates racism and racial hierarchies and furthers a black-white binary in a much more complicated world (Hilton and Rankin-White 2016, 3).

DOCUMENTARY INSIGHTS 6.1. PROTECTING ATHLETES IN SPORT, *ATHLETE A* (2020)

A toxic culture of sexualization of athletes in USA Gymnastics led to one of the most publicized abrogations of human rights in sport: decades of abuse by team doctor Larry Nasser took place within a broader system of exploitation of athletes, protection of the brand and sponsorship agreements, violation of laws on mandatory reporting of sexual abuse by those such as coaches. USA Olympic medal-winning athletes were among those abused by Nasser and complaints were not acted upon by officials and coaches.

The first athlete to report these abuses, anonymously designated "Athlete A" (Maggie Nichols) gives voice to the survivors and exposes the repressive environment of winning at all costs that created the conditions for the criminal abuse by Nasser. The documentary *Athlete A* (2020), directed by Bonni Cohen and Jon Shenk, offers some modest moment of justice to the victims in sharing their story of abuse in sport, https://www.imdb.com/title/tt11905462/.

The challenges of racism continue to bedevil international sport, especially football. In 2023, Spanish police arrested seven fans who were charged with hanging an effigy of Afro-Brazilian Real Madrid footballer Vinícus Júnior off of a highway bridge; allegedly, the fans are backers of club Valencia, hoisted the effigy near Real's training facilities, and are alleged (as is the club) to have ties to right-wing populist parties in the Valencia region.

The incident highlights much deeper issues of racism in Spanish football, racism in football globally (Garland and Rowe 2001), and throughout sport (BBC 2023c). In the following days, the Brazilian national team showed solidarity against racism in football by meeting Guinea in a friendly rally wearing all-black uniforms in support of their teammate Vinícus; the black-clad Brazil side won 4–1, and Vinícus scored the final goal of the match (McVitie 2023).

Sport has, since the very earliest appearance of women's sport in the beginning of the 20th century, been *an arena for claiming gender and sexuality rights*. The 2022 Qatar-hosted FIFA World Cup raised the absence of LGBTQ rights in the country (especially, the dispute over the "One Love" campaign), environmental impacts, and women's rights in the country. See Case Study 6.4.

Beyond contention across cultures, there continues to be need for rights-based claiming, policy development, and, ultimately, more effective

CASE STUDY 6.4. CONTENDING AND CLAIMING RIGHTS: HANDSHAKES (OR NOT) AND KISSES AT THE 2023 U.S. OPEN

The 2022 U.S. Open was replete with symbolic moments, victories, and contestations over human rights. In a memorable moment, women's tennis professional Mara Kostyuk refused the traditional post-match handshake across the net with Victoria Azarenka: Kostyuk is Ukrainian and Azarenka hails from Belarus (which is cooperating with Russia in its prosecution of the war that began in 2022). Kostyuk has lost the second-round match to the Ukrainian in two sets, 6–2, 6–3. Kostyuk later defended the snub and efforts to prevent Azarenka from participating in a charity event to support relief to the war-affected Ukrainians (Futterman 2022).

In 2023, rights again were on the agenda at the U.S. Open at Flushing Meadows. On Court 17 during the 3rd round, two openly gay players—Daria Kasatkina and Greet Minnen—replaced the post-match handshake with a kiss . . . believed to the be the first time when two openly gay players met in a tennis Grand Slam. Minnen, who hails from Belgium, later remarked that although she lost the match, it was a "pleasure" to have made history with Kasatkina, a Russian athlete (Hansford 2023).

realization of gender and sexuality rights in sport. Sexual rights, and especially transgender rights and categorization of transgender athletes, are widely contested in sport, even as nonbinary athletes are known to have competed historically in sport over many decades if not centuries (Rowello and Swift 2022). See Case Study 6.5.

Following a broad-based social movement, a civil rights struggle to obtain recognition for disability rights, the 1989 creation of the International Paralympic Committee—now based in Bonn, Germany—is the outcome of *much-unfinished efforts to extend sport to those with disabilities*, to create an elite category of para sport, and, over time, to achieve parity between "able" and "para" sport. Some sport events, such as the Boston Marathon overseen by the Boston Athletic Association (BAA), have created a wheelchair division for racing wheelchairs in concert with World Para Athletic rules and classification of athletes, essentially integrating able and para events in the same-day competition. The BAA event began in 1975 when it recognized disabled athlete and adaptive-sport pioneer Bob Hall.[1]

CASE STUDY 6.5. DESPITE PROGRESS, PERVASIVE LGBTQ DISCRIMINATION AND EXCLUSION IN SPORT

Since the mid-1970s, international sport has been, historically, a common venue for athletes to come out and openly declare their sexuality, often at great personal, professional, and potentially financial risk. (See the memoire of tennis champion Billie Jean King, *All In: An Autobiography* (King 2021).

Despite these gains, a review of research studies on LGBTQ participation in sports in 2020 by scholars Denison, Bevan, and Jeanes found widespread stigmatization, discrimination, and exclusion in sports.

Taken together, the available quantitative evidence suggests discrimination and homophobia continues to be an issue within sports contexts. The findings by researchers using quantitative methods reflect and are consistent with a rich and detailed range of recent studies by researchers who have examined homophobia, transphobia, and the discrimination experienced by LGBTQ+ people in sport from a qualitative perspective. . . .

Consistent evidence that LGBTQ+ people continue to experience discrimination and exclusion in sport supports the need identified by UN agencies, public health agencies, and scholars for urgent, collaborative, solution-focused research to identify ways to stop discriminatory behaviours and mitigate any harm being caused to members of this population. However, the primary barrier to action seems to be a lack of engagement in this area of diversity by government policy makers who play a powerful role in setting the agendas and focus of sport managers.

In 2023, Swiss para-athlete Marcel Hug and Susannah Scaroni from the United States won the Boston marathon wheelchair division; Hug won his sixth Boston Marathon, and Scaroni is an Paralympic champion, having won a gold medal in the 5,000 m T54 race at the Tokyo Summer Paralympic Games in 2021. See Case Study 6.6.

Article 30 of the UN Convention on the Rights of Persons with Disabilities (CRPD) provides for the right of those with disabilities to participate in cultural life, including sport, and requires states to pursue equal access to sport. The long history of claiming disability rights as civil rights—borne of a global social movement in the civil rights era—the CRPD provides the rights-based framework for contemporary adaptative, or para, sport globally. The Convention and the now 60-year history of Paralympic Games (the first were in 1960 in Rome, featuring 400 athletes from 23 countries) reflect the

CASE STUDY 6.6. HUMAN RIGHTS: A SPOTLIGHT EFFECT AT THE 2022 FIFA WORLD CUP IN QATAR

The 2022 FIFA Qatar World Cup exposed issues of *labor rights in sport* in a particularly deep way, with allegations of up to 6,500 migrant workers killed in the $2 billion frenzied stadium, hotel, and transportation infrastructure for the four-week event and extensive concerns raised globally about Qatar's *kalafa* system of migrant labor. Although labor reforms were adopted by Qatar in the run-up to the games—demonstrating the effectiveness of global labor-rights campaigning—in the end Human Rights Watch reported ongoing labor-rights violations and migrant-worker deaths (often, from working in the life-threatening heat)—well into 2022 as the Games drew closer.

As the 2022 Netflix documentary *FIFA Uncovered* reveals, the Qatar hosting of the World Cup was won through bribery and patronage politics in FIFA's "one country, one vote" system of bid selection for hosting the world's largest mega-event (Human Rights Watch 2022; Norland and Harris 2022).

The president of the Norwegian Football Association, Lise Klaveness, called out FIFA's complicity and Qatar's abrogation of labor and gender rights: "In 2010, the World Cup was awarded by FIFA in unacceptable ways with unacceptable consequences. Human rights, equality, democracy, the core interests of football, were not in the starting 11 until many years later," she said. "These basic rights were pressured on as substitutes, mainly by outside voices" (Kunti 2022).

Yet there was significant pushback from Qatar and other Muslim countries, especially on the LGBTQ rights matter. The extensive criticism of Qatar from mostly Western voices in the media and organizations such as Human Rights Watch, and from some UN member states such as Norway, generated a backlash in Qatar and in many other Muslim countries. As Marri and Al Ansari (2023) argue, to many Muslims in the region, including younger Qataris who might be more amenable to social change, and the leading Qatari official overseeing the World Cup, Nasser al-Khater, received the external pressures as aggressive and overreaching:

> Many believed that the motives for such bias stemmed from a traditional orientalist mentality, which views Eastern peoples as inferior. Some officials, such as Nasser al-Khater, echoed this sentiment and said that the West is unable to accept the idea that an Arab Muslim country is capable of organizing such a high-profile global event.

ongoing approach to disabilities away from solely a medical model of individual recovery and rehabilitation through adaptive sport to a social model that reflects a more holistic role to the discriminatory practices of "ableism" (preference for those with disabilities and a patronizing approach to those with disabilities) and to broader contributions of disabled athletes to society (Martin 2017). See Case Study 6.7.

Disability sports have deeper origins in efforts to provide access to sport for those with vision impairments, and this realm of adaptive sport continues and expands into the contemporary period. In 2001, American Erik Weihenmayer became the first blind person to summit Mt. Everest, and he went on to top all of the "seven summits" (the tallest peak on each continent) in 2008 (on Everest, see the documentary *Invisible Summit*, https://www.imdb.com/title/tt15289630/).

After World War II, sport for disabled veterans through the Stoke-Mandeville Games is where one finds the origins of the contemporary paralympic games and movement organized through the International Paralympic Committee

CASE STUDY 6.7. SURFIN' SAFARI FOR DISABLED ATHLETES: MADE FOR MORE, SOUTH AFRICA

In Durban, South Africa, Made for More is an organization for sports for children with physical disabilities, founded by former schoolteacher Julia van Zyl, who went through her own personal journey working with a young boy whose life was changed for the better through access to sport, and later developed the 2023 Laureus "sport-for-good"–nominated organization (https://www.laureus.com/world-sports-awards/2023/laureus-sport-for-good/made-for-more).

The organization works to provide expansion of coaching and chaplaincy counseling services and training, run for those with disabilities community projects, sports camp, and exercise therapies (https://madeformore.org.za/what-we-do/).

Among the Made for More activities is adaptive surfing, or surf therapy. The sport of para surfing has grown dramatically with adaptation of surfing for those with a wide range of disabilities such as impaired muscle power, restricted range of motion, limb deficiencies or differences, or vision impairment.

See the Made for More Para Surfing Championships South Africa 2021 on Youtube at https://www.youtube.com/watch?v=KApz5-UqtzE.

(IPC), established in 1989. For those with intellectual disabilities, the Special Olympics is a global organization that in 2021 (even in light of the pandemic) engaged more than 3.7 million athletes in 201 country contexts (Special Olympics 2021). See Documentary Insights 6.2.

Critical in the world of disability sport is the need to further integrate and include disability sport into "mainstream sport" to give greater meaning to the concept of inclusivity and to realize the equal-access and opportunity responsibilities articulated in the CRPD. As Florian Kiuppis finds (2018):

> In sport, the view embedded in the CRPD's text, 'to enable persons with disabilities to participate on an equal basis with others' (Art. 30.5) does not per se favour approaches that take diversity and/or heterogeneity as a starting point but allows for segregated contexts in which persons with disabilities can be physically active together with their peers and competitors who have a similar level of functioning. . . .
>
> Unlike in education, where inclusion debates typically discredit segregated structures and glorify supposedly inclusive ones, in sport the individual should be able to choose an activity on a spectrum ranging from separate activities for persons with disabilities to modified activities designed for all.

DOCUMENTARY INSIGHTS 6.2.
FROM THE BATTLEFIELD TO THE
BEIJING 2008 PARALYMPIC GAMES

The documentary film *Warrior Champions: From Baghdad to Beijing* (2009) follows four U.S. military veterans who, deployed to fight the war in Iraq following the 9/11 attacks on the United States, returned with devastating injuries and deep personal traumas. With lost limbs, paralysis, and the psychological wounds of war, they returned from the Iraq theater as many war veterans return from wars worldwide: disabled physically and emotionally.

This inspiriting film featuring now-famous Paralympic athlete Melissa Stockwell follows her and these remarkable athletes as they recover, rediscover their identities as Paralympic athletes, and strive to compete at the Beijing 2008 Paralympic Games.

NAMING, SHAMING, AND BOYCOTTS

Despite the long association of sport with the spirit and realization of human rights, there is equally a long understanding in the regime of international human rights that there are *inadequate mechanisms globally for confronting by all means possible egregious, ongoing, and gross violations of human rights* (Shelton 2000). In sport, reactions to noncompliance can take many forms, from "bearing witness" to abuses and advocacy, to individual, team, or national suspensions and sanctions, to state-based boycotts. Against such considerations are, equally, the rights of athletes to sport and the aspiration, at least, of sport organizations to be in the realm of organizing global cultural cooperation without political intrusion. See Documentary Insights 6.3.

In instances historical and recent, from the 1936 Berlin Olympic Games, to 1956 at Melbourne, to the 1980 and 1984 Cold War Olympics, calls for boycott over alleged abuses by a participating state have been a somewhat constant feature of high-profile global sport competition. At the Beijing Winter Olympic Games, the United States and ten allies including Australia, India, and the UK imposed (for various reasons) a "diplomatic boycott"—preventing official endorsement—but sending athletes to the Beijing games nonetheless. See Case Study 6.8.

Other analysts point out that there is no commonly accepted yardstick for sanctions for human rights abuses in societies globally beyond sport, such that boycotts can be a blunt human-rights compliance-seeking mechanism globally (Weseterbeek and Spaaij 2023).

DOCUMENTARY INSIGHTS 6.3.
AN UNFINISHED JOURNEY, PARALYMPIC
SPORT: *RISING PHOENIX* (2020)

From medical wards to treat wounded prisoners to champions of social justice, Paralympic sport has moved from the margins of sport to the mainstream. *Rising Phoenix* takes the viewer through the very early days of sport for those with disabilities with veterans to today's major global sports event through to the highly acclaimed Rio 2016 Summer Paralympic Games where athletes were so warmly embraced and supported by Brazilian host fans, https://www.imdb.com/title/tt10851618/.

CASE STUDY 6.8. EFFECTIVE SHAMING: THE ANTI-APARTHEID BOYCOTT IN SPORT

Whether boycotts in sport "work" to stem human rights abuses is informed by imposition and effects of the cultural and sport boycott campaign against South Africa during which its ruling white minority regime imposed the repugnant and oppressive system of racial segregation known by its Afrikaans name, *apartheid* (roughly, "separateness"). From the late 1940s, South Africa accelerated its pernicious apartheid politics in both everyday life with unequal segregationist measures in housing, marriage, and sex, and in separate facilities, services, and institutions; and, in "grand" apartheid, the regime sought to define the 10–78 percent Black majority out of citizenship rights and belonging in the country . . . setting up fictitious states or homelands and seeking to get them recognized internationally. The boycott and the conflicts around it created "pitch battles" around the world commensurate with political debates about whether to sanction South Africa for apartheid or to engage the ruling regime in efforts to reform it (Hain and Odendaal 2022).

Resistance to apartheid from within was paralleled with external denunciation over the growing human rights abuses, particularly the Sharpeville Massacre of March 1960, in which Black South Africans were brutally beaten by police . . . and the video made it via television into the homes of people worldwide. In the prior year, the South African Sports Association was formed to promote integrated, nonracial sport, which in turn went to the IOC to urge South Africa's expulsion from the Olympics.

In a long, fascinating history of international intrigue at the IOC, there were violations of the boycott (especially in Rugby, during the infamous 1976 All-Blacks Tour and the Springbok Tour of New Zealand in 1981 . . . in order to play in apartheid South Africa, the Māori members of the All-Blacks tour were granted "honorary white" status).

The sport boycott against South Africa saw the country expelled between 1964 and 1988 in the Olympic Games, and it only returned to international sport in the 1992 Barcelona Games (which released political prisoner Nelson Mandela attended, prior to his becoming president).

Did the sport boycott against South Africa work? The sport and cultural boycott against South Africa did, in fact, play a role in the eventual demise of apartheid. The sport boycott's primary effect was to convince many White South Africans that failure to reform and abandon apartheid was a way toward a more rights-based, inclusive democracy that would leave them, and their beloved country, in a forever-Pariah state status in the international system (Sisk 2013). The case study presents perhaps the best evidence for effectiveness of a sport boycott.

IMPLICATIONS: SPORT, AN ARENA FOR RIGHTS-CLAIMING

In response to efforts to prevent all Russian and Belarussian athletes from participating in sport while the war in Ukraine continues relentlessly and there is no justice for the injustices that have already been done, some human rights specialists have argued that suspension of all athletes from a country is a violation of the individual human rights of athletes, invoking in a way the spirit of the historical Olympic Truce of the ancient games.

UN OHCHR Special Rapporteur Alexandra Xanthaki for cultural rights has argued that in the spirit of participation of sport as a fundamental right, a blanket prohibition on Russian and Belarussian athletes in sport violates principles of universality and nondiscrimination. Xanthaki asserts:

Such blanket prohibition actually undermines peace, rather than promotes it. The practice of sport is an instrument for preventing conflict and promoting long lasting peace and development objectives, as the UN has recognized. In the face of threats to peace and security, we should resist to being lured to further aggression and we should maintain our checks and balances when it comes to restrictions of human rights.

Searching for avenues that allow all athletes who have not committed human rights violations, whatever their nationality, to engage in sports is acting to prevent the further erosion of our common values and promote peace and understanding. (Xanthaki 2023)

She further elaborates that more individual criteria apply to all participants in international sport, i.e., that participation in international sport should be based on individual-by-individual analysis (Xanthaki 2023, 3–4); the cultural rights Special Rapporteur further elaborated that such analysis would exclude "only Russian military members implicated in 'allegations of war crimes, genocide, crimes against humanity or propaganda for war' should be denied neutral status to compete" (Dunbar 2023).

The analysis of sport and human rights points toward thinking about the cumulative effect of advocacy and results such as efforts to advance rights through sports by the World Player's (2019) Association (WPA), which like the IOC in its strategic framework, have begun to get more serious in codifying clearly and flexing sport's power for human rights. Partnerships that embed the IOC within the broader system and architecture, and further bottom-up reform and improvement of national and local human-rights mechanisms are essential.

Yet without significant reform of international sport and its institutions, issues of human rights themselves become politicized, leaving—as is the case with the IOC and Ukraine—sport organizations in the middle. Until then, for progress in realizing human rights, it may be best to look toward the arena for advocacy that sport provides, as in disability access in a very unfriendly Paris, rather than to international instruments and institutions.

QUESTIONS FOR CONSIDERATION

- How is sport a fundamental right for all, and how is sport today often ignored or disrespected as a human right?
- How have the Paralympic Games and movement evolved to advance the rights of those with disabilities?
- What is the role for sport for advancing LGBTQ rights?
- What are the barriers of access to sport, especially for those most marginalized or vulnerable elements of the world population, especially women and girls? How can sport and physical education as a fundamental human right—"sport for all"—be more successfully promoted?

FOR FURTHER INFORMATION

In September 2022, the IOC published its first-ever Strategic Framework on Human Rights in an approach that articulates five focus areas: equality and nondiscrimination, voice, privacy, safety and well-being, and livelihood and decent work. The framework seeks to apply athletes, the institutions of the Olympic games (including the federations and NOCs), workers and value chains in Olympic-related events, and the broader Olympic "communities" to include associated news media, communities living in or affected by Games, and historically marginalized and vulnerable groups (IOC 2022c).

The organizations pledge to a two-year periodic review of its human rights framework and performance.

The transnational Sport and Rights Alliance (https://sportandrightsalliance.org/) is a coalition of organizations that includes civil society groups, labor organizations, advocates for women and children, LGBTQ organizations, journalists, concerned fans, and engaged athletes to advocate for human rights in and around sport. The Alliance, which includes organizations that regularly monitor and advocate for rights such as Amnesty International and Human Rights Watch, organizations such as the WPA and the International Trade Union Confederation, and the Committee to Protect Journalists, and anti-corruption watchdogs such as Transparency International. The Alliance website invites visitors to "take action" and provides opportunities for engagement to defend and advance human rights in and through sport.

The Center for Human Rights in Sport also features a partnership approach through a wide group of partnerships, from entities within the UN such as UN Women and UNICEF to corporate sponsors of sport such as Adidas and FIFA, government partners such as the German Interior Ministry, and global sport federations such as FIBA. The Center's principal aim is to ensure that human rights are embedded in the mission, program, and implementation of organizations throughout the global sport universe. Among the tools developed by the Centre are ways to embed human rights through the "life cycle" of sport mega-events, integrating human rights into sport-related educations, and a tool kit on sports for national human rights institutions in countries around the world.

In 2023, UN Women and UNESCO unveiled a comprehensive handbook in the fight against violence against women and girls in and related to sport, offer practical guidance for sport organizations and the broader network with guidance on context assessment, legal frameworks, prevention, education, reporting, and sport-based interventions to reduce violence (UN Women and UNESCO 2023).

NOTES

1. See the interview with the first wheelchair competitor in the Boston marathon, Bob Nichol, at   https://www.wcvb.com/article/the-history-behind-the-wheelchair-division-of-the-boston-marathon/43556374. Nichol lost his legs in an automobile accident and was influenced to begin wheelchair racing by Bob Hall, a pioneer of adaptive sport in the marathon.

Chapter 7

Sport for Sustainable Development

CHAPTER OVERVIEW

A 2018 study by the World Bank and the United Nations sought to scour the scholarly literature for the underlying causal dynamics that lead to violence, and the ways in which transitions, institutional changes, and strengthening social cohesion can put societies on pathways to peace. Poignantly, the report—*Pathways for Peace: Inclusive Approaches to Preventing Violent Conflict*—identified three key underlying drivers of conflict: inequality, especially when it dovetails with group identity lines of ethnicity, race, or caste; multidimensional exclusion, or reinforcing syndromes of poverty, social, and political discrimination; and grievances, or sentiments of injustice, social wrongs, or group fears (World Bank and UN 2018: 109–40).

Can sport contribute to redressing these underlying drivers of conflict, thus creating the basis of sustaining peace? This chapter considers the ways in which the international political economy of sport may not contribute directly to the aims of inclusive or sustainable development, and that the international political economy of sport is related more to elite sport, retail consumerism, brand identities, and merchandizing than the direct or meaningful contributions to inclusive growth, remediating inequality, or realizing the aims of sport for all.

It is important to focus this analysis on the key issues identified in the Pathways report. First, how can sport-based interventions address persistent poverty and multidimensional inequality, with a focus on breaking the "inter-generational" gap through early childhood engagement and youth-based initiatives toward positive youth identities?

CHAPTER HIGHLIGHTS

- Inclusive human development through sport is seen principally in efforts to use sport for development purposes through public-policy interventions and partnerships. The SDP sector, once seen as marginal or a nice "add-on" to development approaches, is now more mainstreamed across the UN's 2030 Sustainable Development Goals, with a high level of donor alignment and institutionalization.
- Climate change has already begun to affect the world of international sport, with concerns ranging from the effects of extreme heat on athletes during events to the sustainability of current practices of construction frenzies and consumerism around global sport mega-events. Equally, there is pressure on the world of sport itself to be more environmentally conscious and to enable environmental action.
- Questions about the effectiveness of sport-based interventions for development raise three key questions: theories of change, the knowledge base, and approaches to evidence, evaluation, and sustainability of programs and projects.

SPORT AND THE SDGS

International development assistance and aid practitioners have developed a well-evidenced approach to sport for inclusive development and environmental sustainability. In this chapter, we consider the use of sport for development purposes: that is, sport as an *instrument* of explicitly inclusive development outcomes.

Among the *development outcomes that sport programming can foster* are gains in public health, improved educational attainment, progress toward gender equality and women's empowerment, life skills and opportunities for those with disabilities, livelihoods and small-enterprise incubation, and environmentally sustainable large infrastructure projects that jumpstart economic growth although results are not guaranteed and can be highly based on context (The Commonwealth 2019; Schulenkopf and Adair 2013; Schnitzer et al. 2013). The COVID-19 pandemic gave further urgency to the need for innovative ways to use sport toward the SDG aims, with approaches focused on safeguarding participants, promoting human rights of access to sport and freedom from stigmatization such as racism or homophobia, and ensuring integrity in sport. The UN called for using sport to "recover better" from the pandemic's effects (UN DESA 2020).

A 2017 systematic review found a wide range of stakeholders or entities involved in the SDP sector, with nearly 3,200 organizations identified as being involved (culled from a review of databases and documents) with almost 1,000 involved in "grassroots practice" across all global regions (Svenson and Woods 2017; see also Schulenkorf, Sheery, and Rowe 2016). The organizations work in sport-related practice in education, livelihoods, health, and disability services in core development sectors, and about a third relied primarily on football even as most organizations reported using multiple sports or were focused on specific sports including hiking, indigenous sports, and Ultimate Frisbee.

Scholar Richard Giulianotti finds, in review of the origins of the sector and the agenda-setting drives that have led to its creation, that 2005 was a turning point for international organizations, nongovernmental organizations, and official and corporate donors working in the sector: previously, practice was ad hoc, project-based, not well integrated, and not necessarily locally sustainable. Since then, however, he finds that the sector is more aligned with common aims, has developed a knowledge base and robust community of practice, and is much more networked and collaborative with focus on sustainability for local communities (Giulianotti 2011).

The UN's 2015–2030 development agenda, with 17 Sustainable Development Goals (SDGs). Sport, in the SDGs, is seen in the SDG agenda as an enabler or instrument to achieving these goals. Enabling the agenda addresses many of the key issues of global participation in sport and health outcomes, encouraging the new behaviors, and in capacity development for greater awareness of sport's role in development. Practitioners in this area refer to "+sport" and "sport+" approaches to cogently describe what might be alternately termed instrumental and intrinsic approaches to sport-based intervention. Instrumental approaches see sport as a means to a related outcome (for a health outcome, for example), whereas intrinsic approaches emphasize the benefits of sport activities as such (for a peacebuilding outcome, for example).

With the evolution of practice in SDP, there is no longer much serious debate about the claim by the UN that sport is a "catalyst" for development and peace (UN 2022), but rather the question is how to engage more purposefully, design, implement, and demonstrate results from such programming. Much depends on the SDP practice area on well-developed knowledge and theory-of-change constructs, thoughtful and deliberate context analysis and program and project design, and consistent attention to local needs and voices, sustainability, and ethical interventions.

In evaluation of the ways in which sport is a crosscutting activity with the potential for contributing to all of the SDGs, but certainly more central to some than others, it is useful to consider the relationship in terms of *SDGs that are sport-essential and those that are sport-related* to attainment of the sustainable development goals. A large volume of policy-oriented and scholarly literature has evaluated this sector and focused particularly on areas of evidence, scaling up, and long-term effectiveness of what initially began as mostly isolated projects based on donor interests, the preferences and specialization of SDP organization, and local enabling environments.

Research findings back claims for sport-based interventions. A 2018 expert-panel review found a high degree of efficacy for SDP programs related to the SDG goals, both directly and indirectly, although national and regional data (beyond aggregate survey data on the extent of participation in sport) (International Working Group on SDP 2018). See Concept Box 7.1 and Case Study 7.1.

Central to the SDGs, and to the argument that sport goes beyond development outcomes to relate specifically to peace, is the argument that *absent addressing systemic multidimensional poverty, socioeconomic drivers of inequality, group-grievance mobilization, and repression will continue.* The linkage between such socioeconomic marginalization and the denial of rights and drivers of conflict are clearly identified by both nongovernmental and international organization analysis alike (Minority Rights Group 2021,

CONCEPT BOX 7.1. MAPPING SPORT TO THE SDGS: UN DESA

Sport-based interventions are related to eight of the 16 SDGs *directly* and are *indirectly* related to the climate change goals (12, 13, 14, and 15) in the SDGs (UN DESA 2020). The 17th SDG is about strengthening partnerships, which is crosscutting or applicable across all of the development objectives.

SDG 3	Health and well-being
SDG 4	Quality education
SDG 5	Gender equality
SDG 8	Decent work and inclusive growth
SDG 10	Inequality reduction
SDG 11	Sustainable cities
SDG 16	Peaceful societies and inclusive governance

For further analysis and mapping of these SDGs to sport-related results, see The Commonwealth (2019, 19–24).

CASE STUDY 7.1. UNICEF ON SPORT FOR CHILD DEVELOPMENT

The UN Children's Fund (UNICEF) has harnessed the evidence emanating from both natural and social sciences on the overwhelmingly salutary effects of physical recreation, play, and sport on the human brain. Strategically, if there is an interest in employing SDP purposes, linkages are critical. If harmful orientations and mindsets of prejudice, exclusive ethnic- or race-based national constructions, sexism and misogyny, transphobia, or stigmatization of those with disabilities begin with early socialization and childhood acquisition of social identities, the place to start with how sport might contribute to mindsets of empathy, fairness and equity, inclusion, and tolerance should also start with a child-centered focus.

The 2021 UNICEF report "Getting into the Game: Understanding the Evidence for Child-focused Sport for Development" (UNICEF 2021) provides the most compelling evidence to date for the underlying argument about physical activity and sport: through direct and indirect physiological and psychological processes, *sport and play are essential, in fact fundamental, building blocks* of the arguments, assumptions, and high-flying rhetoric about the "beauty," and "power" of sport . . . essentially, that physical recreation and play *can create self-reinforcing feelings and sensations of ecstasy and well-being* similar to art, music, or a captivating sunset.

Social psychology analysis emphasizes the reward system to sentiments such as the emotional aspects of spectacle—from sporting events to rock concerts to political rallies—and associated ecstatic emotions felt by participants. One hundred and fifty thousand fans chanting, stomping, and singing in a major venue such as the Maracanã football stadium in Rio—especially during a rivalry match—produces a swell of contagious, collective emotions; sporting events, especially large mega-events in the international realm, are rightly characterized as media-accelerated spectacles (Tomlinson and Young 2006).

The UNICEF report provides compelling evidence on the linkages between sport, early childhood development, and positive social outcomes such as addressing fear in turbulent contexts (such as refugee settings), exclusion, marginalization, and early childhood trauma or toxic stress. In sum, in the UNICEF review of the evidence base, the core findings are clear.

> Well-designed [sport-for-development, S4D] initiatives are improving the lives of children across the globe. Sport activities increase children's access to, and participation in initiatives and services—including for the most marginalized children—and thus promote equitable outcomes in learning, skills development, inclusion, safety, and empowerment.
>
> Evidence shows that special care should be taken to ensure that sport initiatives do not reinforce sociocultural attitudes and norms that present a risk to children or the initiative's goals. For example, S4D initiative should not: reinforce sporting cultures that can normalize violence and/or equal power relation, exclusiveness, whether because of peer behaviors or limited access, and pervasive structural and social inequalities (UNICEF 2021, 8, 9).

UNDP 2021, Human Rights Council 2022; World Bank and UN 2018). See Case Study 7.2.

Thus, as with the SDGs overall, SDP, priorities are focused on the principle of Leaving No One Behind (LNOB), beginning with those "furthest" behind, in that the principle begins with an approach to reach those most excluded and hardest to reach for proactive efforts to advance inclusion, participation, and influence in the pursuit of greater equity (UN DESA 2017). As the LNOB principles articulate, discriminatory laws and practices are reinforcing and intersectional, such that historical marginalization, as the LNOB principles reflect, "leave particular groups of people further and further behind."

SDP, as *development policy, relies on a wide range of critical theories of change or strategic perspectives* to initiatives, programs, and projects—ideally, derived from lessons learned and cumulative knowledge and experience—and critical understandings about overall development policy, such as the critical nature of local voices, empowerment, and sustainability of initiatives.

Among the most important of these is the importance of physical recreation and play in early-childhood development. Increasingly, research shows that early-childhood development is critical for subsequent life skills for successful coping, social engagement, and personal development. In 2015, the World Bank featured in its annual World Development report a focus on mindsets as related to development, and the report emphasized the very critical importance of early childhood development in social identity formation, individual skills development, and lifelong resilience capacities (World Bank 2015).

CASE STUDY 7.2. AGENDA SETTING
THROUGH THE 2017 KAZAN ACTION PLAN

In global governance networks, a key function of international organization is agenda-setting, or advocacy for a common strategy and collective action on a global-governance issue. The Kazan Action Plan of 2017 adopted by the congress of the United Nations Education, Cultural, and Scientific Organization (UNESCO) is a goal statement by the international community that seeks to align sport-based policies and activities to the goals of the SDGs, notably goals related to expanding global health, education, gender equality, sustainable cities, sustainable environment, combatting climate change effects, and economic development, and fostering peace and inclusive institutions.

The 2017 Kazan Action Plan—organized under the guidance of UNESCO as a statement of sport ministers and officials—is a significant global instrument that collectively expresses a sense of consensus that sport contributes to development and peace, that practice has come a long way in the evolution of SDP programs, evaluations, and related research, and that SDP is critical as a strategy of peacebuilding and social cohesion. At the same time, it acknowledges the key concern about SDP as an approach: it is not yet sufficiently able to "scale," or to add up beyond programs and projects.

Thus, the Plan equally calls for better evidence on how sport-related interventions may be expanded from local-to-national and from isolated programs to broad-based systems and institutions. Sport policy globally was subsequently thus more focused than before to reduce barriers to access to sport, improve strategic program and project design in SDP programs, and to address threats to the integrity of sport (for example, doping, gambling, or political interference).

The Kazan Action Plan is found at https://en.unesco.org/mineps6/ kazan-action-plan.

A leading theory of change in SDP is that sport is a magnet, or in development-intervention jargon, an effective "entry point" for programming in which sport brings a strong attractive power to potential participants or onlookers that can be harnessed by an array of development efforts toward delivery of SDG-outcome programming and delivery; sport can be a strategic tool for engaging communities in collective efficacy, for example in engaging both official local institutions and authorities, and working with informal institution such as traditional or indigenous group leaders. See Case Study 7.3.

Sport has been used for "plus sport" approach to bring disease prevention, vaccination, and reproductive health education and capacity development programming to a community. Mercy Corps International, for example, a major transnational development assistance NGO, reported on its sport-based interventions (tennis and soccer) in Liberia and Southern Sudan (now South Sudan) to prevent HIV/AIDS through programs dubbed "Yes to Soccer" and "Sports for Peace and Life." The project's evaluation, including challenges faced, guidelines for future practice, and monitoring and evaluation results have found that the HIV/AIDS prevention activities were effective in increasing knowledge and protective attitudes against the disease (although the project was unable to assess behavioral change) (Mercy Corps 2017).

CASE STUDY 7.3. SPORT FOR DEVELOPMENT, A WESTERN CAPE PROGRAM EVALUATION

In South Africa's Western Cape, long-standing settlement patterns and policies reaching back into the apartheid era have left deep development demands of access to basic services, livelihoods, community safety, facilitating tourism, and ensuring that large-scale sporting events in cities such as Cape Town have positive economic externalities to disadvantaged communities. In many areas, informal settlement conditions create strong obstacles of access to safe sport, to educational and health opportunities, and to secure livelihoods.

In a wide-ranging, evidence and methods driven analysis of Phase 2 of a multiyear research program on sport and development, University of the Western Cape Interdisciplinary Center for Sport Science and Excellence researchers showed through rigorous program evaluation that sport-based interventions have continued to show "huge benefits in terms of socioeconomic initiatives and impacts (de Coning 2018, 25). Sport-based programs have been used throughout 202 varied communities of the Western Cape province including large peri-urban communities such as Crossroads, Nyanga, Khayelitsha, and Eersterivier.

Sports and recreation activity—including unusual sports such as racing pigeons, a culturally significant activity in some communities, and esports—have served the interests of community protection, livelihoods through both formal and informal employment, and early childhood development, and cross-community relationship building.

National sport associations have been engaged in public-health interventions, for example in Zambia, where HIV/AIDS awareness and prevention was carried out through interventions by the country's national sports organizations (such as the country's netball association, the Netball Association of Zambia). Banda describes how key changes in policy, such as allowing national sport organizations to receive international donor funds directly, make a key difference in the country's multisectoral approach to the disease (2017). Banda found that "sport settings have served as conducive environments through which information about the virus can be disseminated to influence positive and social behaviors that reduce incidences that lead to infection (Banda 2017, 241). See Case Study 7.4.

Programs such as World Bicycle Relief and social enterprises like Portal Bikes in Nepal have realized an important fact about one of the simplest (yet increasingly complex with the advent of electric power), technology in sport: the bicycle. World Bicycle Relief has distributed more than 700,000 bicycles to beneficiaries in developing countries around the world, citing data that owning a bicycle for the poorest in the community can increase personal household income by as much as 35 percent. The organization engages in partnerships, capacity development, sustainability initiatives, healthcare access initiatives, and children's access to schools in Latin America, Africa, and Southeast Asia (World Bicycle Relief 2022).

Portal Bikes in Nepal builds and distributes bicycles built for development. Specializing in cargo bikes and fit-for-purpose multi-person and small-enterprise bikes, the company works with local NGOs focused on empowerment, social cohesion across Nepal's diverse society, ecotourism, and small- and medium-enterprise business development in the cycling industry (Shresttha 2017). See Case Study 7.5.

A common instrumental use of sport in the SDP community is women's empowerment, particularly in contexts where women's sport participation remains comparatively low, such as South Asia. Three examples illustrate:

- Scholar Samantha Nanyakkara found that women have been "trivialized" in sport in the countries of the subcontinent, facing inequities and constraints emanating from personal, social, and cultural barriers. She finds that lack of coaching opportunities, lack of women's representation in current sport federations, and poor facilities all inhibit access to sport in the South Asian countries (Nanayakkara 2012, 1899–1900).
- In research on sport for at-risk adolescent girls in St. Lucia, Sarah Zip evaluated sport participation in programs and conducted study groups among project beneficiaries, administrators, and community leaders. She finds that "female only sport participation encouraged a positive sense of self-efficacy and fostered peer/mentor relationships, [whereas]

CASE STUDY 7.4. JOEL EMBIID,
NBA MVP 2023, A BWB ALUM

When Joel Embiid of the Philadelphia 76ers won the National Basketball Association's Most-Valuable Player (MVP) award in 2023, the award could be considered to be shared for an entire area of development practice—the use of international development assistance to improve livelihoods and prosperous societies globally—known as "sport for development and peace" (SDP). With roots in bilateral development assistance programs of countries which provide significant official development assistance (ODA), such as Norway, the SDP sector today is an extensive network of international humanitarian and development organizations, transnational civil society, and local civil society organizations.

Embiid, a towering center for the 76ers, was born in Cameroon and only came to the United States for secondary school for better recruitment prospects in the professional pinnacle of the sport, the NBA: he got his start playing basketball at age 15 in a Basketball without Borders program in Yaondé, Cameroon, that was funded in part by a foundation of another NBA star that had "given back" through his foundation to make the FIBA, NBA, and BWB camp possible, Luc Mbah a Moute.

At aged 15, Embiid hadn't played much basketball: his father, a military officer and handball athlete, saw a future for his exceptionally tall son in volleyball (MacMullan 2017). Luc, himself, was the product of a Basketball without Borders camp, having had the opportunity at age 16 to train with a coach, Guy Muido, at a BWB program in Johannesburg, South Africa (MacMullan 2017).

Embiid's journey, which he describes as "improbable [that] . . . someone like me . . . probably a negative zero" would rise from beginning a sport at 15 to being an MVP in the NBA can thus be rather directly traced to SDP intervention as a pathway to the highest levels of elite levels in international sport (Africanews 2023).

If anecdotes such as Embiid's counted well as "evidence" for the efficacy of the value of sport for pathways of personal development, and collective development through the broader effects of the Cameroon basketball programs for youth—especially, providing inspiration and a safe place for sport for women and girls—sport unambiguously contributes to development.

For a fictitious story of such pathways to the pinnacle of elite sport, see the novel *Sooley: A Novel* (Grisham 2021).

CASE STUDY 7.5. HAMMERING FOR HUMANISM: LACHLAN MORTON'S FKT ON THE COLORADO TRAIL, 2022

When "alt-" cyclist Lachlan Morton set out on Tuesday, September 6, 2022, in an effort to set the record for the "fastest known time" (FKT) for mountain-bike completion of the exceptionally rugged and challenging Colorado Trail—an 849-km (~530-mile) route that features some 27,400 vertical meters (90,000 feet) of climbing, with the average elevation over 3,140m (~10,300 ft)—he was not riding solely for the record books. Instead, the Herculean ride by the Australian was for humanism (the philosophy of sport, see chapter 5).

A month earlier, fellow professional cyclist and Morton compatriot Sule Kangangi tragically died during the Vermont Overland gravel race in a crash; Kangangi was the captain of Team Amani, a nonprofit East African squad that is devoted to the development of cycling in East Africa and is comprised of riders from Rwanda, Kenya, and Uganda.

Morton rode the Colorado Trail for Sule: his FKT ride attempt was to raise money for the Sule Kangagi Memorial Fund, set up to support Kangangi's surviving wife and children. The ride and associated GoFundMe campaign raised over $80,000 for the Fund.

With Sule's memory in his grieving mind, Morton hammered (cycling slang for intense effort) through the unimaginably difficult route—replete with weather, wildlife, and withering hike-a-bike ascents and treacherous single-track descents—in three days, 10 hours, and 15 minutes, achieving the FKT for the record books (Stuart 2022). The feat was about 70 hours of full-on hammering, with only 12 hours of off-bike time over the three days, finishing at 2 am on day four.

In 2021, Morton rode an "alt tour" of the Tour de France, completing the route (to include transfers) five days ahead of the well-supported race peloton . . . raising funds for World Bicycle Relief, an NGO devoted to providing bikes to the most in need around the world; the 2021 alt-tour feat raised over $700,000 (https://worldbicyclerelief.org/alt-tour/).

Morton's epic Colorado Trail FKT achievement, and his overall humanism, illustrates the underlying motivation of sport for goals beyond sport's sake: in this case, *transnational solidarity* for the family of a fallen friend.

engagement in co-education football supported girls' empowerment and the challenging of gender stereotypes" (Zipp 2017, abstract).

- The global spread of women's sport for empowerment is ongoing. In 2019, Senegal hosted its first ever pro surfing event, and the country's first-ever female professional surfer, Khadjou Sambe, supports the "Black Girls Surf" organization (Bensemra 2020). Although Sambe faced personal struggles to be allowed to surf as a young girl in predominantly Muslim Senegal, she now coaches young girls in sport, mental well-being, and personal resilience.

Blough and Rivat find in their analysis of programs for the French aid agency, AED (Agence Française de Dévelopment) that SDP programs aimed at women's and girl's empowerment are overall in need of "urgent action" to remedy the disparity in access to sport and physical recreation between men and boys and women and girls globally. There is the need for SDP practitioners to relate more fully to gender dynamics in societies to consider issues such as boy's access to traditionally women's sport (such as dance) (Blough and Rivat 2023, 15).

Related work in development has seen prominent athletes and sport organizations working in networks to prevent malaria (e.g., the "Nothing but Nets" campaign) and sport programs to expand the reach of vaccination campaigns or to extend the reach of education or nutrition efforts. The former NBA star from China Yao Ming turned his remarkable physical presence (at 7'6" or 2.3 meters) toward promoting sport for environmental sustainability after injuries ended his professional basketball career. Ming worked to raise awareness on environmental issues, advocating bans on ivory imports and shark-fin harvesting, in collaboration with the NGO WildAid (Denver 2014). See Documentary Insights 7.1.

SPORT AND ENVIRONMENTAL SUSTAINABILITY

One of the most poignant arenas at the intersection of sport is its historical and contemporary troubled *relationship with environmental sustainability*, despite recent efforts to orient sport more directly toward environmental sustainability (as described in chapter 8). Mega-events have notoriously left detrimental environmental legacies, and sport-related tourism has helped precipitate a global crisis of pollution and impact in often fragile ecosystems from lagoons to summits (Atkinson 2016; Tomino, Perić, and Wise 2020).

There is increasing concern emanating from athlete voices on the *environmental effects of globalized sport*, particularly new lifestyle sports among upper middle-class and elite from around the world seeking to reach personal

DOCUMENTARY INSIGHTS 7.1. BOX GIRLS KENYA: AN UPPERCUT TO MARGINALIZATION

In the informal settlement (slum) of Kairobangi, the heroine of the documentary *Box Girl*, Sonko Msoto, is followed on her remarkable journal from a situation of multidimensional poverty as a woman from the impoverished community. This 9-minute documentary is critically acclaimed in its genre as a short film (https://www.imdb.com/title/tt3326942/).

The academy in which the film is set, Box Girls Kenya, engages young women in the community through boxing, and in turn works toward challenging and changing local norms about sport being traditionally reserved for boys and men, or that women can't perform in sports requiring strength and strategy.

Box Girls Kenya pairs boxing-as-sport with life-skills development for the women and girls geared toward peer support, children and women's rights in education, gender roles, and problem-solving and conflict resolution skills (Al Jazeera 2017).

heights and to live most fully commensurately with their means. In surfing, a former countercultural sport that developed in the 1960s, concerns have been raised about the environmental effects of surfboards, which are made of polyurethane and polystyrene, unrecyclable and destined to end up in landfills around the world. So, too, some 8,000 tons of neoprene wetsuits used in the sport end up in landfills annually. Seven-time British champion in women's surfing Lucy Campbell has called out companies and athletes to be more sustainable: "You do want to encourage people to get outdoors," she said, "but at what cost to the planet?" (BBC 2023).

Lifestyle sport companies are turning to technology and approaches such as recycling to address the environmental impact of these sports. The French company Salomon, for example, is working to further expand recycled materials in its line of new skis to prevent plastics made from polyurethane and polypropylene from ending up in a landfill.[1]

The *economic, environmental, and social effects of mega-events* have become better understood, with best practices of generating sustainable development externalities appearing to be increasingly known. For social development, instances such as London 2012 and the Manchester 2002 Commonwealth Games have been carefully evaluated as case studies of mega-events and ostensible positive side effects such as gains in public health and urban renewal . . . including a legacy of space spaces for access to sport (Thompson et al. 2015; Carlsen and Taylor 2003). Such mega-events are getting larger, for example, the South-East Asian (SEA) Games in Phnom Penh, Cambodia, in 2023 featuring 11 countries participating put 581 medals up in sports such as cricket dance, teqball,[2] and Jet-Skiing (Economist 2023).

Increasingly, organizations such as the IOC and sport federations are implementing new and stricter guidelines for environmental best practices at sport events. Yet the economic, environmental, and social costs of global sport mega-events will continue to come under scrutiny as the world's climate crisis grows more dire. See Case Study 7.6.

FROM CATALYST TO CAUSALITIES: DEBATING SDP

This need for evidence that sport-related programming is effective requires thinking beyond project-based monitoring and evaluation of outcomes to look at how sport-based programs fit into, and complement, a broader peacebuilding strategy at the country level. Development *scholars have at times been hesitant to embrace generalized claims of effectiveness of sport-for-peace-and-development* programming—highlighting in the process a distinct lack of evidence linking sport programming to either demonstrable progress in peacebuilding or human development outcomes on a larger scale. Black (2010), for example, recognized the potential for sport to enhance development, but also discerned a "donor discourse" that inflates the potential of sport as a lever or instrument for peace and development programming. Coalter (2010) found that the sport-for-peace-and-development rhetoric promotes an unjustified linkage between donor-funded sport initiatives and development progress.

Like Coalter, there is a deep, yet friendly skepticism found in the SDP practice area—where sport is argued to be a "catalyst" for development—that the community of practice can be sufficiently self-critical, despite the detailed policy planning and log frame-mapping of program activities that has accompanied the Kazan action plan. *Donors, leaders of development organizations, policy officers, and project implementers alike have struggled to show with systematic and comparative evidence the special and long-term efficacy of sport-based programming.* Indeed, it is methodologically difficult to isolate out how sport as such provides unique or especially effective value-added into the community beyond participants in an intervention.

Scholar Holly Collison finds through close-in research on SDP interventions for reconciliation, peacebuilding, and rehabilitation in war-torn Liberia in the early 2010s that within the broader community-level socioeconomic contexts in which these interventions for youth development through football, there is a need for caution about claims of sport's power to transform. She identifies a mutual seduction of sponsors, organizers, and participants for

CASE STUDY 7.6. EVEREST BASE CAMP: THE WORLD'S HIGHEST GARBAGE DUMP

Taken to a global level, awareness about sport's potential negative effects on sustainability has reached new heights. Everest base camp, the ostensible epitome of rarified, purified air and natural sportscape, is now deemed by legendary local indigenous Sherpa athletes as "the world's highest garbage dump." The high-altitude garbage patch can be directly related to the international political economy of ecotourism that brings some 40,000 hikers per year to the Everest base camp along a popular trekking route.

The year 2023 saw the most crowded climbing season at Everest ever, and deadly, with more guided, typically globally wealthy athletes seeking to climb the mountain, causing a myriad of global ecotourism, economic, environmental, and global-local injustice questions; in 2023, a video of the mountain of litter at Everest base camp, taken by Tenzi Sherpa, underscores the "heartbreaking" impact of international sport on the fragile ecosystem (Kim 2023).

Figure 7.1 is a stark symbol of mountaineering mayhem on a "bluebird summit day" (cloud-free) on Everest in 2019.

Figure 7.1. Crampons and Crowds: A Traffic Jam at 8,000m/26,000', Mt. Everest, 2019. A long queue of crampon-clad mountain on Mount Everest just below Camp 4, in Nepal, on a "bluebird" (cloud-free) summit day, May 22, 2019. Credit: AP Photo/ Rizza Alee, File.

sports programming and a complex environment that limits program impacts. In Liberia, she finds:

> SDP organisations proclaim that sport unites and aids the processes of reconstruction, reconciliation and rehabilitation in post-conflict societies, yet the issues facing Liberian youth have little to do with these areas. The limited access to adulthood is what deprives Liberian youth of independence, status, power and acknowledgement.
>
> Gaining opportunities for employment, meaningful recognised education and reducing barriers between the generational categories would better address the youth problem in Liberia than football programmes. It may be the case that current SDP projects and the adoption of such practices by internal agencies and individuals encourages and affirms youths as youths: playing football is the most visible indicator of youth identity. (Collison 2016, 224)

This embedded analysis of SDP programs reinforces the need for local understandings of the efficacy and design of sport programming, evaluation of the effects of sport programming on key target populations such as the displaced, ex-combatants, and to think more holistically about the contribution of sport programs to national unity and broader social cohesion. That is, there is the need for more Southern, and more beneficiary, voices in determining what constitutes evidence for effective SDP interventions. These issues are further explored in chapter 8.

Despite these cautionary notes, *scholarly evidence demonstrates in more narrow studies positive outcomes from utilizing sport and play to enhance development and peacebuilding initiatives.* Lyras and Welty-Peachey, in a comparative analysis of sport programming in Haiti and Cyprus, developed an evaluative framework for project-level analysis that consists of five components—an assessment of a program's impact, its organizational structure, the role of sport in society, and education and cultural enrichment elements. The authors develop a structured theoretical rubric with which to analyze individual programs, and simultaneously present evidence-based research from case studies including the Doves Project in Cyprus and the World Scholastic Athletic Games (WSAG) in order to demonstrate levels of effectiveness. After applying this framework to projects in these two country-level case studies, the authors conclude that the most effective programs incorporate elements from each of these five core components. In particular, they find that:

> The blend of sport with cultural enrichment activities (e.g., arts, dance and music) and global citizenship education, global issues awareness, human rights and environment) can provide a framework for personal development, cross-cultural acceptance and collaboration, and social change.

These components can then be used to identify factors that facilitate and inhibit positive change, set objectives and assess social, psychological, and societal change across time and space. (Lyras and Welty Peachey 2011: 313)

Although sports bodies like FIFA and the Olympic Games have programs to address sport for development and peace, these activities are a small sliver of vast resources—athlete, administrator, and coaches' salaries, event expenses, travel, marketing, and branding—that are involved with elite sport.

There is little available data on the annual amount of official development assistance (ODA) for SDP, with best estimates at about $150 million/year in initiatives funded by traditional ODA donors (i.e., members of the OECD "Paris Club" who report collectively on ODA).

Among the research areas that are critical for next-generation work in SDP is to understand how much—or, in fact how little—sport-related interventions are funded to scale to have a strong impact on outcomes such as development. There is much attention to evidence in sport-for-development, but this attention from policymakers and scholars does not appear commensurate with the actual investment in sport-related development as a total share of global development assistance.

IMPLICATIONS: FURTHERING EVIDENCE

SDP has made *tremendous strides in the knowledge and evidence base on the efficacy of SDP programming* more broadly, and sport-for-peacebuilding specifically. Civil society implementing groups have made strides in developing project-specific monitoring and evaluation (M&E) specific to sport programming. In addition to development outcomes—enhancing quality education, improving health, and supporting child and youth development—sport programming has been a part of efforts to prevent, manage, and mitigate conflict.

There is equally the need to dive deeper into the wide array of sport, and combinations of sport, games, and curricular activities, that are common features of SDP interventions. Particularly, ways to provide evidence on direct outcomes has progressed well within this development community of practice, yet there is the need for further evidence on two important fronts: measuring indirect outcomes, like how a project might be perceived within a broader community context or by important stakeholders, and long-term effects or the extent to which SDP activities have the often purported life-changing and lifelong consequences for participants or communities.

Providing great evidence on indirect outcomes requires further integration of sport-based initiatives with overall SDG-attainment monitoring, and seeking to solve a puzzle that has long affected this community of practice: What is the specific, causal mechanism-informed, value added of "sport-based" as an activity as such? What is it about physical activity-based interventions that are special, different, or putatively "catalytic?" In the initial, more formative years of the SDP area of practice in the early 2000s, there was widespread concern about a lack of evidence on sport's contribution to development and peace, or its purported power as an instrument of improving livelihoods, fostering coexistence between former enemies, or having a lasting impact on broad-based social cohesion.

While evidence-based concerns linger, the evolution of monitoring and evaluation frameworks, synthetic research by international organizations such as UNICEF, and more "co-creation" of knowledge with local practitioners and scholars (Nicholls, Giles, and Sethna 2010), has led to a current context in which there are few debates about whether sport can contribute to development and instead, even further evidence-gathering on the most effective approaches, methods of local assessment and engagement, and building in evaluation linkages across sectors to extend up-scaling community effects and for longitudinal analysis.

The question going forward, as reflected in the Kazan SDP partnership plan, is to further expand, or scale, sport-for-peace-and-development. Without having ever scaled sport-based interventions in an integrated or holistic approach to a country or context, it is a given that there are few integrated national, regional, or global analyses of long-term benefits and outcomes of SDP interventions.

QUESTIONS FOR CONSIDERATION

- How has the international development community begun to more systematically mainstream sport into education and health programing in developing countries, and to what effect?
- Can the system of international sport, dependent on team travel, mega-events, and widespread marketing campaigns, reach environmentally neutral or even positive externalities?
- Sport programming has a certain feel-good quality, replete with heartwarming anecdotes and global athlete-inspired or -involved initiatives, but to what extent does evidence exist that sport programming is scalable and effective as an instrument of development?

FOR FURTHER INFORMATION

- The UN's SDG Fund developed a practice-oriented tool kit for the SDP sector in its 2018 publication "The Contribution of Sports to the

Achievement of the Sustainable Development Goals: A Toolkit for Action" (SDG Fund 2018). The tool kit itself consists of well-detailed mapping of the SDGS and sub-indicators to sport activities, theories of change, guidance for practice, and recommendations for programming and further development of the SDP sector.

• For those seeking to formulate projects, programs, and initiatives in sport for development, the Commonwealth updated in 2019 its comprehensive tool kit for practitioners. "Measuring the Contribution of Sport, Physical Education and Physical Activity to the Sustainable Development Goals: Toolkit and Model Indicators (version 3.1)" provides knowledge and practice guidance for sports-based interventions, a results-based management approach to program and project implementation, and a menu of indicators and approaches for quantifying results on the social and economic value of sport-based interventions (The Commonwealth 2019).

• UN DESA has conducted a deep analysis of the effects of climate change on sport, and how sport can in turn affect the trajectory of climate change, in a policy brief that provides an overview of current knowledge and lessons learned in sport and environmental sustainability internationally. A 2022 Brief finds that "sport is a key social platform that can reach and influence millions of people and raise awareness on climate change, promote a culture in favour of climate action, and champion sustainable behaviors" (UN DESA 2022b, 1).

• Finally, the International Council of Sport Science and Physical Education ICSSPE) has developed a toolkit for sport-based interventions for development by grassroots sport leaders. "Let's Get Moving Together" was developed by participants from Namibia, South Africa, Zambia, and Germany (ICSSPE and UNESCO 2022).

NOTES

1. The company released its first fully recycled Nordic ski in 2023; see https://www.salomon.com/en-us/blog/wse-sustainability-ambitions.

2. Teqball and para teqball are played with a ball on a curved table, with elements of kick-style volleyball (*sepak takraw*); the sport is governed by the International Teqball Federation (ITF), https://www.fiteq.org/.

PART V

Sustaining Peace

Humanitarianism, Peacebuilding, and Social Cohesion

Chapter 8

Sport for Humanitarian Action, Peacebuilding, and Social Cohesion

CHAPTER OVERVIEW

Persistent and worsening armed conflict in the international system continues to present the most grave and immediate threats to international peace, with new escalations to civil war in Sudan in 2023 and the alarming "return" of international war between sovereign states in the Russian aggression against Ukraine in 2022. The OECD survey of fragile contexts around the world—countries experiencing violence, deep multidimensional poverty, and chronic humanitarian needs—estimates there are more than 500 million people in more than 60 countries at risk of extreme poverty, displacement, food insecurity, and vulnerability to further violence. New conflicts in Azerbaijan, Sudan, and Israel in 2023 raise ongoing concerns about atrocities in conflict.

Youth aged 15–24 are some 20 percent of people in these contexts, and the OECD reporting finds that more than a quarter of these youth have no access to employment, education, or training and are thus especially vulnerable to recruitment into violent extremism. Moreover, 64 percent of the world's displaced populations are found in these fragile-state environments, many of whom are internally displaced within their own countries (OECD 2022, 17).

The principal aims of sport-for-peace interventions in fragile- and conflict-affected contexts are to symbolize and advance reconciliation and a "new relationship" among contending social forces, to promote social reintegration and to redress the root causes of conflict that are often found in youth disaffection, unemployment, and vulnerabilities to gangs, crime, or

insurgency, and to create the conditions for sustaining peace through community security and social cohesion.

CHAPTER HIGHLIGHTS

- In settings where delivery of humanitarian assistance is urgent,
  sport-based initiatives and sport facilities have been used to improve the
  effectiveness of delivery of essential relief such as food, medicine, or
  vaccines and programs and projects for psychosocial support to address
  trauma-induced mental health challenges.
- In situations of displacement, sport has emerged as an important instrument for reaching vulnerable youth with opportunities for respite from
  conflict, a safe place for community gathering, and for mental health and
  psychosocial well-being.
- Sport-based approaches have been shown to be effective in community
  security and the bottom-up conditions of social cohesion that are neces-
  sary to sustain peace.

SPORT IN HUMANITARIAN ACTION

As a consequence of long-running wars, criminality and armed violence,
natural disasters, and discrimination, the world faces a deeply intransigent
humanitarian crisis: some 370 million people globally need humanitarian
assistance (OCHA 2022). There are more than 110 million people living in
a situation of forced displacement with more than 80 percent of those living
in conditions of low resource environments with limited access to healthcare
services, employment, safe and reliable food and water, and access to public services (UNHCR 2022). With one in 23 people globally depending on
humanitarian assistance and protection and with uneven economic growth,
continued conflict and fragility, pandemics and disease, and climate emergencies, the number is expected to grow dramatically by 2026 (OCHA 2022).

In situations of complex humanitarian emergencies, delivery of assistance
to meet fundamental or basic human needs is urgent. The UN and its specialized agencies, in partnerships with nongovernmental assistance providers,
approach assistance in such contexts through the "Global Cluster for Early
Recovery" that organizes aid to deliver urgent, live-saving relief . . . *early
critical interventions* occur in the humanitarian assistance phase while focusing on ways to enhance resilience and recovery for affected populations.
The approach emphasizes two important principles: local ownership of relief
priorities and an understanding of the social and economic conditions, and

engagements that address vulnerabilities to new crises and that reduce future risk by strategically providing relief in a way that enhances local capacities, preparedness, and recovery. Activities in the early recovery phase include both meeting essential human needs of livelihood through cash payments or other resources, shelter and housing for safety and protection, water and sanitation, and mental health and psychosocial support.

Humanitarian action is about providing critical relief to affected populations and about addressing their needs in contexts of violence and fragility, displacement, or other situations where human security is at imminent risk. While in humanitarian action the first-order needs of shelter, food, water and sanitation, and social protection are paramount, sport has been used as an effective means of delivering such assistance.

Like with development, *sport is both an important instrument or enabler of effective humanitarian action, as well as an effective approach to programming to enhance mental health* and psychosocial well-being. International humanitarian actors engaged in relief in situations of crisis have employed sport as an effective approach to meeting essential-needs delivery objectives such as distribution of food and medicines, as a way to provide psychosocial benefits to displaced and other highly vulnerable people, as a means of fundraising and building awareness for humanitarian causes, and in efforts to address acute vulnerability and human insecurity.

In conditions of crisis, *sport-related infrastructure such as stadiums have been used effectively for delivery of humanitarian assistance.* Such "sportscapes" are often sites of common community location, can accommodate the management of people, and provide opportunities for communication, delivery of assistance, security, and for effective delivery of assistance.

In Haiti, for example, following the 2010 earthquake, relief organizations strategically used soccer stadiums as distribution points for early-recovery assistance. With protection from Brazilian peacekeepers deployed in the United Nations Assistance Mission for Haiti (MINUSTAH), aid groups were able to distribute food, shelter materials, medicines (see Figure 8.1). So, too, when disaster struck again in 2021 in another earthquake, it was through local soccer stadiums that relief organizations were able to deliver assistance and organize temporary housing for families who lost homes even though over time conditions at the stadium become dire as needs and bad weather conditions outstripped the ability of assistance provider to stay ahead of the expansive needs (Beaubien and Balaban 2021). See Case Study 8.1.

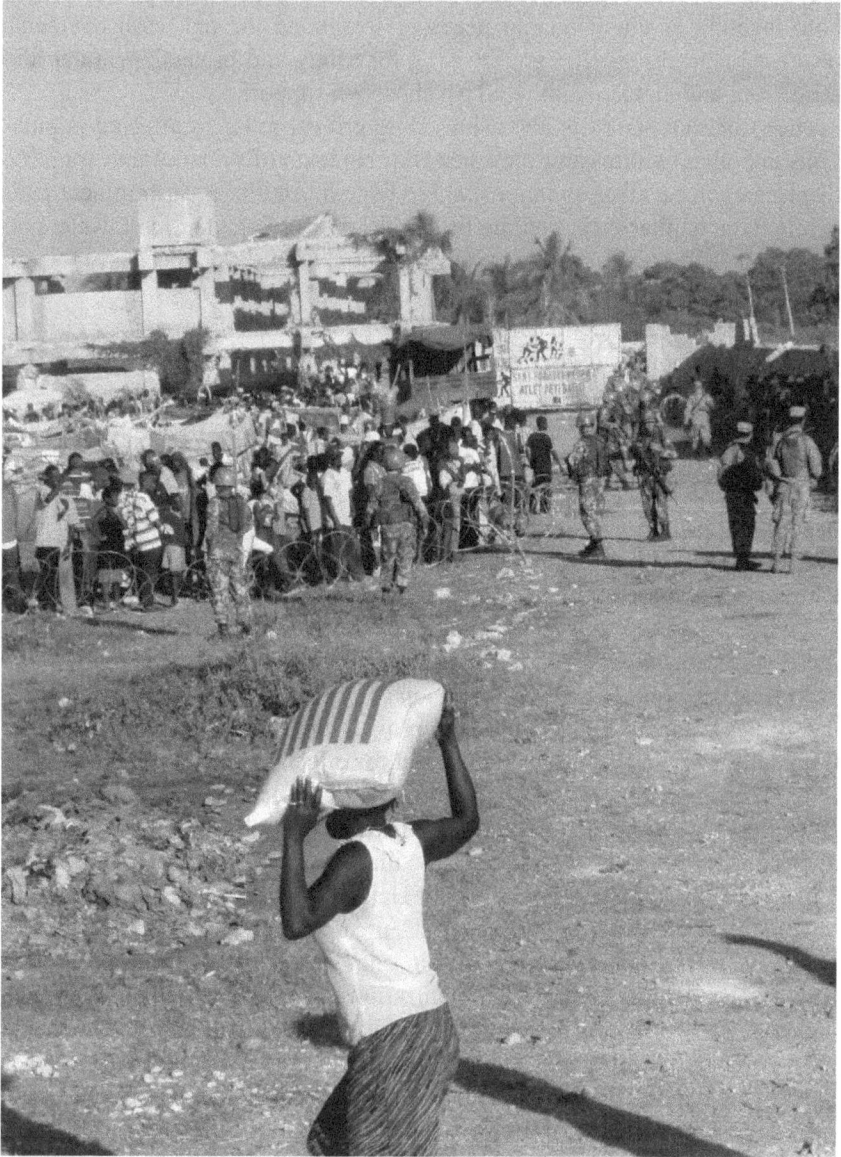

Figure 8.1. Sport Infrastructure for Humanitarian Relief: Aid Distribution at the Football Field after the Haitian Earthquake, 2010. *Credit: Fletcher D. Cox.*

CASE STUDY 8.1. SPORT AND CIVILIAN PROTECTION IN UN PEACE OPERATIONS: UNMISS

The United Nations Assistance Mission in South Sudan (UNMISS) was deployed as a multidimensional peace operation in 2011 after the independence of the country and has continued to work to protect civilians and facilitate peacebuilding in the wake of the 2013 civil war and the 2018 peace agreement. Despite the agreement, the country continues to face communal conflict and an ongoing crisis of displacement with 2.2 million internally displaced and another 2.3 million displaced as refugees (IDMC 2022).

An UNMISS quick impact project with a local community partner in the ethnically diverse community of Yei saw peacekeepers and local partners construct a football pitch, locker facilities, and a perimeter wall in the town square. The community has seen challenges from returning displaced persons, and there was a need for facilities to conduct peace meetings, common social activities, and for places for youth.

Lauro Ohiyo, an UNMISS protection officer, said that through the small-scale intervention "We managed to create a secure space for youth and the larger community to congregate, be it for a football tournament, community dialogue, or a cultural event. When communities come together it helps promote peace, forgiveness, and reconciliation, thereby encouraging more returns" (*UN News* 2023).

PSYCHOSOCIAL INTERVENTIONS: REACHING VULNERABLE YOUTH

Sport is employed in contexts of humanitarian crisis as a *critical means of mental health and psychosocial intervention*. Sport-based activities can provide a respite, contribute to physical development and social skills capacity development for children, and address the emotional needs of beneficiaries. In Yemen, for example, the UEFA Foundation for Children supported a project in Ibb governorate through the Italian relief agency Helpcode for children 6–15 from nearly 2,000 displaced families to improve access to sport for respite and trauma relief and to provide important education and skills development to help them cope with the crisis context.[1] Projects such as these seek to address the need for personal resilience, coping capacities of those affected, including perseverance, flexibility, ingenuity, self-esteem, and to build "social and cultural capital" (Spaaij 2012).

Sport-based interventions are *a nonclinical approach to individual and community-level coping capacities* in complex emergencies, harnessing the process of sport to contribute to physical strength and endurance, mental well-being, and collective work together in the context of a community. A common objective is to restore or enhance emotional and psychological health, activities tailored to local traditions, with benefits to participants in three ways:

- Safety and safe access to sport, play, or recreation, especially for women and children;
- Periods of respite, taking attention away from the experience of loss; and as an
- Opportunity to reinforce educational methods, such as empathy, tolerance, and respect.

Humanitarian actors seek to address *physical health—food, medicines, shelter, maternal and child nutrition and care, water, and sanitation—and mental health and psychosocial well-being, focusing on trauma resilience and recovery.* Many displaced people and migrants have experienced exceptional trauma along deeply insecure routes and may continue to live in circumstances of vulnerability to interpersonal or community violence. The United Nations High Commissioner for Refugees (UNHCR), with sponsorship from the International Olympic Committee, has used sport to help refugee children regain "lost childhood" through volleyball programs in countries such as East Timor, Nepal, South Sudan, and Yemen.[2]

And sport-related interventions at the level of individual needs may well be the very basis of "peacebuilding." As scholar Mari Fitzduff finds in her analysis of the linkages between neuroscience and the underlying drivers of violence:

> Young men in particular need positive "heroic" opportunities. Young men, who are the main perpetrators and the main victims in all conflicts, need opportunities to use their biopsychological energies and tendencies for either better or worse purposes. Curbing their attraction to joining illegal violent groups often requires creating alternative and positive opportunities for their energies and their ideals through, for example, employment, civil society action, or marriage and children. . . . It also means minimizing the inequities and exclusion that they may feel, which are often used to justify their violence. (2021, 147)

Sport-based mental health interventions seek to address these drivers directly: they typically seek outcomes such as reductions in anxiety, depression, and post-traumatic stress disorder with symptoms such as flashbacks, nightmares, and anhedonia (indifference to what would normally cause pleasure). Among the approaches that have shown particularly effective for these purposes is the use of action sports such as BMX cycling, parkour, skateboarding, and surfing that involve some degree of risk, skills, and countercultural aspects that are new and different in contrast to traditional sports such as football.

Building sport through skateboarding has been a highly successful endeavor in war-affected contexts such as Palestine and Uganda and skateparks have been built in countries such as Jamaica, Peru, and Morocco; organizations such as SkatePal in Palestine and Concrete Jungle Foundation have been at the forefront of skateboard-related initiatives for youth resilience and capacity development. This approach is well-documented by scholar Holly Thorpe, who examined a wide range of sport-based interventions in contexts such as Afghanistan, Cambodia, and South Africa with names such as "Chill," "Surfers for Peace," and "Surfaid International" (Thorpe 2016).

Perhaps the most well-known of these organizations is "Skateistan" which operates in many of these countries and is working to employ action sports such as skateboarding for children to provide safe spaces, new skills, and opportunities for social interactions across lines of division in society; the organization focuses on participants from low-income households, those with disabilities, and those facing social discrimination such as young girls or minority youth in line with the "Child Protection Policy" to reduce risks and enhance outcomes in the programming (Skateistan 2019). In the late 2000s, the organization Skateistan had thousands of participants in Afghanistan, but was affected by the return of the repression of sport (especially for girls) in 2021; after suspending the program when the regime changed, the organization continues to operate there and is using sport-based interventions to address issues of food security, distributing food parcels to families through the participants in their programming (Skateistan 2022). See Case Study 8.2 and Figure 8.2.

Thorpe finds that, although attention must be paid to inclusivity and access, "action sports [such as skateboarding] can complement the SDP movement by offering alternative learning experiences that encourage self-expression and creating thinking, and, when supported appropriately, can develop a different set of physical and social skills among children and youth" (2016: 109).

Sport-based interventions are used to assist especially vulnerable populations to promote livelihoods, status, and dignity. For example, sport can be used as an intervention tool for marginalized youth to reduce their

CASE STUDY 8.2. PEER VIOLENCE REDUCTION: RIGHT TO PLAY IN HYDERABAD, PAKISTAN

Right to Play has been at the forefront of developing M&E tools and is a leader in the community of practice in articulating measurement strategies for sport-programming impact. In its M&E approach, the organization employs quasi-experimental methods (such as random controlled trials, RCT), survey sampling of participants, longitudinal child-by-child level outcome tracking, and learning studies to assess community-level impact.

To address the challenges of peer violence in schools in Hyderabad, Pakistan—a community which has seen violence among kids, with 85 percent of girls and 95 percent of boys having experienced peer violence (either as victim or perpetrator)—Right to Play Pakistan together with Aga Khan university scholars conducted an evaluation of a sport-based violence reduction program in schools. The program—designed as a cluster-randomized controlled trial—used sport activities to engage 8,000 participants in 40 schools on critical thinking on negative emotions, resilience, conflict resolution, and gender discrimination (Karmaliani et al. 2020).

Evaluation of the program showed impressive results. The children who participated experienced lower victimization and perpetration at schools up to two years after the intervention. Figure 8.1 shows the results of the peer violence measure used in the evaluation, which was found to provide a "significant reduction" in peer violence and other measures such as reduced depression (Karmaliani et al. 2020, 6).

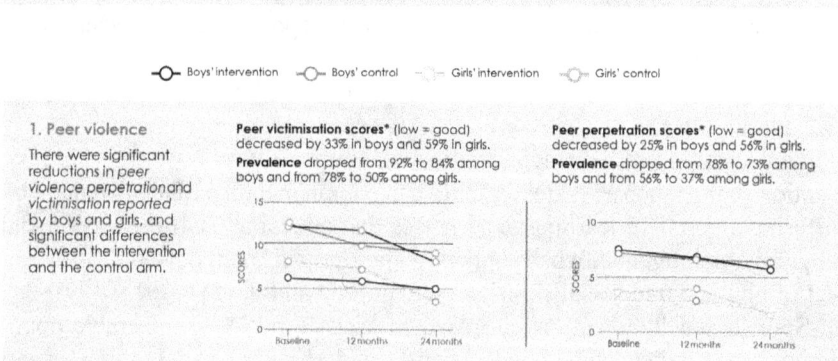

Figure 8.2. RCT Findings: Reduced Peer Violence in Hyderabad. Credit: Right to Play. The project was supported by UKAid.

vulnerability to lives of crime, gangs, and, in some contexts, recruitment into insurgent organizations.

The UN's Office of Drugs and Crime (UNODC) features a significant program to evaluate and advocate for the use of sport-based intervention for preventing violent extremism (PVE). The program, "Line Up, Live Up" seeks to leverage the popularity of sport to further values that work against radicalization and recruitment of youth by extremist groups. Developed together with UNESCO and UN DESA, the program's technical guide offers analysis of five areas of intervention: providing safe spaces for youth, fostering feelings of social inclusion, empowerment through skills training, education, and skills for personal resilience (UNODC 2020). The program also features a practical guide for coaches and facilitators, and an e-learning course on sport-for-PVE.

UNODC finds that sport-based interventions have been effective in three key areas of PVE programming: sport to reduce vulnerability to crime and recruitment into criminal organizations, the use of sport in correctional settings to prevent further radicalization and for rehabilitation and readiness for release and reintegration, and efforts to use sport-related values of respect, empathy, and inclusion as a counter to extremist ideologies (UNODC 2020, 13). Importantly, the sport-for-PVE approach stems from findings from research on radicalization that concepts such as injustice, uncertainty, and emotional responses to social discrimination are the root-cause drivers of extremism, and that these sentiments that lead to anger, frustration, and ultimately willingness to commit violence can be addressed by programs to ameliorate trauma, depression, and hopelessness through self-empowerment. An example of these programs is the UNESCO-affiliated Peace Initiative Framework (PIN) organization in Kano, Nigeria, which is engaged in efforts to bring together youth in the area from different ethnic and religious backgrounds that pairs sport activities with peace studies curriculum in workshops and seminars.[3]

Sport-for-PVE programs have inherent risks, however, and without careful context assessment, community trust-building, and protective measures for participants such programs must be particularly well-considered and designed. As the UNODC guide affirms, "If poorly designed and managed, sporting events or projects can actually contribute to marginalization by strengthening the very social divisions and inequalities they are expected to bridge" (UNODC 2020, 35).

With this guidance in mind, well-designed programming has shown effectiveness. In war-torn Liberia, organizations such as Mercy Corps have used sports such as kickball to reach young women with programs that seek to enhance communication skills, problem-solving, and leadership, part of the organizations Liberal Life Skills and Sports Development Initiative, which enrolled nearly 5,000 participants with a majority of the beneficiaries being young women (Sambolah 2023). See Documentary Insights 8.1.

DOCUMENTARY INSIGHTS 8.1 RECOVERY
CHAMPIONS: *THE FLYING STARS* (2014)

The Flying Stars, directed by Ngardy Conteh and Allan Tong, takes the viewer into the complexities of an SDP program for disabled football players in Sierra Leone, many of whom—including the documentary's protagonist, Bonor—were disabled in the country's brutal civil war from 1991 to 2002, many from landmines.

The documentary shows the remarkable courage of the athletes who play in the Single Leg Amputee Sports Association (SLASA). A form of adaptive football, athletes play with crutches and other protection, working with partners such as SwissLimbs and the National Rehabilitation Center of Sierra Leone; amputee soccer is fast, physically demanding (especially balance), and brimming with emotional intensity.

Although the courage, resilience, and sport-prowess of the participants comes through in the bear-witness documentary, so, too, does the enormity of the life challenges the participants, or beneficiaries, continue to face in the wake of war. Bonor, the protagonist, struggles off the pitch: his life of disability in a tough Freetown, Sierra Leone, is a daily existential challenge while he wrestles with the demons stemming from bodily and mental trauma in conflict, https://www.imdb.com/title/tt3790398/.

The International Committee of the Red Cross (ICRC), together with the Red Crescent Movement, has expanded its use of sport for those with disabilities, recognizing that sport-based interventions are critical for recovery and rehabilitation, and these programs have also been critical to global awareness raising on the costs of war by providing pathways to participation in the Paralympic Games for athletes. In 2019, the ICRC ran a wheelchair basketball tournament in South Sudan, which included extensive pre-tournament training, physical therapy and orthopedic treatment, and mental health support. An important objective of the program is to reduce stigmatization of those with disabilities more widely in South Sudan and to create avenues for social inclusion (ICRC 2019). See Figure 8.3.

Sport-based programs have emerged as an integral component of humanitarian relief and humanitarian action in protection, food security, and personal and community resilience in settings of forced displacement.

Figure 8.3. Champions of Recovery: Amputee Football in Sierra Leone Amputees play in a football game, part of the activities planned in observance of the International Day of Peace, organized by the United Nations Mission in Liberia (UNMIL), September 21, 2008. *Credit: United Nations Photo Library Collections, Reference # UN7646672.*

Sport for those forcibly displaced, refugees, and IDPs. At the forefront of practice in this area is the United Nations High Commissioner for Refugees and the intergovernmental International Organization for Migration. Refugee and displaced populations represent those communities who are often most negatively affected by violence and conflict, most likely to be traumatized, and most in need of international assistance for health, education, and livelihoods. IDPs and refugees are also likely in need of health-related interventions such as vaccination campaigns, disease prevention, and mental health interventions.

Since 2016, the IOC and UNCHR have worked to organize and field the Olympic and Paralympic refugee teams (Refugee Olympic Athletes Team, EOR) and in 2017 created the Olympic Refugee Foundation to institutionalize the opportunities for athletes from conflict-affected countries who would not otherwise have a pathway for participation; refugee athletes participated in the Rio 2016 Summer Games and the Tokyo 2020 Games with athletes with countries of origin such as Afghanistan, Cameroon, the Democratic Republic of Congo, Iran, South Sudan, Syria, and Venezuela. See Case Study 8.3.

To raise public awareness and to mobilize action, international humanitarian relief organizations have turned to the *global-public star power of athletes and other celebrities to advance to educate and for resource mobilization* or fundraising. Through the UN's Goodwill Ambassador program, directors

CASE STUDY 8.3. SPORTS AND HUMANITARIAN ASSISTANCE (SAHA II) PROJECT LEBANON

Lebanon has experienced years of compounding crises of conflict, governance, and economic stress since the end of the civil war in 1990 in the peace agreement known as the Taif Accord. The conflict reinforced and strongly exacerbated tensions along confessional lines and called into question a common or shared Lebanese identity. Since 2011, Lebanon's fragile social fabric was further tested with the influx of some 1.1 million refugees, roughly equal to 25 percent of the Lebanese population.

An already fragile context has led to widespread scarcity of basic resources and public services, and regional conflicts have led to increased frictions and sporadic violence in Lebanon. UNDP documents Lebanon's stark demographic transition and the impact on youth in the country, finding that approximately 27 percent of Lebanon's population are youth aged 15–29, and that of these 24 percent are Syrian, 6 percent are Palestinian, and 71 percent are Lebanese of various subgroups (Lebanon has 18 official subgroups or "confessions," among them Christians, Druze, Shi'a, and Sunni) (UNDP 2016).

Right to Play, the Netherlands Football Association (KNVB), and the transnational humanitarian assistance organization War Child implemented the SAHA II project in stressed local environments in contexts such as Tripoli which sees continued vulnerability in the face of the socio-economic pressures. The program is designed to connect Palestinian and Syrian refugee communities to better connect them with local Lebanese communities.

The football-oriented program uses sport teams and tournaments as a respite from conflict and for building community-level connections among youth in positive ways that emphasize values of leadership and cross-cultural support, human-rights based approaches, gender equality and prevention of gender-based violence, and livelihood skills to include potential work in sport-related jobs. The program seeks sustainability through encouraging development of youth peace committees in affected communities and works to follow humanitarian principles through community-level engagement as stakeholders in the football program.

Phase II of the project, which engaged some of the top football stars from the Netherlands, ran from 2015 to 2019, was supported by the government of the Netherlands, and is presented on video: https://www.youtube.com/watch?v=IueuImIfvkE.

of specialized agencies of the UN tap sport superstars to participate in programs and to communicate key messages of crisis consequences, needs, and the urgency of humanitarian assistance. Tennis champion Maria Sharapova represented the UNDP for a decade in efforts to champion the needs of those recovering from the Chernobyl nuclear reactor disaster and other contexts of acute humanitarian need; in 2021 UNDP enlisted former Ivory Coast national team captain and Chelsea football legend Didier Drogba in HIV/AIDS prevention, human rights, and women's empowerment campaigns.[4]

Sport-based interventions in such settings must first be *aligned with humanitarian principles* of nondiscrimination and inclusion, have an apolitical focus, be based on local cultures, customs, and community needs, and they should build on and not supplant or overwhelm local capacities. Importantly, there is the need to avoid what in development practice jargon is known as "project-itis": short-term efforts, often following short-term donor or funding cycles, that fail to be sustainable over time and which raise expectations of participants without the ability to continue to support them over the long term.

The most important consideration of sport-based initiatives for humanitarian action is the need for any engagement to be strongly consistent with the long-standing, well-developed "Do No Harm" principles (The Sphere Project 2011) of providing relief and support in situations of conflict, displacement, and acute human needs. José Barrena's mapping of sport and humanitarian action principles finds that one of the most important ethical criteria for such interventions is inclusivity. He finds that program designers should be acutely aware of the need to create and administer programs with the widest possible accessibility (Barrena 2009 119).

> Sport is not only for a few individuals of the community with high motor and sport skills. . . . SHA [sport for humanitarian action] must be based on a sport for all approach where any individual can participate regardless of race, social class, gender and disabilities. This becomes particularly important when an SHA intervention seeks not only individual but community outcomes.

The "Do No Harm" imperative is more fully articulated, with program and project design examples and frameworks, in the major tool kits on sport and humanitarian action described at the end of this chapter (for further information and engagement). The principles are important not only in the design of programs for humanitarian relief or mental-health aims, but equally in contexts where the aim of interventions is to address the need for peacebuilding in transitions from war, and in programs to strengthen social cohesion: in all these contexts, children, youth, and adult participants' life experiences and social contexts must be strongly considered in order to reduce risk and enhance outcomes.

PEACEBUILDING: OVERCOMING ENMITY, SUSTAINING PEACE

In fragile and conflict-affected contexts, where social cohesion is fractured and societies are deeply vulnerable to recurrent violence, sport programming appears to offer a unique instrument to help societies restore disrupted lives and relationships, advance education, health, and livelihood outcomes, and to give opportunities for recovery by individuals and societies. Since the early 1990s, drawing on perspectives from the growth of the field of peace research, peacebuilding has become the central concept for transitions from violence to conditions of peace. At the UN, peacebuilding norms, knowledge and practice are embodied in the mandates and work of the UN Peacebuilding Support Office, the Peacebuilding Commission, and the Peacebuilding Fund. See Concept Box 8.1.

The UN Secretary-General's 2023 Our Common Agenda initiative empha-sizes—in an agenda-setting policy brief titled "A New Agenda for Peace"—that the conditions for sustaining peace in the long run are found not just in the effectiveness of securitized responses such as peace opera-tions, but in the end there is need for innovative and novel approaches to "whole-of-society" approaches that are informed by comprehensive national-level violence-prevention strategies (UN 2023: 19). "The scale of threats that we face require all-of-society approaches at the national level, and all-of-humanity approaches at the international level," the UN argues (UN 2023: 32).

Peacebuilding focuses principally on both the official, governmental side of transitions from war or community-level conflict, such as nego-tiation and peace agreements, truth and reconciliation commissions, military transformations to demobilize and integrate insurgent groups, truth-finding and truth-telling, language and autonomy recognitions for marginalized minorities, new constitutional dispensations that create new norms, institu-tions. Equally, though, peacebuilding is oriented toward "whole-of-society" approaches, opening arenas for dialogue, and local-level initiatives such as the creation of "local peace architectures" or arenas for community dialogue, monitoring, and violence prevention (Cox and Sisk 2017; Giessmann 2016).

Strategically, peacebuilding and social cohesion efforts are oriented toward renewing or establishing the social contract: trust in society across divisions and mechanisms such as networks that stem crises from escalat-ing into violence (McCandless 2019; UNDP 2020). Within the literature on

CONCEPT BOX 8.1. THEORIES OF CHANGE
IN SPORT-BASED PEACEBUILDING
AND SOCIAL COHESION

Theories of change in *sport for peacebuilding and social cohesion* focus on efforts to break down stereotypes, develop a perspective of empathy and mutual understanding (known as perspective-taking), representing social cohesion through carefully constructed symbolism, ritual, and intervention design, and the development of sport participants (athletes, coaches, media, celebrities) directly involved in peacebuilding and social cohesion networks.

- Sport and *cross-cultural contact*. Traditional approaches are grounded in "contact theory" by which exposure to those of different orientations, identities, ethnic or racial identities, or nationalities learn of others through contact. By getting to know others, the theory would suggest, they appreciate the similarities of life experience and may bond across lines of conflict; experience suggests that contact-theory approaches need to grapple with locally specific cultural relevance to be effective (Schulenkorf and Sherry 2021).

  This approach often involves perspective-taking, or engaging with participants to help see another's perspective, experience, and the effects of conflict on their lives. In Iraq, a program sponsored by the Abdul Latif Jameel Poverty Action Lab sought to promote and evaluate theories of change involving contact and perspective-taking. Scholar Salma Moussa randomly assigned Christians who had displaced in conflict with Muslim, or with fellow Christians, in a two-month soccer league. The results of the field experiment were compelling in support of the contact thesis and perspective-taking approach: those participants who had participated in mixed teams reported that they were 318 percent more likely to train with Muslims six months after the experience, although the program showed less affirmation that this would extend to other areas of life such as mixed social events (Moussa 2020).
- *Representing a shared destiny*. The literature suggests the need for varied and more context-specific theories of change that emphasize the importance of "representation," and the deliberate use of

symbolic politics to state, reflect, and reify the core concept of a shared and common destiny.

In Kenya, for example, a foundation created by long-distance track and road runner—the first African woman to hold the marathon world record—Tegla Loroupe, organizes peace initiatives through sport throughout the country's at-times conflict-affected Rift Valley, including convening an annual 10-km Peace Race from 2003 to 2012. UNHCR Kenya organized with the Loroupe Foundation a Race for Peace event in Kapenguria, Kenya, near the border with Uganda, which featured celebrity participation by Pur Biel, a South Sudanese refugee and member of the inaugural 2016 Olympic Refugee Team. Biel first participated in a sport event himself through a Louroupe Foundation program in 2015 (his biography appears at https://olympics.com/en/athletes/yiech -pur-biel).

peacebuilding, an important sport-related perspective is that of the conflict-transformation approach (Lederach 2005). In essence, this perspective reflects that peacebuilding is critical across two important subdimensions:

- Elite-led processes (such as peace agreements) must be buttressed by peacebuilding efforts at mid- and grassroots levels of society.
- Peacebuilding processes must extend over long periods of time, and that the principal strategic objective of peacebuilding efforts is to create the conditions for sustaining peace though integrated networks, institutions, and key grassroots, mid-level and leadership stewardship of a shared or common destiny of living together.

Peacebuilding and efforts to strengthen social cohesion on issues of national identity, trust in the state, trust in society, economic interdependence, and development of a country or context's (sense of shared or common destiny [UNDP 2020]). Research and policy reflection in the area of social cohesion is informed by a new set of international agendas for peacebuilding and development, such as the World Bank's 2013 study of the societal dynamics of fragility which equally positions social cohesion as creating the essential enabling conditions for inclusive and sustainable economic development (Alexandre et al. 2013). Organizations such as SCORE have done well to operationalize the social cohesion concept by developing its political, social, and economic dimensions and conducting country-level assessments.[5] In sum, sport-based peacebuilding is designed to engage in carefully designed efforts to *symbolically represent peace, perhaps most effectively—but not only—at the community level.* See Table 8.1.

Conceptually, peacebuilding can be understood in three ways: relationships, interests, and capacities for a society to be able to be resilient in the face of new stress and to grapple with the consequences of prior conflicts (Aall 2016). Sport for peacebuilding, mapped in relation to this perspective, offers three principal ways in which sport has been used as a strategic approach to advance the three peacebuilding and social cohesion aims. In aggregate, sport-based programs have sought to advance peacebuilding and have shown effectiveness in key areas such as youth intervention and at grassroots (Spaaij 2013; Meir and Fletcher 2019).

In sport-related peacebuilding programs, a nagging concern is that they are often premised or structured on putting the challenging task of extending the effects beyond the program to the communities concerned on the shoulders of the participants themselves . . . expecting that they are able and can safely advocate for change in the broader community is a lot to expect of participants in an intercommunal sport program (Moustakas 2022). Moreover, there is the need for more longitudinal analysis to assess whether such programs have very long-lasting effects on individuals and communities (Clarke, Jones, and Smith 2021).

Table 8.1. Sport-for-Peacebuilding Programming: A Sample

Country or Region	Program	Local Organization	Supporting Organization
Balkans	Region-wide hockey league and tournaments	Balkan Ice Hockey Union	International Ice Hockey Federation
Colombia	*Football with Principles*	Talentos Foundation, Government, University of Cordoba	GiZ
Rwanda and wider Great Lakes Region	Caravanami (Peace Caravan)	Esperance— Football for Peace	GIZ
South Africa	Youth Development Through Football	Department of Sport and Recreation South Africa (SRSA)	GIZ/EU
Tajikistan	Girls Empowerment	Tajikistan National Taekwondo Federation	UNDP/UN Women

In *relationship-building*, sport-based interventions have been used in these contexts to work toward overcoming long-standing or seemingly intractable intergroup conflict dynamics in countries and contexts that have experienced fragility. For example, in Nepal, internationally funded nongovernmental organization Search for Common Ground developed a soccer-themed situation comedy that focuses on the lives of youth in coping with the post-conflict environment.[6] In Nepal, as well, nongovernmental organizations such as the Nepal Peacebuilding Initiative have organized soccer matches between mixed teams of ex-insurgents and police in the restive regions of the Terai. A program under the aegis of the Office of Presidential Adviser of the Peace Process in the Philippines engaged in partnership with related UN agencies to engage with non-state armed groups for sport activities to buttress as the peace process and to prevent escalation of violence in Muslim-majority Mindanao (UN 2018, 17).

Scholars John Sugden and Alan Tomlinson explore sport-based interventions in Northern Ireland, Israel-Palestine, and South Africa, arguing for the need for "critical pragmatism" on how effective these programs can be (Sugden with Tomlinson 2016). Working to go beyond the hyperbole about sport's potential to contribute to peace, they find that under the right conditions and understandings about the local context, and how sport is situated within broader and often rapidly changing environments of political power; overall, they do find that while "Sport may not change the world, but children playing with their enemies might" (Sugden and Tomlinson 2016, 131).

Scholars Kristine Höglund and Ralph Sundberg conclude similarly in their study of sport and reconciliation in South Africa: "The impact at the national level reconciliations and symbols appears to be limited, because of the fleeing nature of symbolic events" (2008, 815). See Documentary Insights 8.2.

Too, Alan Bairner, in evaluating sport-based efforts to overcome sectarian divisions and a history of sectarian-based sport organizations finds them limited: in his assessment of the role of sport in the Northern Ireland peace process, he finds that political institutions that cement sectarian-oriented governance have limited efforts—for example, through the "Football for All" campaign—to build crosscutting sport organizations and teams. "Sport is often used in nation-building processes," he observes; "In this case, however, it may be that the nation-building process must precede the football nation-building process" (Bairner 2013, 229; see also Hassan 2016). See Documentary Insights 8.3.

A well-documented case is the development of Open Fun Football Schools (OFFS) programs in the wake of conflicts in the Balkans, in contexts such as Kosovo. In a mixed-methods analysis using quantitative data to determine the extent of OFFS participation and qualitative data of program and beneficiary interviews, scholars Karsniqi and Besnik sought to determine

DOCUMENTARY INSIGHTS 8.2.
SPORT AND PEACEBUILDING IN SOUTH
SUDAN: *FOR THE SAKE OF PEACE* (2022)
AND *SCORING FOR PEACE* (2013)

South Sudan has seen conflict: prior to its remarkable independence from Sudan, it had faced years of insurgency, neglect, exploitation, and deprivation from famine and disease. Since indpendence, internal conflict has brought new human security threats and challenges to the postindependence generation of South Sudanese who aspire to a secure future with freedom from threats and existential challenges.

This riveting documentary takes the viewer into the world of football in a refugee camp, and shows how the putative power of football is equally the power of resilience and dedication to peace by footballers and the community across local divisions of tribe and youth identities.

Scoring for Peace is set in war-torn Burundi and features the Great Lakes Cup, a tournament organized by the World Bank in 2012 to in part help ex-combatants returning from war reintegrate well into their communities. The documentary features former child soldiers and fighters from Burundi, Democratic Republic of Congo (DRC), Rwanda, and Uganda. This moving and compelling documentary invites viewers to learn directly from the participants the power of sport in their quest for recovery and reintegration.

For the Sake of Peace can be found at https://www.imdb.com/title/tt20222582/?ref_=tt_mv_close and Scoring for Peace at https://www.imdb.com/title/tt3975632/.

the efficacy of intergroup-contact theory approaches to advance positive cross-ethnic interactions and empowerment of minority youth. They found in their analysis that:

OFFS in Kosovo contributed significantly to positive social change, not only when it comes to peacebuilding, but also in terms of social inclusion of other minorities (such as Roma, Bosnians, and Turks. . . . Our study found evidence in support of the Intergroup Interaction Theory and Social Change Theory that sport programs (OFFSs) contribute to change in the perception through interactions and play. This was confirmed by all participants who changed their initial perceptions about each other's ethnicity. Their initial negative perceptions have changed over time when participants played together, enjoyed football and

DOCUMENTARY INSIGHTS 8.3.
BEITAR JERUSALEM F.C.: A DIFFICULT
SEASON FOR DIVERSITY

FC Beitar Jerusalem, a popular football team in Israel, was the only club in the country's Premier League to sign an Arab player . . . two footballers from Chechnya brought to the club in a questionable, secret deal involving a Russian-Israeli oligarch. The events that ensued in the club's difficult 2012–2013 season reveals and underscores the undercurrents of racism and bigotry among the club's fans, the close of sport with money and politics, and the ways in which sport may seek to promote diversity but instead struggles to cope with the underlying divisions and enmity within society.

The acclaimed documentary *Forever Pure* (2016) captures these events and the social context that can limit sport's potential for contributing to inter group harmony. See: https://www.imdb.com/title/tt5529828/.

> friendship with lots of other social aspects of the OFFSs. (Krasniqi and Besnik 2019, 155)

In Sri Lanka, scholar Nico Schulendkorf examined programs to promote reconciliation in western regions that are highly diverse across Sinhalese, Tamil, and Muslim communities in areas experiencing economic marginalization and few opportunities for community sport events. The programs sought to engage participants in imagining ways to live together, and through the sporting events efforts were made to encourage a common identity through national-level flaps, anthems, and jerseys. In this way, Schulenkorf reports,

> Inter-community sport events have the capacity to function as active and exciting vehicles for inclusive social change. . . . Positive contact experiences allowed for the establishment of interpersonal friendships and the creation of positive social identities along national lines, organizational lines, common interests, and imagined factors. (Schulenkorf 2010, 291)

Cárdenas finds in a comparative study of sport for peacebuilding interventions in Colombia and Northern Ireland that sport-for-peace in Northern Ireland is indeed burdened by overarching politics and sectarianism, whereas in Colombia the overall peace process creates more of an enabling environment for such interventions (Cárdenas 2016). In another study, Cárdenas finds in a comparative case-study review of sport and peacebuilding programming at individual, community, and national relationship-building levels that programming has been effective in serving as a cultural shared interest, provides a space for contact and interaction (with, ideally, with a humanizing effect) and a platform for communication of peace-supporting communities (Cárdenas 2019, 385).

Colombia's experience is likely to inform the sport-for-peacebuilding field for years to come as it has become a laboratory of innovation in the practice of using sport to build peace in the wake of some 50 years of civil war. Organizations like La Paz FC have used football to build bridges with the country's largest erstwhile rebel force, the FARC. . . . "We want to change rubber guerilla boots for football boots," organizer and human rights lawyer Félix Mora explains (Gamba 2018). Martial arts, cycling, white-water rafting, indigenous sport, and, of course, football, have all been part of a widespread effort involving a network of partners and stakeholders to symbolize and represent peace locally, to address ongoing concerns of violence, and to advance common needs for environmental protection, livelihoods, community security, and reintegration of ex-combatants. A 2015–2019 program, Paz en Movimiento (peace in movement) for example, brings together various ministries of the Colombian government together with local partners in the country's fragile border readers to provide training in coaching following the Fútbol con Principios (football with principles) methodology.[7]

Both practitioner and scholarly communities of practice who analyze the societal basis of peace have homed in on the role of *integrated, inclusive civil society*—particularly, crosscutting organizations that bridge across social divides—is foundational for sustaining peace. In the practitioner literature, this perspective is captured well in UNDP's focus on the role of "insider mediators" for peacebuilding and social cohesion. The organization finds:

> What distinguishes insider mediation from other forms of mediation is that it involves credible figures, groups or institutions internal to a conflict, who are able to use their influence to play a role—often largely behind the scenes or in undefined capacities—which directly or indirectly influences the trajectory of conflict in a constructive manner. Credibility and influence are central to the concept and practice of internal mediation. (UNDP 2016, 7)

In this vein, Peace and Sport, a Lausanne-based organization founded by former Pentathlon world champion Joël Bouzou, implemented sport-for-peace programs in Burundi, Colombia, Côte d'Ivoire, Haiti, Israel-Palestine, the Democratic Republic of Congo, and Timor Leste. The organization also administers the "Champions for Peace" program that facilitates the involvement of elite athletes in peacebuilding work. The program's charter commits the elite athletes—some 110 have been designated as of mid-2023—to affirm their personal belief that "sport can be a tool for their personal development, education and social integration and that sport played in a structured way, with identical rules for all, can nurture inter-community dialogue, social solidarity and sustainable peace."[8] See Case Study 8.4 and Figure 8.4.

Strengthening women's networks for peace is an essential part of most social cohesion programs of development actors, even as programming is often scattered and uncoordinated in many conflict-affected environments. Research on women and peacebuilding have highlighted the limits, and opportunities, for focusing on women as the key source of bridge-building in conflict-affected contexts (Berry 2018). Sport programming has also been

CASE STUDY 8.4. BRIDGING CIVIL SOCIETY: EFFECTIVENESS IN SPORT FOR PEACE IN THE WESTERN CAPE

Scholar Marion Keim found in her evaluation of the community-coalition project Kicking for Peace, implemented by a group of 40 NGOs in the Western Cape, that long-standing projects such as this (since 2006) have shown demonstrable results in early childhood intervention for development outcomes and social skills for conflict resolution and community-level peacebuilding (Keim 2018, 444).

She finds that

> It has been proven crucial for the Network to involve parties from all cultural groups. The Western Cape Network for Community Peace and Development, a unique grassroots network, is the only one as far as we know that brings together South Africa's disenfranchised black populations with white and colored groups. . . .
>
> The project's success depends on being able to reach across socio-historical and cultural divides that have demarcated South African communities for decades. By initiating the project through a network of 40 NGOs and other entities, the project can reach more deeply into communities and achieve greater participation than a single NGO might achieve.
>
> Every hour spent in sport and life skills training is an hour not spent in activities that undermine youth's lives, such as drugs, gangsterism, and crime. The model is easily replicable in other provinces with the potential to serve millions of children.

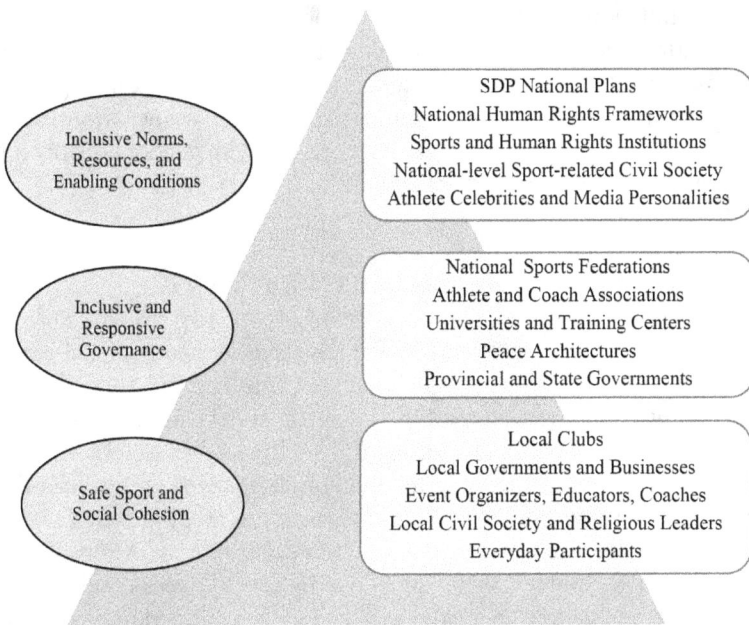

Figure 8.4.   **A Holistic Approach to Sport-Related Peacebuilding in a National Context.** *Source: The author, drawing on the social pyramid depiction of the conflict transformation approach in Lederach (2005).*

especially effective in *engaging women and girls in conflict-affected settings.* Yet such approaches require exceptional sensitivity in communities where traditional values of male participation in sport are strong, and where women face daily life challenges that limit the sustainability of efforts to use sport for empowering women's ability to act in society as peacebuilders through sport. The findings of study of sport-based programs for peacebuilding in Gulu, northern Uganda, for example, argue for caution as sport-for-women in the community is considered an "indulgence."

Where the participation of girls is often a requirement of externally funded programmes and is somewhat accepted by family members and neighbours, programme organisers and the women who participated in the research noted the resistance they faced amplified when those programmes ended. . . .

Coaches and organizers also indicated that similar sentiments were expressed by parents who stopped their daughters from partaking in sport. These barriers severely constrain the participation, inclusion and belonging of female participants. In this way [*sic*] sport reproduces and reinforces gendered social dynamics. (Abonga and Brown 2022, 246)

With these limitations in mind, however, donors have sought to develop women-and-girls oriented sport programming to develop a cadre of women to engage in peacebuilding efforts in their social networks. For example, Japan has sponsored the "Ladies First" program that brought women from South Sudan for athletics events in Tanzania that is paired with gender equality and peacebuilding capacity development activities.[9]

IMPLICATIONS: REFLECTIVE PRACTICE

Those who work to design, implement, and advocate for sport-related peace-building have engaged in extensive practice, not least because there is much hyperbole about the "power of sport" in this area of development assistance but without the concomitant evidence of its effectiveness. Too, sport in conditions of fragility, conflict, and involving marginalized and traumatized communities *requires carefully designed interventions that are based on significant local engagement, understanding, and partnerships.* Attempting to "intervene" in such complex social situations inherently faces challenges of cultural context, adaptations to local norms and values, the conditions needed for local ownership and sustainability, difficult choices on gender dynamics and women and girls' inclusion, and long-term, demonstrable results (Giulianotti 2011; Collison et al. 2017).

Going forward is the need for reflective practice and innovation in sport-for-peacebuilding efforts, to take evidence and lessons learned of individual-level and community-level positive outcomes for ways to manage risk, design and implement programs, and advance evaluation methods. Going forward, the problem of *"scaling up," or expanding, the use of sport* for these specific, bottom-up social development aims faces its most serious problem in garnering sufficient resources for the aspirations of a better sport regime to be realized. The need for further evidence on sport's contribution to peacebuilding is hampered by the fact that other than in some country-case contexts such as Colombia, where its effectiveness is widely acknowledged, sport has not been sufficiently embraced, prioritized, and integrated across other areas of practice as a tool for peacebuilding and social cohesion.

The Olympic Refuge Foundation's Think Tank polled its membership on lessons learned and best practice for sport-based programs in contexts of fragility. The survey revealed these themes as critical for practice in harmony with humanitarian principles (Olympic Refuge Think Tank 2022).

- First, sport programming should be designed to potentially foster a wide range of outcomes at various levels, such that they are informed by and integrated into understandings of local social dynamics that in which individual participants are embedded. The concept of safety and protection is foremost: safe environments, safe activities, safety to deal with trauma and stress.

- Second, awareness of the cultural context is critical, from gaining access and understanding the root causes of barriers to participation, or how participants interact within families, peer groups, and community leaders.
- Third, programs and projects must be designed at the outset for sustainability, with approaches that emphasize building sport organizations, and moving to embed or institutionalize sport-related programs in local or public service delivery.
- Fourth, there remain significant gaps in the evidence base. Those who advocate for sport-based programming should adopt the most rigorous evaluation methods to demonstrate results.
- Finally, risk mitigation in sport-for-peacebuilding comes from careful engagement with local stakeholders, including parents and community leaders, who are best able to identify potential program or participant risks and offer ways these may be mitigated.

QUESTIONS FOR CONSIDERATION

- What role can sport-based initiatives play in facilitating the delivery and distribution of humanitarian assistance, and how does the "sport as a magnet" metaphor offer potential aid-delivery entry points for humanitarian assistance providers?
- What are the most effective ways in which sport can be used to prevent conflict, to build peace, and to heal the wounds of war?
- What are lessons learned in community-based initiatives to use sport for conflict prevention and post-conflict peacebuilding?

FOR FURTHER INFORMATION

"Tool kits" from international organizations provide those who seek to understand, support, design, and implement sport-based interventions in conflict-affected contexts, understanding that these programs are fraught with potential program risk, risk to beneficiaries, and their inherent selectivity given the scope of need around the world. All told, these tool kits offer one-stop shopping for researchers, practitioners, donors, and government stakeholders on sport-for-peacebuilding, including overviews of theories of change, lessons learned, and templates for activities, evaluation, and communication.

- The International Committee of the Red Cross (ICRC) offers detailed and highly accessible practical guidance for sport interventions to support mental health and psychosocial wellness in conflict-affected contexts. *Moving Together: Promoting Psychosocial Well-being through Sport and Physical Activity* (2014) is designed for program designers and facilitators (ICRC 2014). See: https://pscentre.org/?resource=moving -together-english&wpv_search=true&selected=single-resource.
- The UNHCR/IOC/Terre des Hommes *Sport for Protection Toolkit: Programming for Young People in Forced Displacement Settings* defines the sport-for-protection orientation, provides tools for risk analysis, and offers practitioner checklists and planning templates (UNHCR, IOC, and Terre des Hommes 2019). See: https://www.unhcr.org/en-us/ publications/manuals/5d35a7bc4/sport-for-protection-toolkit.html.
- UNODC's 2020 tool kit on sport for PVE, *Preventing Violent Extremism through Sport: A Technical Guide*, provides program principles, design guidance, and evaluation tools for social inclusion, education, and youth empowerment (UNODC 2020). See: https://www.unodc.org/documents /dohadeclaration/Sports/PVE/PVE_TechnicalGuide_EN.pdf.

NOTES

1. The Helpcode project is described at: https://helpcode.org/en/projects/ education-through-sports-in-yemen.

2. See the article on the UNHCR program at: http://www.unhcr.org/45e82c444. html.

3. The Initiative's activities are described at: https://www.peaceinitiativenetwork. org/.

4. Additional UNDP celebrity ambassadors and advocates are listed at: https:// www.undp.org/goodwill-ambassadors-and-advocates.

5. The SCORE conceptual approach and methods along with case-study reports on various countries are found at: https://www.scoreforpeace.org/.

6. For further information on the Search program, titled "The Team," see http:// www.sfcg.org/programmes/nepal/.

7. The project, sponsored by GiZ, is described at: https://www.giz.de/en/ worldwide/ 59683.html#:~:text=The%20Colombian%20Government%20 already%20uses,the%20Sport%20for%20Development%20programme. See also the Colombia overview of sport and peacebuilding from the GiZ: https://www.sport-for-development.com/ imglib/downloads/Factsheets/giz2020-en-factsheet-sport-for-development-colombia.pdf.

8. The Charter is at: https://www.peace-sport.org/wp-content/uploads/2017/09/Champion_For_Peace_Charter.pdf.

9. The project is described at: https://www.jica.go.jp/Resource/english/news/field/2020/20200428_01.html.

PART VI

Conclusion

Chapter 9

Imagining More Effective
Sport-for-Peace

CHAPTER OVERVIEW

The death of Ukrainian boxing champion Oleksandr Onyschchenko in the trench-warfare battle for Bahkmut in 2023 overshadows any pretense that the Paris 2024 Games can represent a proverbial celebration of humanity . . . a "Master of Sports," junior champion, Carpathian Cup winner, and member of the Ukraine national boxing team, Onyschenko is but one of 262 Ukrainian athletes killed in the Russian invasion of his country (Kyiv Independent 2023). How many Ukrainian athletes would have won medals at the Paris 2024 Summer Olympic Games? How can humanity's universalism be celebrated through sport when such universalism clearly doesn't exist in the trenches of Bakhmut? If Russian veterans from the war participate in the Paralympic Games, even as putatively neutral athletes, will Ukrainian athletes be forced into sharing a podium with the living symbols of the aggression and atrocities they have suffered in war?

A cloud of war and human suffering in this turbulent world hangs over international sport and the Paris 2024 Games and beyond as a persistent reminder of the deep disconnections between international sports and peace. The Ukraine War, among others, underscores the utter inability of international sport to contribute to a more peaceful and inclusive world, instead harking back to the pre–World War II spectacle of hatred and nationalism that was the 1936 Berlin Games. The outbreak of war between Israel and Hamas in October 2023 underscored the vulnerability of the Paris Games to global turbulence, raising new questions about whether Israel should participate, the participation of athletes from war-torn Gaza or the West Bank (Palestine, a recognized NOC, began participating in the Olympics in 1986), and whether and how the devastating conflict raises new questions of boycotts and exclusions.

Without deep, systemic reform international sport cannot contribute to peace as its original designers, and modern-day proselytizers, contend. This conclusion presents a series of potential reforms, some more radical and some more incremental, to improve the "global regime" of international sport. Among the more far-reaching recommendations are to create an avenue for qualification to participate in the Olympic Games outside of national processes, a seemingly seditious idea to states such as China, Russia, or Iran who may see Uighur, political, or youthful dissidents competing in the international arena as individuals, rather than "representing" nation-state authority.

Global sport institutions and networks remain insular, with the need to expand inclusivity within—particularly, athlete equity, rights, and voice—and to be more fully transparent and accountable in interactions with international-community partners and local stakeholders. International sport needs to be further democratized, more equitable, and brought into the other universe of organizations that collectively in a globally inclusive structure address other global issues, from confronting harms of climate change to realizing sport's contribution to the SDGs.

Imagining a better global sport regime and stimulating debate and discussion on a better system of organizing and advancing international sport is the purpose of these concluding observations and recommendations.

REPRIORITIZING SPORT FOR PEACEBUILDING AND SOCIAL COHESION

There is an evident need to reorient the regime of sport-for-peacebuilding and social cohesion to situate such policymaking, programming, and intervention activities toward knowledge and practice in the fields of conflict analysis, dispute system resolution design, and architectures for peace. For bottom-up peacebuilding sport-related interventions should be focused on, first, amplifying and reinforcing the role of national sport institutions as specifically and directly engaged in local-level peacebuilding and social cohesion. The gap between sport, well-known for commercialism and development, and its direct and tangible relations to bottom-up and "everyday peace" in countries and contexts is underappreciated. Extensive work is required in developing better methods of assessment, of the role of sport in national strategies of social cohesion, inclusive governance, and human rights, and the ways in which sport at the local and community level is networked and may be scaled up effectively to provide clear evidence and local knowledge on the underlying causal processes by which sport-related interventions are effective.

At least one area of certainty stemming from the literature on social cohesion is the critical role of inclusive institutions *and* of related civil societies if social organizations such as sport institutions are to contribute to bonding and bridging social cohesion. Sports of sport-related programming for peacebuilding should give special scrutiny to this factor: How inclusive and authentically represented and responsive are sports institutions that govern sport at national and local levels? How integrated is sport-related civil society and in what ways does it fully seek to respond to the challenges of all segments of society in realizing access to and the potential individual and community benefits of sport? Few countries or contexts have deep data and understandings on these critical questions. One approach to remedy these issues would be to *encourage the design and adoption of "national action plans" or NAPs for sport peacebuilding and social cohesion,* as has been done in the area of women, peace, and security. NAPs are strategies for policy, but they are equally context-driven dialogue on objectives, approaches, and concerns.

In national planning processes, social cohesion has increasingly been included as an outcome of public policies in education, health care delivery, and in infrastructure planning, as a crosscutting issue that also features direct efforts to promote cohesion, for example through dialogue processes. In Iraq, for example, UNDP's "Support for Social Cohesion in Iraq" program is a major five-year initiative to improve trust in governance vertically, and trust in society horizontally, in Iraq. The 2020–2025 program builds on significant prior work on reconciliation and social cohesion in Iraq that had been implemented since 2017, and furthers the strategy of facilitating locally driven solutions, conflict sensitivity, and building capacities for sustaining peace, and building up institutional frameworks and local mechanisms for preventing conflict.[1] Integrating and *improving capacity for national-level delivery of SDP programming* requires expansion and further development, in Iraq and elsewhere.

One avenue for expanding local capacities for developing and delivering sport-related programming is the creation of an UN-overseen *SDP Trust Fund* supported by recurring revenue from global sports events, broadcasting rights, and voluntary contributions of broadcasters, merchandizing corporations, athletes, sport organizations, 'and other engaged contributors. A precedent for such a fund may be the UN's Peacebuilding Fund, which seeks to mobilize and direct resources to the most innovative approaches to peacebuilding in situations of greatest need.

Sport's contribution to social cohesion continues to be challenged by threats to sport participations—athletes, officials and coaches, fans, and fandoms—from racism, homophobia, and other hate speech. Efforts to tame toxic misogyny, nationalism, and gender-based abuse—particularly of girl and women athletes (UN Women 2023)—underscores the vulnerability of sport to the ill winds of mindsets around the world. In 2022, MMA-organization Ultimate Fighting Championship (UFC, a $21 billion corporation after a 2023 merger with the WWE, Chapman 2023) promulgated a rule to ban national flag displays by athletes at events. In Scottish football, efforts have been imposed to tame sectarianism (albeit with mixed effects), Waiton 2018). With the outbreak of war between Israel and Hamas in 2023, the Champion League's Celtics struggled to censor a fan base championing the Palestinian cause from the stands, eventually revoking season passes for the most stridently protesting "Green Brigade" fans (*The Guardian* 2023).

What appears *insufficient in SDP practice are approaches, programs, and issues in integrating sport-related issues into national human rights institutions, monitoring, and related reporting of countries, regional, and international organizations* and regularizing sport-related abuses in annual mandatory state reporting and global surveys. Among the human-rights issues that should be more regularly addressed are inequitable in sport and the corrupt influences of money, confronting environmental irresponsibility and exploitation, furthering mechanisms for monitoring and sanctioning speech, and continuing and expanding confrontation against gender and sexuality norms that restrict human rights and which undermine the platitudinous claims of "sport-for-all."

REFORMING GLOBAL SPORT GOVERNANCE

The critical fact that governance of international sport lives principally outside of other regime networks on health, education, and peace at the overarching authority of the UN, the regime lacks an ability to deal with two critical problems: harm in sport, and disconnection between elite sport and the aims of widespread, global participation in sport. While the global governance regime purports to be principally oriented toward social development, it is a governance system that is more suited to serve elite sport and the business of sports entertainment than in realizing the aims of mass participation in sport globally in pursuit of social development aims.

Make the Olympic Truce more than a "scrap of paper." Several steps may be taken toward this end, principally its movement from a UNGA resolution to a resolution of the United Nations Security Council. This, in turn, would animate the work of the UN peacemakers in peacemaking and gaining humanitarian access, to humanitarian workers to provide a known and reliable window for the provision of relief, and to UN country offices worldwide to organize key aims such as vaccination, food security and shelter efforts, and to leverage the temporary peace during the truce period into long-term conflict termination to pave the way for peacebuilding and social cohesion.

As the 2023 dispute over the Paris 2024 truce resolution underscores, amid geopolitical polarization there is little likelihood that the Olympic Truce is much more than a proverbial "scrap of paper" . . . an ambiguous pledge that is not intended to be honored.

International sport organizations would do well to soul-search and develop a publicly available set of clear criteria that define and clarify the relationship between sport and human rights. Such criteria should describe remedies including suspension, expulsion, or other sanctions against rights-abusing regimes or contexts in which human rights abuses occur. Particularly, consistent guidelines are needed in relation to the conditions under which human-rights abuses by a country in terms of international aggression, or violation of global norms such as the Responsibility to Protect, generate sport-related sanctions by sport-related international organizations. Creating clarity of criteria and creating international sport organizations as "agencies of restraint" on human rights, needs re-adaptation in a rapidly changing world. Sanctions for human-rights abuses continue to be context-specific consideration for global sport organizations, sewing confusion and expectations that only the most egregious violations—such as blatant international aggression in the case of the 2022 Ukraine invasion—will generate more than a toothless "diplomatic boycott" with at best some interpretative symbolic effect.

A principal reform that has been advocated for improving support is *a global institution devoted to creation of an integrated system of monitoring, reporting, investigation, and sanctions around harm in sport.* Even more radical proposals suggest bringing the IOC into the panoply of global organizations under the auspices of the United Nations (much like was done with the erstwhile independent International Organization for Migration, IOM). Other more incremental proposals for reform including extending the authority of the Olympic Athletes' Commission, imposing greater "sunshine" rules for disclosure of IOC and federation monies, and *create a commission to design and launch a specialized UN-based organization devoted to sport and peacebuilding.* In this analysis, the UN's lack of a centralized institutional entity that focuses specifically on SDP hampers the organization's effectiveness; while UN DESA is effective at being supportive, the lack of a dedicated specialized agency that could further bring the universe of international sport organizations within the global-governance framework of the UN limits sport's ability to contribute to human rights and peacebuilding.

If power is the Achilles' heel of international sport, the time has come to revisit deeply the prevailing norm of national recognition that pervades what should be a universalistic cultural event without prejudice of national identity as the most symbolically portrayed social identity: through flags, anthems, logos, and color associations. That the overarching imagery, organization, and representation-assigning nature of most international sport events—an integral to the symbolic representational story of the Olympics—of athlete or team's national identity is anachronistic . . . *prejudicing national identity above all others a relic of the nationalistic age of the 19th century, when the era of modern international sport began, that continues to haunt international politics today.*

While progress has been made—the advent of categories for "neutral" athletes, such as those designated "Olympic Athletes from Russia," or the Olympic Refugee Team (EOR)—the norm of national recognition runs against a world of globalized societies, multiple citizenships, and transnational identities. A first step in this direction would be *the creation of a "Non-National Olympic Committee"* with the same privileges and relationship with the IOC as current NOCs and which would allow a pathway for any athlete or para-athlete to pursue participation—as a human right that extends to an individual, not countries—without being associated with or specifically representing any nation as such.

REVISITING A CLICHÉ

Does sport contribute to peace? Sport does appear to have deep, abiding, perhaps neuro-scientifically explicable power for individuals, small groups of the like-minded, communities, nations, and transnationally.

The putative power of sport, however, is equally the basis for its capture and manipulation for political aims and for pursuing dominance and superiority internationally. The slow and uneven evolution of sports historically has left an international system of sport that is ill-structured and insufficiently prepared to realize its potential for peace in today's turbulent world. Yet at the same time, from the individual and community level up, and further integration into institutions, policy, and international governance priorities, sport has immensely untapped potential to contribution to the underlying drivers of peace: human rights, equitable and inclusive development, urgent humanitarian action, and in peacebuilding and strengthening social cohesion.

So perhaps the former South African president's now-clichéd words (see the Introduction) about sport's mystical powers for advancing peace are affirmed in evidence of sport-based effectiveness in human rights, development, and sustaining peace. But the mechanisms sport-for-peace need further articulation. The mechanism Mandela used so effectively was to harness the power of sport deftly for symbolic political power: to help reconcile a society deeply divided by the repugnant laws of the white-minority, brutally enforced system of racial segregation, apartheid. In 1995, Mandela himself purposefully and strategically chose sport to symbolically represent peace as the country transitioned toward a "New South Africa."

At the final game of the 1995 Rugby World Cup, symbolizing in part the emergence of the country from the sport boycott, Mandela appeared on the pitch wearing the jersey of the white captain, Francois Pienaar, in a moment that defines the relationships between peace and sport in a nutshell. The PBS documentary film *The Long Walk of Nelson Mandela* (PBS 1999b) features interviews with those involved in 1995 and original footage of the historical moment (in contrast to the Hollywood version depicted in the film *Invictus*, 2009). "How was rugby perceived by Black people?" South Africa rugby team leader Morne du Plessis rhetorically asks. "Maybe a game played by the white oppressors, a game that was used by the governing party and the government of the time as highlighting how good were as a country."

Mandela flipped the script on sport, politics, and peace. Symbolically, the rugby captain's jersey reconciliation gesture could not have been more significant, and it gave the fans across the country's polarized social spectrum an evident, unexpected moment of a shared sense of community and destiny. When South Africa won the World Cup against the favored New Zealand squad, by three points in extra time (15–12), it marked a momentary milestone of unity amid a society engulfed in uncertainty, violence, and inequality, issues which continue in South Africa today. Pienaar and Mandela together hoisted the World Cup trophy.

While Mandela's 1995 iconic peacebuilding symbol's long-lasting effects may not be measurable, the moment was undeniably tangible. *The Long Walk* documentarians report that in that moment "the whole country went wild;" Mandela later remarked, "It was the happiest day of my life" (PBS 1999b, 1:46:20–40).

NOTES

1. For background on the context and the results of InterAction field research on the challenges of social cohesion in Iraq, see InterAction, "Moving forward together, Leaving no one behind: From stigmatization to social cohesion in post-conflict Iraq." 2018, at: https://www.interaction.org/wp-content/uploads/2018/10/interaction_moving_forward_together_leaving_no_one_behind_iraq_mission_report.pdf.

Bibliography

Aall, Pamela. 2016. "Building Interests, Relationships and Capacity: Three Roads to Conflict Management." In Chester A. Crocker, Pamela Aall, and Fen. O. Hampson (Eds.), *Managing Conflict in a World Adrift.* Washington, DC: United States Institute of Peace Press.

Abonga, Francis, and Charlotte Brown. (2022, January). "Restoration and Renewal through Sport: Gendered Experiences of Resilience for War-Affected Youth in Northern Uganda." *Civil Wars* 24 (203): 230–253.

Adams, Kirby. (2020). "The Bond between Paralympian Oksana Masters and her Mother Began in a Ukrainian Orphanage." *Louisville Courier Journal*, May 7. https://www.courier-journal.com/story/life/2020/05/07/paralympian-oksana -masters-and-her-mother-share-powerful-bond/4818915002/.

AFP. (2023). "Germany Holds Munich Massacre Probe 50 Years On." *Barron's*, April 21. https://www.barrons.com/news/germany-holds-munich-olympics-massacre -probe-50-years-on-56690ff8.

Africanews. (2021). "Tokyo 2020: Burkina Faso Claims First Ever Olympic Medal." *Africanews*, May 8. https://www.africanews.com/2021/08/05/tokyo-2020-burkina -faso-claims-first-ever-olympic-medal//.

Africanews. (2023). "Joel Embiid Reacts to MVP Award." *Africanews*, May 5. https: //www.africanews.com/2023/05/04/joel-embiid-reacts-to-nba-mvp-award//.

Alexandre, Marc, Alys Willman, Ghazia Aslam, and Michelle Rebosio. (2013). *Social Dynamics and Fragility: Engaging Societies in Responding to Fragile Situations.* Washington, DC: The World Bank.

Al Jazeera. (2023a). "French Open: 'I Don't Support War,' Belarusian Sabalenka Says." Al Jazeera, June 6. https://www.aljazeera.com/news/2023/6/6/french-open-i -dont-support-war-belarusian-sabalenka-says.

Al Jazeera. (2023b). "Photos: Voices from the Stands at India v Pakistan Asia Cup Cricket Match." Al Jazeera, September 12. https://www.aljazeera.com/gallery/2023 /9/12/photos-voices-from-the-stands-at-india-v-pakistan-asia-cup-cricket-match.

Al Jazeera. (2017). "The Boxing Girls of Kenya" (Photo Gallery). March 8. https:// www.aljazeera.com/gallery/2017/3/8/the-boxing-girls-of-kenya.

Al-Khateeb, Zac. (2023). "Highest Paid MLS Players: Where Messi's Inter Miami Contract Ranks in the 2023 Season." *The Sporting News*, June 8. https://www

.sportingnews.com/us/soccer/news/messi-inter-miami-contract-highest-paid-mls
-players-2023/ysvnxds4zbaldqgfvvzu2rc5.

Al Marri, Abdulrahman, and Hind Al Ansari. (2023). "World Cup in Qatar: Human Rights and Normalization." Carnegie Endowment for International Peace, January 26. https://carnegieendowment.org/sada/88890#:~:text=In%20addition%20to %20championship%20matches,support%20for%20the%20Palestinian%20cause.

Alter, Joseph S. (2018). "Wrestling with the History of Yoga as Sport." *India International Center Quarterly, 44*(3&4), 252–265.

American Psychological Association. 2018. "APA Guidelines for Psychological Practice with Boys and Men." Washington, DC: APA. https://www.apa.org/about/ policy/boys-men-practice-guidelines.pdf.

Anderson, Mark. (2023). "Slap Fighting: The Next Big Thing, or Unsporting Stupidity?" AP News, March 8. https://apnews.com/article/power-slap-league-dana -white-ufc-concussion-99fda5fc571e015145ef420a36d1d9ed.

Anishchuk, Alexei. (2014). "Putin to Sochi Athletes: Mission Accomplished." Reuters, February 24. https://www.reuters.com/article/uk-olympics-putin/putin-to -sochi-athletes-mission-accomplished-idUKBREA1N0OQ20140224.

AP. (2022). "Iranian Athlete who Competed without Hijab Returns to Iran," PBS, October 19. https://www.pbs.org/newshour/world/iranian-athlete-who-competed -without-hijab-returns-to-tehran.

AP. (2023). "Russia's Sports Exile Persists 1 Year after Invading Ukraine." AP News, February 22. https://apnews.com/article/russia-ukraine-winter-olympics-sports -tennis-war-and-unrest-af3684913e1268cfaffa5bb08e38b731.

Arbena, Joseph L. (1990). "Generals and *Goles*: Assessing the Connection between the Military and Soccer in Argentina." *The International Journal of the History of Sport* 7 (1), 120–130.

Armour, Nancy. (2023). "The IOC Needs to Read the Room on Allowing Russian Athletes at Paris Olympics." *USA Today*, February 22.

Arnold, Richard. (2018). "Sport and Official Nationalism in Modern Russia." *Problems of Post-Communism 65* (2), 129–141.

Around the Rings. (2021). "One in Seven Olympic Committees are Directly Linked to Governments." *Around the Rings*. July 12. https://www.infobae.com /aroundtherings/ioc/2021/07/12/one-in-seven-olympic-committees-are-directly -linked-to-governments/.

Atkinson, Will. (2016). "Sport and Sustainability." In *The Routledge Handbook of Sport and Politics*, Abingdon, UK: Routledge.

Bairner, Alan. (2013). "Sport, The Northern Ireland Peace Process, and the Politics of Identity." *Journal of Aggression, Conflict, and Peace Research 5*(4): 220–229.

Bairner, Alan, John Kelly, and Jung Woo Lee. (2016). "Editors' Introduction." In Alan Bairner, John Kelly, and Jung Woo Lee (Eds.), *The Routledge Handbook of Sport and Politics*, Abingdon, UK: Routledge.

Banda, Davies. (2017). "Sport for Development and Global Public Health Issues: A Case Study of National Sports Associations." *AIMS Public Health 4*(3): 240–257.

Barrena, Jose Antonio León. (2009). "Sport for Humanitarian Action: A Do No Harm Approach." Bilbao: Duesto Yearbook on Humanitarian Action and Human Rights.

Bas, Daniela, Pegah Zohouri Haghian, with Suki Hoagland. (2022, January). "Addressing Climate Change through Sport." UN DESA Policy Brief 128. UN DESA. https://www.un.org/development/desa/dpad/publication/un-desa-policy-brief-no-128-addressing-climate-change-through-sport/#:~:text=National%20governments%20and%20international%20organizations,as%20a%20tool%20for%20climate.

BBC. (2012). "London 2012 Olympics: Saudi Arabia Women to Compete," July 12. https://www.bbc.com/news/world-middle-east-18813543.

BBC. (2021). "Laurel Hubbard: First Transgender Athlete to Compete at Olympics." June 21. https://www.bbc.com/news/world-asia-57549653.

BBC. (2022a). "Elnaz Rekabi: Family Home of Iranian Climber Demolished." December 3, 2022. https://www.bbc.com/news/world-middle-east-63847173.

BBC. (2022b). "Mexico Revives a 3,000-Year-Old Ball Game." BBC Reel. June 15. https://www.bbc.com/reel/video/p0cdy0t3/mexico-revives-a-3-000-year-old-ball-game.

BBC. (2023a). "Surf Champ Lucy Campbell Says Her Sport Must be Greener." BBC, May 16. https://www.bbc.com/news/science-environment-65563622.

BBC. (2023b). "Vinicus Jr Case Opens Wider Racism Debate in Spain." BBC, May 23. https://www.bbc.com/news/world-europe-65685661.

Beaubien, Jason, and Samantha Balaban. (2021). "Haitians Who Lost their Homes are Living in a Muddy Soccer Field." National Public Radio. August 19, 2021. https://www.npr.org/2021/08/19/1029437808/haitians-who-have-lost-their-homes-are-living-on-a-muddy-soccer-field.

Bellinger, Robert. (2015). "The Origins and Development of Ultimate Frisbee." *The Sport Journal, 18*(1). https://thesportjournal.org/article/the-origins-and-development-of-ultimate-frisbee/.

Bensemra, Zohra. (2020). "Senegal's First Female Pro Surfer Draws Others in her Wake." Reuters. August 27, 2020. https://www.reuters.com/article/us-senegal-women-surfing-widerimage-idINKBN25N0PY.

Bensinger, Ken. (2018). *Red Card: How the US Blew the Whistle on the World's Biggest Sports Scandal.* New York: Simon & Schuster.

Berry, Marie. (2018). *War, Women, and Power: From Violence to Mobilization in Rwanda and Bosnia-Herzegovina.* New York: Cambridge University Press, 2018.

Bisharat, Andrew. (2016). "Why are so many BASE Jumpers Dying?" *Adventure,* National Geographic Society, August 30, 2016. https://www.nationalgeographic.com/adventure/article/why-are-so-many-base-jumpers-dying.

Black, David R. (2010). "The Ambiguities of Development: Implications for Development through Sport." *Sport in Society, 13*(1): 121–29.

Blough, David, and Emmanuel Rivat. (2023, March). "Sport for Development and Peace: A Scientific and Bottom-up Approach to Impact Measurement." Paris: AED. https://www.afd.fr/en/ressources/rt69_sport_development_projects_blough_rivat_habchi_valot.

Bourdieu, Pierre. (1979). "Symbolic Power." *Critique of Anthropology, 4*(13–14), 77–89.

Boykoff, Jules. (2016). *Power Games: A Political History of the Olympics.* New York: Verso.

Brennan, Elliot. (2022). "Saudi Minister says Hosting Olympics is the 'Ultimate Goal, Rejects Sportswashing Allegations." Inside the Games. August 22. https://www.insidethegames.biz/articles/1127216/saudi-minister-olympics.

Brockman, Nobert. (2006). "Bikila, Abebe." In *African Biographical Dictionary*, 75. Toronto: Grey House Publishing.

Brück, Matthias. (2022). "Shankar Donetsk: A Football Club Fleeing War." *Deutsche Welle*. April 20. https://www.dw.com/en/shakhtar-donetsk-a-football-club-fleeing-war/a-61520819.

Brymer, Eric, and Robert Schweitzer. (2017). "Evoking the Ineffable: The Phenomenology of Extreme Sports." *American Psychological Association*. https://psycnet.apa.org/record/2017-12269-005.

Buckhorn, Göran. (2018). "So . . . About Vikings and their Helmets." *Mystic Seaport Museum Magazine*, May 23. https://www.mysticseaport.org/news/so-about-vikings-and-their-helmets/.

Burke, Jason. (2016). "Ethiopian Olympic Medallist [sic] Sees Asylum after Marathon Protest." *The Guardian*, August 22. https://www.theguardian.com/world/2016/aug/22/ethiopian-olympic-medallist-feyisa-lilesa-seeks-asylum-after-marathon-protest-oromo-rio.

Bush, George W. (2022). "Remarks by the President at the Opening Ceremonies of the 2022 Olympic Winter Games." https://georgewbush-whitehouse.archives.gov/news/releases/2002/02/20020209-2.html.

Cara, Marianne, and Ashley Mauritzen. (2015). "Semiotics of Olympic Logos: The Meaning-making Process." *Research World*, September 8. https://archive.researchworld.com/semiotics-of-olympic-logos-the-meaning-making-process/.

Cárdenas, Alexander. (2016). "Sport and Peace-Building in Divided Societies: A Case Study on [sic] Colombia and Northern Ireland," *Peace and Conflict Studies, 23* (2): https://nsuworks.nova.edu/pcs/vol23/iss2/4.

Cárdenas, Alexander. (2019). "Sports and Peace Building." In Joseph Macguire, Mark Falcous, and Kaite Liston (Eds.), *The Business and Culture of Sports: Politics, Economy, Environment, Volume 2: Sociocultural Perspectives*. London: Macmillan Reference.

Carlsen, Jack, and Anne Taylor. (2003). "Mega-Events and Urban Renewal: The Case of the Manchester 2002 Commonwealth Games." *Event Management, 8*(1), 15–22.

Carusa, Raul, and Marco Di Domizio. (2013). "International Hostility and Aggressiveness on the Soccer Pitch: Evidence from the European Championship[s] and World Cups for the Period 2000–2012." In Håvard Mokleiv Nygård, and Scott Gates. "Soft Power at Home and Abroad: Sport Diplomacy, Politics and Peacebuilding" *International Area Studies Review, 16*(3), 235–43.

Chapman, Michelle. (2023). "WWE No Longer a Family Affair after Merger with UFC." AP. April 3. https://apnews.com/article/wwe-mcmahon-endeavor-ufc-f0323725f13c6bbdbd39d18321f26ecf?user_email=cb3a1dc473ed3a2deb2c1e0de9934d

94ae4e7e96a8fcaadd928becff116824db&utm_medium=Sports_Wire&utm_source =Sailthru&utm_campaign=SportsWire_April3&utm_term=Sports%20HQ.

CISM. (2023). "Climbing for Peace: Damavand, Iran." August 8. https://www .milsport.one/news/august-2023-082023/climbing-for-peace-damavand-tehran-iri -summary-news.

Clarke, Felicity, Aled Jones, and Lee Smith. (2021). "Building Peace through Sports Projects: A Scoping Review," *Sustainability, 13*(2129).

Cleophas, Francois. (2021). "Sport and Physical Culture on the Edges of the Imperial Project." In Francois Cleophas (Ed.), *Critical Reflections on Physical Culture at the Edges of Empire.* Stellenbosch: African Sun Media.

Coakley, Jay. (2015). "Assessing the Sociology of Sport: On Cultural Sensitivities and the Great Sport Myth," *International Review for the Sociology of Sport, 50*(4–5), 402–406.

Coalter, Fred. (2002). "Sport and Community Development: A Manual." Research Report No. 86. Edinburgh: Sportscotland.

Coalter, Fred. (2010). "The Politics of Sport-for-Development: Limited Focus Programmes and Broad Gauge Problems?" *International Review for the Sociology of Sport, 45*, 295–314.

Collison, Holly. (2016). *Youth and Sport for Development: The Seduction of Football in Liberia.* Springer: Berlin/Heidelberg, Germany.

Collison, Holly, Simon Darnell, Richard Giulianotti, and P. David; Howe, eds. (2018). *Routledge Handbook of Sport for Development and Peace*, Abington: Routledge.

Collison, Holly, Simon Darnell, Richard Giulianotti, and P. David; Howe. (2017). "Sport for Social Change and Development: Sustaining Transnational Partnerships and Adapting International Curriculums to Local Contexts in Rwanda." *The International Journal of the History of Sport, 33*(15): 1685–99.

The Commonwealth. (2019). "Measuring the Contribution of Sport, Physical Education, and Physical Activity to the Sustainable Development Goals: Toolkit and Model Indicators," London: The Commonwealth Secretariat.

Cottingham, Michael, Ashlyne Vineyard, Fernanda Velasco, and Beradine Asias. (2017). "Meeting Expenses of Wheelchair Rugby: Strategies Employed to Procure Funding by Teams and Players." *Palestra, 31*(1): 16–22. https://grants.hhp.uh.edu/ cottingham/docs/Wheelchair%20Rugby%20article.pdf.

Cox, Fletcher, and Timothy D. Sisk. (2017). "Peacebuilding: A Social Cohesion Approach," in Fletcher D. Cox and Timothy D. Sisk (Eds.), *Peacebuilding in Deeply Divided Societies: Toward Social Cohesion.* London: Palgrave.

Dampf, Andrew, and Graham Dunbar. (2023). "IOC's Bach says Olympics on History's Side in Russia Issue." AP, February 12. https://apnews.com/article/ zelenskyy-politics-sports-europe-poland-393997c287f33cdf6bfd20cbce783839.

Darnell, Simon. (2012). *Sport for Development and Peace: A Critical Sociology.* London: Bloomsbury.

Darnell, Simon, Rusell Field, and Burce Kidd. (2019). *The History and Politics of Sport-for-Development: Activists, Ideologues, and Reformers.* London: Palgrave Macmillan.

Davies, Joe. (2020). "Ancient Indian Wrestling Tradition of Kushti is Dying Out . . . Because Competitors are Expected to be Celibate and Avoid Booze." *Daily Mail,* September 14. https://www.dailymail.co.uk/news/article-8730217/Ancient-Indian -wrestling-tradition-dying-competitors-expected-CELIBATE.html?ito=email _share_article-image-share.

Davies, Shawn, Thérése Petterson, and Magnus Öberg. (2022). "Organized Violence 1998–2021 and Drone Warfare." *Journal of Peace Research, 59*(4), 593–610.

DeBosscher, Veerle et. al. (2009). "Explaining International Sporting Success: An International Comparison of Elite Sport Systems and Politics in Six Countries," *Sport Management Review 12*(3), 113–136.

De Coning, Christo, ed. (2018, August). "The Case for Sport in the Western Cape: Socio-Economic Benefits and Impacts of Sport and Recreation," Interdisciplinary Centre of Excellence for Sport Science and Development, University of the Western Cape. https://www.icsspe.org/content/grassroots-sport -toolkit.

Delaney, Tim. (2015). "The Functionalist Perspective on Sport." In Richard Giulianotti, ed. *The Routledge Handbook of the Sociology of Sport.* London and New York: Routledge.

Dennis, Michael, and Jonathan Grix. (2012). *Sport under Communism: Behind the East German 'Miracle.'* London: Palgrave.

Dension, Erik, Nadia Bevan, and Ruth Jeanes. "Reviewing Evidence of LGBTQ+ Discrimination and Exclusion in Sport." *Sport Management Review, 24* (3), 389–409.

Denver, Simon. (2014). "Yao Ming Aims to Save Africa's Elephants by Persuading China to Give up Ivory." *Washington Post*, September 4. https://www .washingtonpost.com/world/ex-rocket-yao-ming-aims-to-save-africas-elephants --with-china-campaign/2014/09/03/87ebbe2a-d3e1-4283-964e-8d87dea397d6 _story.html.

Dichter, Heather L. (2022). "Sport and Politics." In Murray G. Phillips, Douglas Booth, and Carly Adams (Eds.), *Routledge Handbook of Sport History.* London and New York: Routledge.

Dixon, Ed. (2022). "Tokyo 2020 Pushes IOC to US $7.6bn Revenue for 2017/2021 Cycle." *The Guardian*, May 23. https://www.sportspromedia.com/news/ ioc-financial-results-2021-revenue-tokyo-2020-olympics/?zephr_sso_ott=qthEMf.

Donnelly, Peter. (2006). "The Sociology of Sport." In *21st Century Sociology: A Reference Handbook.* Ed. Clifton D. Bryant and Dennis L. Peck. Vol. 2: Specialty and Interdisciplinary Studies. 21st Century Reference Series. Thousand Oaks, CA: SAGE Publications, 205–213.

Dörr, Luisa. (2022). "ImillaSkate: An Indigenous Bolivian Skateboard Collective-photo Essay." *The Guardian*, February 8.

Druckman, Daniel. (1994). "Nationalism, Patriotism, and Group Loyalty: A Social Psychological Perspective." *Mershon International Studies Review, 38* (1): 43–68.

Durham, William H. (1979). *Scarcity and Survival in Central America: Ecological Origins of the Soccer War.* Stanford: Stanford University Press.

The Economist. (2016). "Look Inside China's Secretive Olympic Training Camps." https://www.youtube.com/watch?v=8-OGKGmxSbw.

Edelman, Robert, and Mikhail Prozumenshikov. (2018). "The Soviets Navigate the Olympics: Troubled Waters." Cold War International History Project e-Dossier No. 68. https://www.wilsoncenter.org/publication/the-soviets-navigate-the-olympics-troubled-waters.

Edwards, Harry. (2017). *The Revolt of the Black Athlete* (50th Anniversary Edition). Champaign-Urbana: University of Illinois Press.

English, Colleen. (2017). "Toward Sport Reform: Hegemonic Masculinity and Reconceptualizing Competition," *Journal of the Philosophy of Sport, 44*(2): 183–198.

Euronews. (2023). "Protests for Disabled Rights held in France ahead of Paris Olympics and Paralympics." *Euronews*, April 8. https://www.euronews.com/2023/04/27/protests-for-disabled-rights-held-in-france-ahead-of-paris-olympics-and-paralympics.

Euronews. (2022). "Beijing Olympics: China's Choice of Uyghur Torchbearer Causes Controversy." *Euronews*, May 2. https://www.euronews.com/2022/02/05/beijing-olympics-china-s-choice-of-uyghur-torchbearer-causes-controversy.

Ferris-Rotman, Amie, and Sayed Hassib. (2012). "In war-ravaged Afghanistan, Combat-Sports Reign." Reuters, February 19. https://www.reuters.com/article/uk-afghanistan-olympics/in-war-ravaged-afghanistan-combat-sports-reign-idUKTRE81J09320120220.

Field, Russell. (2022). "Sport and Activism." In Murray G. Phillips, Douglas Booth, and Carly Adams (Eds.), *Routledge Handbook of Sport History*. London and New York: Routledge.

FIFA. (2023). "One Month On: 5 Billion Engaged with the FIFA World Cup Qatar," January 18. https://www.fifa.com/tournaments/mens/worldcup/qatar2022/news/one-month-on-5-billion-engaged-with-the-fifa-world-cup-qatar-2022-tm.

Finlay, Mitchell James et al. (2021). "The Association between Competitor Level and the Physical Preparation Practices of Amateur Boxers." *PLoS One, 16* (9), 1–13.

Firstpost. (2023). "Explained: Brazil's Iconic Football Jersey, Its Link to Far-Right Jain Bolsonaro and the 8 January Riots." January 10.

Fitzduff, Mari. (2021). *Our Brains at War.* Oxford: Oxford University Press.

Flindall, Rory Alexander. (2020). "Portraying 'Paralympism'? An Analysis of the Evolution of Paralympic Athlete Media Representations since the 1980s." *Diagoras: International Academic Journal on Olympic Studies 4,* 75–101.

Futterman, Matthew. (2022). "Ukrainian Refuses Hand of Belarussian Opponent." *New York Times.* September 22.

Gajek, Eva Maria. (2016). "The Rome and Munich Olympics, 1960, 1972." In Alex Bairner, John Kelly, and Jung Woo Lee (Eds.), *The Routledge Handbook of Sport and Politics*. Abingdon, UK: Routledge.

Gamba, Laura. (2018). "Colombia Conflict: Swapping the Battlefield for the Football Pitch." *BBC News.* May 22. https://www.bbc.com/news/world-latin-america-44142503.

Garfield, Leanna. (2018). "War Tore Apart the City that Hosted the 1984 Olympic Games—Here's What the Abandoned Venues Look Like Today." *Business Insider*,

February 7. https://www.businessinsider.com/winter-olympics-abandoned-venues-sarajevo-bosnia-2018-2.

Garland, Jon, and Michael Rowe. (2001). *Racism and Anti-Racism in Football.* London: Palgrave.

Garner, Ian. (2023a). *Generation Z: Into the Heart of Russia's Fascist Youth.* London: Hurst.

Garner, Ian. (2023b). "Russia's Frighteningly Fascist Youth." *Foreign Policy*, May 21.

Ghildiyal, Rakesh. (2015). "Role of Sports in the Development of an Individual and Role of Psychology in Sports." *Mens Sana Monographs, 13*(1): 165–170. www.ncbi.nlm.nih.gov/pmc/articles/PMC4381313/.

Ghobarah, Hazem Adam, Paul Huth, and Bruce Russet. "Civil Wars Kill and Maim People—Long After the Shooting Stops." *American Political Science Review, 97*(2): 189–202.

Giessmann, Hans. J. (2016). "Embedded Peace. Infrastructures for Peace: Lessons Learned." New York: UNDP.

Giulianotti, Richard. (2011). "The Sport, Development and Peace Sector: A Model of Four Policy Dilemmas." *Journal of Sport Policy, 40* (4): 757–776.

Giulianotti, Richard. (2015). "Introduction." In Richard Giulianotti (Ed.), *Routledge Handbook on the Sociology of Sport*, xix–xxiii. Abingdon: Routledge.

Gonzales, Roger. (2020). "New FIFA Indictment Confirms Bribes Paid to Vote for World Cups in Qatar and Russia." CBS Sports, April 7. https://www.cbssports.com/soccer/news/new-fifa-indictment-confirms-paid-bribes-to-vote-for-world-cups-in-qatar-and-russia/.

Gray, Colin. (2006). *Freedom's Fury.* Wolo Entertainment. https://www.imdb.com/title/tt0322332/.

Grix, Jonathan. (2015). *Sport Politics: An Introduction.* New York: Springer.

Grix, Jonathan, Paul Michael Brannagan, and Donna Lee. (2019). "Sports Mega-Events and the Concept of Soft Power." In Jonathan Grix, Paul Michael Brannagan, and Donna Lee (Eds.), *Entering the Global Arena: Emerging States, Soft Power Strategies and Sport Mega Events.* Singapore: Palgrave Pivot.

The Guardian. (2022). "Jim Thorpe Reinstated as Sole Winner of 1912 Olympic Gold Medals." *The Guardian*, July 15. https://www.theguardian.com/sport/2022/jul/15/jim-thorpe-restored-olympic-gold-medals-decathlon-pentathlon.

The Guardian. (2023). "Celtic Ban Green Brigade Fans' Group from Attending Home Matches." *The Guardian*, October 31. https://www.theguardian.com/football/2023/oct/31/celtic-ban-green-brigade-fans-group-from-attending-home-matches.

Guterres, António. (2019). "Hatred 'a Threat to everyone,' Declares Guterres Calling for Global Effort to End Xenophobia and 'Loathsome Rhetoric.'" UN News, April 4. https://news.un.org/en/story/2019/04/1037531.

Guterres, António. (2020). "Secretary General Denounces "Tsunami' of Xenophobia Unleased amid COVID-19, Calling for All-Out Effort against Hate Speech." United Nations Office of the Secretary General, May 8. https://www.un.org/press/en/2020/sgsm20076.doc.htm.

Guttman, Allen. (1992). *The Olympics, A History of the Modern Games.* Champaign-Urbana, Illinois: University of Illinois Press.

Guttman, Allen. (1993). "The Diffusion of Sports and the Problem of Cultural Imperialism." In Eric Dunning, Joseph A. Maguire, and Robert E. Pearton, *The Sports Process: A Comparative and Developmental Approach.* Champaign-Urbana: Human Kinetics.

Hain, Peter, and Andres Odendaal. (2022). *Pitch Battles: Sport, Racism, and Resistance.* Lanham, MD: Rowman & Littlefield.

Hansford, Amelia. (2023). "US Open: LGBTQ+ Players Make Tennis History in Grand Slam." *PinkNews.* September 3. https://www.thepinknews.com/2023/09/03/tennis-us-open-daria-kasatkina-greet-minnen/.

Hartmann, Douglas. "Sport and Social Intervention." In Richard Giulianotti (Ed.), *The Routledge Handbook of the Sociology of Sport.* London and New York: Routledge.

Hassan, David. (2016). "Sport in a Divided Northern Ireland: Past and Present," in *The Routledge Handbook of Sport and Politics.* Abingdon, UK: Routledge.

Henderson, Simon. (2013). "The Olympic Project for Human Rights: Genesis and Response." In *Sidelines: How American Sports Challenged the Black Freedom Struggle.* Lexington: University of Kentucky Press.

Hobsbawn, Eric. (1983). "Mass-Producing Traditions: Europe, 1870–1914." In Erica Hobsbawn and Terence Ranger, eds. *The Invention of Tradition.* Cambridge: Cambridge University Press.

Höglund, Kristine, and Ralph Sundberg. (2008). "Reconciliation through Sports? The Case of South Africa." *Third World Quarterly, 29*(4): 805–818.

Houlihan, Barrie. (1994). *Sport and International Politics.* Hertfordshire: Harvester Wheatsheaf.

Houlihan, Barrie. (2015). "Political Science, Sociology, and the Study of Sport." In Richard Giulianotti (Ed.), *The Routledge Handbook of the Sociology of Sport.* London and New York: Routledge.

Howe, P. David. (2015). "Disability and Sport: The Case of the Paralympic Games." In Richard Giulianotti (Ed.), *The Routledge Handbook of the Sociology of Sport.* London and New York: Routledge.

Huber, Martin Fritz. (2022). "How Jasmin Paris Conquered the Barkley Marathons 'Fun Run.'" *Outside Magazine*, March 15. https://www.outsideonline.com/health/running/culture-running/people/jasmin-paris-barkley-marathons/.

Human Rights Watch. (2023). "Saudi Arabia: Events of 2022." World Report 2023. https://www.hrw.org/world-report/2023/country-chapters/saudi-arabia.

Human Rights Watch. (2022). "Qatar: Rights Abuses Stain FIFA World Cup." November 14. https://www.hrw.org/news/2022/11/14/qatar-rights-abuses-stain-fifa-world-cup.

Human Rights Watch. (2020a). "Japan: Child Abuse in Pursuit of Olympic Gold Medals." Human Rights Watch, July 20. https://www.hrw.org/news/2020/07/20/japan-child-abuse-pursuit-olympic-medals.

Human Rights Watch. (2020b). "China: Repression Threatens Wider Olympics: Letter to the International Olympic Committee Urges Human Rights Risk Assessment."

December 22. https://www.hrw.org/news/2020/12/22/china-repression-threatens-winter-olympics.

Hurst, Whitney. (2010). "India and Pakistani Players Unite to Reach U.S. Open Final." CNN. September 10. https://edition.cnn.com/2010/SPORT/09/10/india.pakistan.tennis/index.html.

Hussein, Abid. (2023). "'Indian Hostility' Looms over Asia Cup's Stripped-back Host Pakistan." Al Jazeera, August 29. https://www.aljazeera.com/sports/2023/8/29/cricket-pakistan-asia-cup-2023-hosts-india.

Hylton, Kevin, and Alexandra J. Rankin-Wright. (2016). "'Race,' Sport, and Politics." In Alan Bairner, John Kelly, and Jung Woo Lee (Eds.), *The Routledge Handbook of Sport and Politics*. Abingdon, UK: Routledge.

Kaufman, Stuart. (2001). *Modern Hatreds: The Symbolic Politics of Ethnic War*. Ithaca, NY: Cornell University Press.

Kunti, Samidra. (2022). "Norwegian FA Boss Klaveness bursts the FIFA and Qatar Human Rights Feel-good Bubble." Inside World Football, March 31. https://www.insideworldfootball.com/2022/03/31/norwegian-fa-boss-klaveness-bursts-fifa-qatar-2022-human-rights-bubble/.

ICRC. (2019). "ICRC Preparing for Major Expansion of Sports Programmes for People with Disabilities." International Committee of the Red Cross, December 3. https://www.icrc.org/en/document/icrc-preparing-major-expansion-sports-programs-people-disabilities.

ICRC. (2014). "Moving Together: Promoting Psycho-Social Well-Being through Sport and Physical Activity." https://pscentre.org/?resource=moving-together-english&wpv_search=true&selected=single-resource.

ICSSPE and UNESCO. (2022). "Let's Get Moving Together: A Toolkit for Grassroots Sport Leaders." https://www.icsspe.org/content/let%E2%80%99s-get-moving-together-toolkit-grassroots-sport-leaders.

IEP. (2022). "Global Peace Index 2022: Measuring Peace in a Complex World." Institute for Economics and Peace. https://www.visionofhumanity.org/wp-content/uploads/2022/06/GPI-2022-web.pdf.

Ingle, Sean. (2021). "Modern Pentathlon Votes to Ditch Horse Riding after Tokyo Olympic Turmoil." *The Guardian*, November 2. https://www.theguardian.com/sport/2021/nov/02/modern-pentathlon-votes-to-ditch-horse-riding-after-tokyo-olympic-turmoil.

Ingle, Sean. (2022). "Russian Gymnast with 'Z' Symbol on Podium Next to Ukrainian Faces Long Ban." *The Guardian*, March 7. https://www.theguardian.com/sport/2022/mar/07/shocking-behaviour-russian-gymnast-shows-z-symbol-on-podium-next-to-ukrainian-winner.

IOC. (2020). "The Olympic Charter." International Olympics Committee, July 17. https://stillmed.olympic.org/media/Document%20Library/OlympicOrg/General/EN-Olympic-Charter.pdf.

IOC. (2021a). "Tokyo 2022: Audience & Insights Report." International Olympics Committee. https://library.olympics.com/Ils/digitalCollection/DigitalCollectionThumbnailHandler.ashx?documentId=1327776&size=LARGE&fallback=https

%3a%2f%2flibrary.olympics.com%2fui%2fskins%2fCIOL%2fportal%2ffront
%2fimages%2fGeneral%2fDocType%2fENUM_LARGE.png.

IOC. (2021b). "Annual Report 2021: Faster, Higher, Stronger—Together."
Lausanne: International Olympic Committee. https://stillmed.olympics.com/media
/Documents/International-Olympic-Committee/Annual-report/IOC-Annual-Report
-2021.pdf?_ga=2.77075997.981478691.1685120340-378726175.1685026438.

IOC. (2022a). "Olympic Winter Games Beijing 2022 Watched by More than 2 Billion
People." International Olympics Committee, October 20. https://olympics.com
/ioc/news/olympic-winter-games-beijing-2022-watched-by-more-than-2-billion
-people.

IOC. (2022b). "IOC EB Urges All International Federations to Relocate or Cancel
their Sports Events Currently Planned in Russia or Belarus." International
Olympics Committee, February 25. https://olympics.com/ioc/news/ioc-eb-urges
-all-ifs-to-relocate-or-cancel-their-sports-events-currently-planned-in-russia-or
-belarus.

IOC (2022c). "IOC Strategic Framework on Human Rights." International Olympics
Committee, September.

https://stillmed.olympics.com/media/Documents/Beyond-the-Games/Human-Rights/
IOC-Strategic-Framework-on-Human-Rights.pdf#_ga=2.264467215.1073227638
.1694803368-1500324480.1694108056.

IOC. (2023a). "Statement on Solidarity with Ukraine, Sanctions against Russia and
Belarus, and the Status of Athletes from These Countries." International Olympics
Committee, January 25. https://olympics.com/ioc/news/statement-on-solidarity
-with-ukraine-sanctions-against-russia-and-belarus-and-the-status-of-athletes.

IOC. (2023b). "Factsheet: Women in the Olympic Movement." International
Olympics Committee, April 14. https://stillmed.olympics.com/media/Documents/
Olympic-Movement/Factsheets/Women-in-the-Olympic-Movement.pdf.

IPC. (2022). "IPC President Andrew Parsons' Beijing 2022 Opening Ceremony
Speech." International Paralympic Committee, March 4. https://www.paralympic
.org/feature/ipc-president-andrew-parsons-beijing-2022-opening-ceremony
-speech.

IPC. (2023). "IPC Statement Following IOC Executive Board Decision." International
Paralympic Committee, January 25. https://www.paralympic.org/news/ipc
-statement-following-ioc-executive-board-decision.

Irak, Dağhan. (2020). "Football in Turkey during the Erdoğan Regime." *Soccer and
Society, 21*(6), 680–691.

Johnson, David. (2013). "The Frisbee: A Political-Economic History of a
Counter-Culture Icon." *Journal of Sport & Social Issues, 37*(2): 106–126.

Judah, Tim. (2008). *Bikila: Ethiopia's Barefoot Olympian*. London: Reportage Press.

Kamareva, Nina, and Jonathan Grix. 2019. "'War and Peace' at the 1980 Moscow and
2014 Sochi Olympics: The Role of Hard and Soft Power in Russian Identity." *The
International Journal of the History of Sport, 35*(14): 1–21.

Kanal, Samarth. (2022). "Timeline: How the FIA Cost Cap Story Unfolded as Redbull
and Aston Martin Enter Agreements over Breaches." Formula 1, October 22. https://

www.formula1.com/en/latest/article.timeline-how-the-fia-cost-cap-story-unfolded
.6yAhD5hKoRuUTqhU1wYuGY.html.

Karmaliani, Rozina, Judith McFarlane, Hussain Maqbool Ahmed Khuwaja, Yasmin Somani, Shireen Shezad Bhamani, Tazeen Said Ali, Nargis Asad, Esnet D. Chirwa, and Rachel Jewkes. (2020). "Right to Play's Intervention to Reduce Peer Violence among Children in Public Schools: A Cluster Randomized Controlled Trial." *Global Health Action, 13*(1).

Kassing, Jeffrey W., and Lindsey Meân, eds. (2017). *Perspectives on the U.S.-Mexican Soccer Rivalry: Passion and Politics in Red, White, Blue, and Green.* London: Palgrave.

Keim, Marion. (2018). "Kicking for Peace (2015)." In Christo de Coning (Ed.), "The Case for Sport in the Western Cape: Socio-Economic Benefits and Impacts of Sport and Recreation." Belleville: Interdisciplinary Centre of Excellence for Sport Science and Development.

Keles, Oguzhan, (2021). "Examining the 'Pocket Hercules'—Naim Suleymanoglu: His Life and Career in Olympic Weightlifting and International Sport" (2021). Thesis, University of Western Ontario. Electronic Thesis and Dissertation Repository. 7704. https://ir.lib.uwo.ca/etd/7704.

Keyes, Helen et al. (2023). "Attending Live Sporting Events Predicts Subjective Wellbeing and Reduces Loneliness." *Frontiers of Public Health, 10.*

Keys, Barbara. (2022). "Sport and Emotion." In Murray G. Phillips, Douglas Booth, and Carly Adams (Eds.), *Routledge Handbook of Sport History.* London and New York: Routledge.

Kim, Soo. (2023). "Mountaineer Shows Piles of Garbage at Mount Everest in Shocking Viral Video." *Newsweek*, June 1. https://www.newsweek.com/mount -everest-garbage-pollution-mountain-guide-climbers-viral-video-1803916.

King, Billie Jean. (2021). *All In: An Autobiography.* New York: Alfred A. Knopf.

Kobierecki, Michal Marcin. (2016). "Ping-Pong Diplomacy and its Legacy in the [*sic*] American Foreign Policy." *Polish Political Yearbook 45*, 304–16.

Kobierecki, Michal Marcin and Piotr Strożek. (2017). "Sport as a Factor in National Branding: A Quantitative Approach." *International Journal of the History of Sport, 34*(7–8): 697–712.

Konopka, Lukasz. (2015). "Exercise vs Competitive Athletics in Youth: A Neuroscience Perspective." *Croatia Medical Journal, 56*(6): 581–582.

Krüger, Arnd. (2002). "The Unfinished Symphony: The Olympic Games from Coubertin to Samaranch." In James Riordan and Arnd Krüger (Eds.), *The International Politics of Sport in the 20th Century.* Abingdon, UK: Routledge.

Krüger, Arnd. (2003). "Germany: The Nazi Propaganda Machine." In Arnd Krüger and William Murray (Eds.), *The Nazi Olympics: Sport, Politics and Appeasement in the 1930s.* Champaign-Urbana: University of Illinois Press.

Kyiv Independent. (2023). "Ukrainian Boxing Champion dies in Combat Near Bakhmut." *Kyiv Independent*, May 25. https://kyivindependent.com/ukrainian -boxing-champion-dies-in-combat-near-bakhmut/.

LaFeber, Walter. (1999). *Michael Jordan and the New Global Capitalism.* New York: Norton.

Large, David Clay. (2016). "The Olympic Spirit is Unbridled, Rabid Nationalism." *Foreign Policy*, August 12. https://foreignpolicy.com/2016/08/12/the-olympic-spirit-is-unbridled-rabid-nationalism/.

Lederach, John Paul. (2005). *The Moral Imagination: The Art and Soul of Building Peace.* Oxford: Oxford University Press.

Lee, Jong Woo Lee, and Alan Bairner. (2016). "Sport and Communism: The Examples of North Korea and Cuba." In *The Routledge Handbook of Sport and Politics*, Abingdon, UK: Routledge.

Lee, Woojun, and Cunningham, George. B. (2019). "Moving Toward Understanding Social Justice in Sport Organizations: A Study of Engagement in Social Justice Advocacy in Sport Organizations." *Journal of Sport and Social Issues, 43*(3): 245–63.

Lessa, Carlos. (2008). "Nation and Nationalism based on the Brazilian Experience." *Estudos Avançados, 22*(62): 237–356.

Leveille, Rohan. (2023). "Game Changer: How Sports are Part of Saudi Arabia's Bigger Plan." *Brown Political Review*, March 15. https://brownpoliticalreview.org/2023/03/game-changer-how-sports-are-part-of-saudi-arabias-bigger-plan/.

Levinson, David, and Gertrud Pfister. (2016). *Berkshire Encyclopedia of World Sport* (3rd ed.). Great Barrington, MA: Berkshire Publishing Group.

Library of Congress. "Soccer." In *Sports Industry: A Resource Guide*. Retrieved May 3, 2023, from https://guides.loc.gov/sports-industry.

Lin, Tzu-Wei, and Yu-Min Kuo. (2013). "Exercise Benefits Brain Function: The Monomine Connection." *Brain Science, 3*(1): 39–53.

Llewellyn, Matthew, and Toby C. Rider. (2018). "Sport, Thatcher and Apartheid Politics: The Zola Budd Affair." *Journal of Southern African Studies, 44*(4): 575–592.

Long, Jonathan, and Karl Spracklen, eds. (2011). *Sports and Challenges to Racism.* London: Palgrave Macmillan.

Lu, Zhouxiang, and Fan, Hong. (2019). "China's Sports Heroes: Nationalism, Patriotism, and Gold Medal." The *International Journal of the History of Sport, 36*(7–8): 748–63.

Lu, Zhouxiang. (2016). "Sport and Politics: The Cultural Revolution in the Chinese Sports Ministry, 1966–1976." *The International Journal of the History of Sport, 33*(5): 569–585.

MacGinty, Roger. (2003). "The Political Use of Symbols of Discord and Accord: Northern Ireland and South Africa." *Civil Wars, 4*(1): 1–21.

MacMullan, Jackie. (2017). "Cameroon Calling." ESPN, May 8. https://www.espn.com/espn/feature/story/_/page/presents19316766/the-key-joel-embiid-rise-luc-mbah-moute.

Mahomed, S., and Dhai, A. (2019). "Global Injustice in Sport: The Caster Semenya Ordeal—Prejudice, Discrimination, and Racial Bias." *SAMJ: South African Medical Journal, 109*(8): 548–551.

Malm, Christer, Johan Jakobsson, and Andreas Isaksson. (2019). "Physical Activity and Sports—Real Health Benefits: A Review with Insight into the Public Health of Sweden." *Sports (Basel), 7*(5): 1–28.

Marshall, Alex. (2016). *Republic or Death! Travels in Search of National Anthems.* London: Windmill Books.

Marin, Jeffrey J. (2017). "Models of Disability." In Jeffrey J. Martin (Ed.), *Handbook of Disability Sport and Exercise Psychology.* Oxford: Oxford Academic.

McCandless, Erin. (2019). "Forging Resilient Social Contracts and Sustaining Peace: Summary of Findings of New Comparative Research," *Journal of Peacebuilding and Development, 14*(1): 90–95.

McKay, Duncan. (2003). "Torture of Iraq's Athletes." *The Guardian.* February 1, 2003. https://www.theguardian.com/sport/2003/feb/02/athletics.duncanmackay1.

McVitie, Peter. 2023. "Brazil Shows Support for Vinicus Junior with All-Black Kit in Anti-Racism Campaign during Guinea Friendly." Goal.com, June 17. https://www.goal.com/en-gb/news/brazil-support-vinicius-all-black-kit-anti-racism-campaign-guinea-friendly/blt2668a8d61fae0f3c.

Mercy Corps. (2007). "Commitment to Practice: A Playbook for Practitioners in HIV, Youth and Sport." November 1. Portland: Mercy Corps. https://www.mercycorps.org/research-resources/commitment-practice.

Meyers, Dvora. (2012). "The Rise (and Fall?) of the Little-Girl Gymnast." *The Atlantic*, July 24. https://www.theatlantic.com/entertainment/archive/2012/07/the-rise-and-fall-of-the-little-girl-gymnast/260123/.

Mills, Daniel. (2023). "Rugby Relations: Australia's Best Diplomacy Asset in the Pacific." Australian Strategic Policy Institute, March 6. https://www.aspistrategist.org.au/rugby-relations-australias-best-diplomatic-asset-in-the-pacific/.

Minority Rights Group. *Peoples under Threat 2021: Authoritarianism.* London: Minority Rights Group International, December 16. https://minorityrights.org/publications/put-2021/.

Montillo, Roseanne. (2017). *Fire on the Track: Betty Robinson and the Triumph of Early Olympic Women.* New York: Crown Publishing Group.

Moussa, Salma. (2020). "Building Social Cohesion between Christians and Muslims through Soccer in Post-ISIS Iraq." *Science, 369*(6505): 866–870.

Moustakas, Louis. (2022). "Sport for Social Cohesion: Transferring from the Pitch to the Community?" *Social Sciences, 11*(513): 1–15.

Mulvaney, Nick. (2008). "China's 100-Year Dream, A Cure for the Sick Man of Asia." Reuters, August 7. https://www.reuters.com/article/us-olympics-china/chinas-100-year-dream-a-cure-for-the-sick-man-of-asia-idUSPEK33620320080807.

Murray, Stuart. (2018). *Sports Diplomacy: Origins, Theory, and Practice.* Aberystwyth: Routledge.

Musumeci Guiseppe. (2021). "Why Would You Choose to Do an Extreme Sport?" *Journal of Functional Morphology and Kinesiology, 26*(3): 65.

NBC. (2002). "The 2002 Olympic Winter Games: Olympic Highlights." NBC (DVD).

Næss, Hans Erik. (2022). *The Neutrality Paradox in Sport: Governance, Politics, and Human Rights after Ukraine.* London: Palgrave.

Nanayakkara, Samantha. (2012). "Crossing Boundaries and Changing Identities: Empowering South Asian Women through Sport and Physical Activities." *The International Journal of the History of Sport, 29*(13): 1885–1906.

Neuroscience News. (2023). "More Steps and Moderate Physical Activity Cuts Dementia and Cognitive Impairment Risk." *Neuroscience News*, January 25. https://neurosciencenews.com/exercise-dementia-aging-22363/.

New York Times. (1973). "Abebe Bikila, Track Star, Dies at 46." *New York Times*, October 26. https://www.nytimes.com/1973/10/26/archives/abebe-bikila-46-track-star-dies-only-man-to-win-olympic-marathon.html.

Nicholls, Sara, Audrey R. Giles, and Christabelle Sethna. (2010). "Perpetuating the 'Lack of Evidence' Discourse in Sport for Development: Privileged Voices, Unheard Stories and Subjugated Knowledge." *International Review of the Sociology of Sport, 46*(3): 249–264.

Nordland, Rod, and Rob Harris. (2022). "Critics Say Qatar's World Cup Plans Include Labor Abuse." *New York Times*. November 25. https://www.nytimes.com/2022/11/25/world/middleeast/qatar-world-cup-criticism.html.

Norwegian Ministry of Foreign Affairs. (2005). "Strategy for Norway's Culture and Sports Cooperation with the Global South." https://www.regjeringen.no/globalassets/upload/kilde/ud/rap/2005/0022/ddd/pdfv/265661-culture.pdf.

Nygård, Håvard Mokleiv, and Scott Gates. (2013). "Soft Power at Home and Abroad: Sport Diplomacy, Politics and Peacebuilding." *International Area Studies Review, 16*(3): 235–43.

OCHA. (2022). Global Humanitarian Overview 2023. New York: United Nations Office of the Coordinator of Humanitarian Affairs (OCHA). December 21. https://reliefweb.int/attachments/22b19cd1-a60a-4d9e-bde1-bd82a95009e8/GHO-2023-EN_FINAL.pdf.

OECD. (2022). States of Fragility 2022. Paris: OECD. https://www-oecd-ilibrary-org.du.idm.oclc.org/development/states-of-fragility-2022_c7fedf5e-en.

Okane, Caitlin. (2023). "This Sherpa Set a World Record with 27 Summits of Mt. Everest. Then, He Topped Himself with 28." *CBS News*, May 23. https://www.cbsnews.com/news/sherpa-mount-everest-record-27-summits-just-completed-28th-kami-rita/.

Olive, Noemie, and Lucien Libert. (2023). "Surrounded by Marathon Medals, an 83-year-old Dreams of Paris." Reuters, May 2. https://www.reuters.com/sports/athletics/surrounded-by-marathon-medals-an-83-year-old-dreams-paris-2023-05-02/.

Olympic Refuge Think Tank. (2022). "Realising the Cross-Cutting Potential of Sport in Situations of Forced Displacement." *BMJ Global Health* 7:e008717: 1–4.

O'Reilly, Norm, et al. (2014). "Urban Sportscapes: An Environmental Deterministic Perspective on the Management of Youth Sport Participation." *Sport Management Review, 18*(2): 291–307.

Orwell, George. (1968). "The Sporting Spirit." In *In Front of Your Nose: The Essays of George Orwell* (1946–1950), George Orwell (author), Sonia Orwell (author), and Ian Angus (editor). Boston, MA: Harcourt. (Online at: https://www.orwellfoundation.com/the-orwell-foundation/orwell/essays-and-other-works/the-sporting-spirit/.)

Osborne, Anne C. (2013). "Performative Sport Fandom: An Approach to Retheorizing Sport Fans." *Sport in Society, 16*(5): 672–681.

Park, Kwangho, Gi Yong Koo, and Minkil Kim. (2023). "The Effect of the United Nations Resolution for Olympic Truce for Peace Based On Functionalism." *Journal of Human Sport and Exercise, 18*(1): 107–125.

Patil, Anushka. (2022). "A Russian Gymnast was Given a One-Year Ban for Wearing the Pro-War 'Z' Symbol at Competition." *New York Times*, May 19. https://www.nytimes.com/2022/05/19/world/russian-gymnast-z-medal.html.

PBS. (1999a). "Red Files: Interview with Olga Korbut." https://www.pbs.org/redfiles/sports/deep/interv/s_int_olga_korbut.htm.

PBS. (1999b). "The Long Walk of Nelson Mandela." *PBS Frontline*. https://www.pbs.org/wgbh/pages/frontline/shows/mandela/.

Pender, Keiran. (2022). "History Will Judge IOC and FIFA as Opportunistic Hypocrites over Russian." *The Guardian*, March 3. https://www.theguardian.com/sport/2022/mar/03/history-will-judge-ioc-and-fifa-as-opportunistic-hypocrites-over-russia.

Perottet, Tony. (2004). *The Naked Olympics: The True Story of the Ancient Games.* New York: Random House.

Pettersson, Thérése, and Magnus Öberg. (2020). "Organized Violence, 1989–2019." *Journal of Peace Research, 57*(4): 597–613.

Pfister, Gertrud, and Susan Bandy. (2015). "Gender and Sport." In Richard Giulianotti (Ed.), *The Routledge Handbook of the Sociology of Sport*. London and New York: Routledge.

Phillips, Murry G., Doulas Booth, and Carly Adams, eds. (2022). "Indigenous Sport History: Introduction." *Routledge Handbook of Sport History*. London and New York: Routledge.

Pink, Brian. (2008). "Defining Sport and Physical Activity: A Conceptual Model," Information Paper 414, Australian Bureau of Statistics. https://www.abs.gov.au/AUSSTATS/abs@.nsf/Lookup/4149.0.55.001Main+Features12008?OpenDocument.

Pop, Christiana. (2013). "The Modern Olympic Games—A Globalized Cultural and Sporting Event." *Procedia: Social and Behavioral Science, 92*: 728–34.

Portugal, Eduardo et al. (2013). "Neuroscience of Exercise: From Neurobiology Mechanisms to Mental Health." *Neuropsychobiology, 68*: 1–14.

Quin Pollard, Martin, and Tony Munroe. (2022). "Exclusive: China's Long, Strange Olympic Hockey Trip Ends, Next Step Uncertain." Reuters, February 18. https://www.reuters.com/lifestyle/sports/exclusive-olympics-chinas-long-strange-olympic-hockey-trip-ends-next-stop-2022-02-18/.

Radnofsky, Caroline. (2021). "Norway's Beach Handball Team Wins Fight Over Sexist Uniform Rules." *NBC News*, November 1. https://www.nbcnews.com/news/world/norways-beach-handball-team-win-fight-sexist-uniform-rules-rcna4218.

Reitschuler, Boris. (2014). "Sochi is to Putin What Berlin in 1936 Was to Hitler, Says Garry Kasparov." *The Guardian*, February 7. https://www.theguardian.com/sport/2014/feb/07/sochi-vladimir-putin-hitler-berlin-garry-kasparov#:~:text=In%20Sochi%2C%20it%20was%20Putin,It's%20a%20one%20man%20circus.%22.

Reuters. (2023). "Saudi Crown Prince Says He Does Not Care about 'Sportswashing' Claims." September 21. https://www.reuters.com/world/middle-east/saudi-crown -prince-says-he-does-not-care-about-sportswashing-claims-2023-09-22/.

Reuters. (2022). "Cricket-Australia targets PNG, Vanuatu in Cricket Diplomacy Project." August 19. https://www.reuters.com/article/cricket-australia -diplomacy/cricket-australia-targets-png-vanuatu-in-cricket-diplomacy-project -idUKKBN2PQ01K.

Reynolds, Tim. (2023). "In the Basketball-crazed Philippines, the World Cup Will be a Shining Moment." *The Journal*, August 22. https://www.the-journal.com/articles /in-the-basketball-crazed-philippines-the-world-cup-will-be-a-shining-moment/.

RFE/RL. (2021). "Turkmenistan Honors its First Olympic Medalist." August 21. https://www.rferl.org/a/turkmenistan-honors-olympic-medalist/31421806.html.

Rider, Toby C. (2016). *Cold War Games: Propaganda, The Olympics, and U.S. Foreign Policy.* Champaign-Urbana: University of Illinois Press.

Rider, Toby C., and Matthew P. Llewellyn. (2015). "The Five Rings and the 'Imagined Community': Nationalism and the Modern Olympic Games." *SAIS Review*, 35(Summer/Fall): 21–32.

Right to Play. (2018). "Preventing Violence Among and Against Children in Schools in Hyderabad, Pakistan: Evidence Brief." Toronto: Right to Play, September. https: //www.whatworks.co.za/documents/publications/211-right-to-play/file.

Rosenau, James. (1990). *Turbulence in World Politics: A Theory of Change and Continuity.* Princeton: Princeton University Press.

Round, Richard. (2004). *Inside the Olympic Games: A Behind-the-Scenes Look at the Politics, the Scandals, and the Glory of the Games.* New York: Wiley.

Rowello, Lauren. (2022). "Nonbinary Runners Have Been There the Whole Time." *New York Times*, April 26. https://www.nytimes.com/2022/04/30/sports/nonbinary -runners-races.html.

Russel, Stuart, Douglas Barrios, and Matt Andres. (2016). "Getting the Ball Rolling: Basis for Assessing the Sports Economy." Harvard University Center for International Development. CID Working Paper No. 321, July. https://growthlab .hks.harvard.edu/files/growthlab/files/cidwp_321_assessing_sports_economy.pdf.

Sambolah, Jakob. (2023). "Goal!: Sports, Community, and Supporting Young People." Mercy Corps. March 30. https://www.mercycorps.org/blog/goal-sports -community-young-people.

Scarborough, Vernon, and David L. Wilcox. (1993). *The Mesoamerican Ballgame.* Tucson: University of Arizona Press.

Schantz, Otto. (2008). "Pierre de Coubertin's 'civilizing mis-sion.'" *Proceedings: International Symposium for Olympic Research*, annual 2008. *Gale Academic OneFile*, https://go.gale.com/ps/i.do?p=AONE&u=anon ~e34a5dac&id=GALE|A197599058&v=2.1&it=r&sid=googleScholar&asid =e8aee029mental%20Approach.%20Champaign.

Schnitzer, March, Max Stephenson, Jr., Laura Zaonotti, and Yannis Stivachtis. (2013). "Theorizing the Role of Sport for Development and Peacebuilding." *Sport in Society*, 16(5): 595–610.

Schulenkorf, Nico. (2010). "Sports Events and Ethnic Reconciliation: Attempting to Create Social Change between Sinhalese, Tamil, and Muslim Sportspeople in War-Torn Sri Lanka." *International Review for the Sociology of Sport, 45*(3): 251–309.

Schulenkorf, Nico, and Daryl Adair, eds. (2013). *Global Sport-for-Development: Critical Perspectives.* London: Palgrave Macmillan.

Schulenkorf, Nico, and Emma Sherry. (2021). "Applying Intergroup Contact Theory to Sport-for-Development." *Sport Management Review, 24*(2): 250–70.

Schulenkorf, Nico, Emma Sherry, and Katie Rowe. (2016). "Sport for Development: An Integrated Literature Review." *Journal of Sport Management, 30*(1): 22–39.

Schwenker, Christopher. (2023). "Competitors Challenge Zwift's Dominance in Virtual Cycling as UCI Accepts Bids for Future Esports World Championships." *Cycling Weekly*, May 15. https://www.cyclingweekly.com/news/competitors-challenge-zwifts-dominance-in-virtual-cycling-as-the-uci-accepts-bids-for-future-esports-world-championships.

Seippel, Ørnulf. (2017). "Sports and Nationalism in a Globalized World," *International Journal of Sociology, 47*(1): 43–61.

Shevchenko, Vitaly. "Why Putin Cares about Russia's Athletes Competing Abroad." BBC, April 16. https://www.bbc.com/news/world-europe-65241285.

Shipley, Amy. (2003). "IOC Panel Proposes Sanctions for Iraq." *Washington Post*, May 8. https://www.washingtonpost.com/archive/sports/2003/05/08/ioc-panel-proposes-sanctions-for-iraq/e6b60554-13c8-40ec-9ce7-83c75b1fb603/.

Shrestha, Shreejana. (2017). "Superbike: Cargo Bikes Ease Daily Chores, Save Money, and Transform Businesses." *Nepali Times*, November 3–9. http://archive.nepalitimes.com/article/Nepali-Times-Buzz/superbike-superbusiness,4010.

Sisk, Timothy D. (2013). "Enabling Liberation: International Influences on Democratic Transition in South Africa." In Kathryn Stoner and Michael McFaul (Eds.), *Transitions to Democracy.* Baltimore: Johns Hopkins University Press.

Skateistan. (2022). "A New Chapter in Afghanistan." January 11. https://skateistan.org/blog/a-new-chapter/afghanistan.

Skateistan. (2019). "Annual Report 2019." https://skateistan.org/sites/default/files/2020-07/Skateistan%20Annual%20Report%202019.pdf.

Spaaij, Ramón. (2013). "Sport, Social Cohesion and Community Building: Managing the Nexus." In Peter Leisink, Paul Boselie, Maarten van Bottenburg, and Dian Hosking (Eds.), *Managing Social Issues.* Cheltenham: Edward Elgar Publishing.

Special Olympics. (2021). "Reach Report 2021." Colorado Springs: Special Olympics. https://resources.specialolympics.org/governance/reach-report.

The Sphere Project. (2018). "The Sphere Project: Humanitarian Charter and Minimum Standards in Humanitarian Response, 2018 Edition." Geneva: The Sphere Project. https://spherestandards.org/wp-content/uploads/Sphere-Handbook-2018-EN.pdf.

Stevenson, Christopher. (1999). "Becoming an International Athlete: Making Decisions about Identity." In Jay Coakley and Peter Donnelly (Eds.), *Inside Sports.* London: Routledge.

Sugden, John, and Alan Tomlinson. (2016). *Sport and Peace-Building in Divided Societies: Playing with Enemies.* Abingdon, UK: Routledge.

Svensson, Per, and Hilary Woods. (2017). "A Systematic Overview of Sport for Development and Peace Organizations." *Journal for Sport Development,* 5(9): 36–48.

Syrgios, Angelos. (2009). "Olympic Truce: From Myth to Reality." In Konstantinos Georgiadis and Angelos Syrigos (Eds.), *Olympic Truce: Sport as a Platform for Peace.* Athens: The International Olympic Truce Centre.

Thiel, Ansgar, and Jan Ove Tangen. (2015). "Niklaus Luhmann, System Theory, and Sport." In Richard Giulianotti (Ed.), *The Routledge Handbook of the Sociology of Sport.* London and New York: Routledge.

Thompson, Claire et al. (2015). "'Everyone Was Looking at You Smiling': East London Residents' Experiences of the 2012 Olympics and Its Legacy on the Social Determinants of Health." *Health & Place, 36*(November): 18–24.

Thorpe, Holly. (2016). "Action Sports for Youth Development: Critical Insights for the SDP Community." *International Journal of Sport Policy and Politics, 8*(1): 91–116.

Thorpe, Holly. 2014. *Transnational Mobilities in Action Sport Cultures.* London: Palgrave Macmillan.

Tomino, Ana Chesulich, Marko Perić, and Nicholas Wise. (2020). "Assessing and Considering the Wider Impacts of Sport-Tourism Events: A Research Agenda Review of Sustainability and Strategic Planning Elements." *Sustainability, 12*(22), 4473.

Tomlinson, Alan. (2000). "Carrying the Torch for Whom?" In Kay Schaffer and Sidonie Smith (Eds.), *The Olympics at the Millennium: Power, Politics, and the Games.* New Brunswick: Rutgers University Press.

Tomlinson, Alan. (2004). "Pierre Bourdieu and the Sociological Study of Sport: Habitus, Capital, and Field." In Richard Giulianotti (Ed.), *Sport and Modern Social Theorists.* London: Palgrave Macmillan.

Tomlinson, Alan, and Christopher Young. (2006). "Culture, Politics, and Spectacle in the Global Sports Event—An Introduction." In Alan Tomlinson and Christopher Young (Eds.), *National Identity and Global Sports Events: Culture, Politics, and Spectacle in the Olympics and World Cup.* Albany: Suny University Press, 1–13.

Totten, Mick. (2016). "Sport Activism and Protest." In Alan Bairner, John Kelly, and Jung Woo Lee (Eds.), *The Routledge Handbook of Sport and Politics.* Abingdon, UK: Routledge.

Towler, Christopher C., Nyron N. Crawford, and Robert A. Bennett III. (2020). "Shut Up and Play: Black Athletes, Protest Politics, and Black Political Action." *Perspectives on Politics, 18*(1), 111–127.

Tremblett, Giles. (2004). "The Cheats." *The Guardian,* September 15, 2004.

Umaña-Taylor, Adriana J. et al. (2014). "Ethnicity and Racial Identity during Adolescence and into Young Adulthood: An Integrated Conceptualization." *Child Development, 85*(1): 21–39.

UN. (2023a). "A New Agenda for Peace." Our Common Agenda Policy Brief 9. Political and Peacebuilding Affairs, July 20. https://dppa.un.org/en/a-new-agenda -for-peace.

UN. (2023b). "Traditional Resolution on Sport for Peace Put to Vote in General Assembly by Russian Federation for 'Politicizing' Olympic Games Next Summer." United Nations, November 21. https://press.un.org/en/2023/ga12565.doc.htm.

UN. (2021). "Sport for Development and Peace: Building a Peaceful and Better World Through Sport and the Olympic Ideal." UN General Assembly Resolution 76/13, December 6. https://undocs.org/en/A/RES/76/13.

UN. (2022). "Sport: Catalyst for a Better, Stronger Recovery." A/77/161, July 15. https://www.un.org/development/desa/dspd/sport-development-peace/unsg -report2022.html.

UN DESA. (2020). "Recovering Better: Sport for Development and Peace: Re-Opening Recovery and Resilience after COVID-19." UN DESA, December 15. https://www.un.org/development/desa/dspd/recovering-better-sport-for -development-and-peace.html.

UN DESA. (2017). "Reaching the Furthest Behind First is the Answer to Leaving No One Behind." UN DESA, July 14. https://www.un.org/development/desa/en/news/ sustainable/reaching-furthest-behind.html.

UNDP. (2022). "Uncertain Times, Unsettled Lives: Shaping our Future in a Transforming World." United Nations Development Programme, September 8. https://hdr.undp.org/content/human-development-report-2021-22.

UNDP. (2021). "Multidimensional Poverty 2021: Unmasking Disparities by Ethnicity, Caste, and Gender." United Nations Development Programme, October 7. https:// hdr.undp.org/content/2021-global-multidimensional-poverty-index-mpi#/indicies /MPI.

UNDP. (2020). "Strengthening Social Cohesion: Conceptual Framing and Programming Implications." United Nations Development Programme, February 27. https://www.undp.org/publications/strengthening-social-cohesion-conceptual -framing-and-programming-implications.

UNDP. (2016). "Supporting Insider Mediation: Strengthening Resilience to Conflict and Turbulence." United Nations Development Programme, August 8. https:// www.undp.org/publications/supporting-insider-mediation-strengthening-resilience -conflict-and-turbulence#.

UNICEF. (2019). "Getting into the Game: Understanding the Evidence for Child-Focused Sport for Development." UNICEF and the Barça Foundation, March.

UNHCR, IOC, and Terre des Hommes. (2019). "Sport for Protection Toolkit: Programming with Young People in Forced Displacement Settings." UNHCR. https://www.unhcr.org/media/sport-protection-toolkit.

UN Human Rights Council. (2023). "Report of the Independent International Commission of Inquiry on Ukraine." A/HRC/52/62, March 15. https://www.ohchr .org/sites/default/files/documents/hrbodies/hrcouncil/coiukraine/A_HRC_52_62 _AUV_EN.pdf.

UN Human Rights Council. (2022). "Intersection of Race and Gender Discrimination in Sport: Report of the UN High Commissioner for Human Rights." A/HRC/44/26, June 15.

UN Interagency Task force on Sport for Development and Peace. (2003). Sport for Development and Peace: Towards Achieving the Millennium Development Goals. UN DESA. https://digitallibrary.un.org/record/503601?ln=en.

UNODC. (2021). "Global Report on Corruption in Sport: Illegal Betting and Sport." United Nations Office on Drugs and Crime. https://www.unodc.org/res/safeguardingsport/grcs/9_22-03221_SPORTS_CORRUPTION_2021.pdf.

UNODC. (2020). *Preventing Violent Extremism through Sport: Technical Guide.* Vienna: United Nations Office at Vienna. https://www.unodc.org/documents/dohadeclaration/Sports/PVE/PVE_TechnicalGuide_EN.pdf.

UN News. (2022). "'We Know No Divisions:' UNMISS Project helps Build Peace Through Sports in Culturally Diverse Yei." United Nations Peacekeeping, June 6. https://peacekeeping.un.org/en/we-know-no-divisions-unmiss-project-helps -build-peace-through-sports-culturally-diverse-yei.

UN Security Council. (2022). "Youth and Peace and Security: Report of the Secretary-General." S/2022/220, April 27. https://www.un.org/peacebuilding/policy-issues-and-partnerships/policy/youth.

UN Women and UNESCO. (2023. "Tackling Violence against Women and Girls in Sport: A Handbook for Policy Makers and Sports Practitioners." https: //www.unwomen.org/en/digital-library/publications/2023/07/tackling-violence -against-women-and-girls-in-sport-a-handbook-for-policy-makers-and-sports -practitioners.

United Nations Alliance for Civilizations. (2022). "Thematic Paper: The Contribution of Sport to the Youth, Peace and Security Agenda." March 16. https://www .unaoc.org/resource/thematic-paper-the-contribution-of-sport-to-the-youth-peace -and-security-agenda/#:~:text=The%20thematic%20paper%20was%20developed ,S%2F2022%2F220.

United Nations and World Bank. (2011). *World Development Report 2011: Conflict, Security and Development.* Washington, DC: World Bank. https://openknowledge .worldbank.org/bitstream/handle/10986/4389/9780821384398_overview.pdf ?sequence=8&isAllowed=y.

Violette, Louis. (2020). "Abebe Bikila: *Portrait d'un Champion Olympique en Témoin de son Temps." Sport History Review* 51, 278–99.

WADA. (2019). "WADA Executive Committee Unanimously Endorses Four-Year Period of Non-Compliance for the Russian Anti-Doping Agency." World Anti-Doping Agency, December 9. https://www.wada-ama.org/en/news/wada-executive -committee-unanimously-endorses-four-year-period-non-compliance-russian-anti.

Westerbeek, Hans, and Rámon Spaaij. (2023). "Boycotts in Sport May Not Advance Human Rights, but They Do Harm Individual Athletes." *The Conversation*, April 11. theconversation.com/boycotts-in-sport-may-not-advance-human-rights-but-they-do-harm-individual-athletes-185208.

Wong, Edward, and Julian E. Barnes. (2022). "China Asked Russia to Delay Ukraine War Until After Olympics, U.S. Officials Say." *New York Times*, March 2. https:// www.nytimes.com/2022/03/02/us/politics/russia-ukraine-china.html.

World Bank. (2015). *World Development Report 2015: Mind, Society, and Behavior.* Washington, DC: The World Bank.

World Bank and United Nations, (2018). *Pathways for Peace: Inclusive Approaches to Preventing Violent Conflict.* Washington: International Bank for Reconstruction and Development/World Bank. https://openknowledge.worldbank.org/handle /10986/28337.

World Bicycle Relief. (2022). "2022 Impact Report." https://worldbicyclerelief.org /2022-impact-report/.

World Health Organization. (2022). "Global Status Report on Physical Activity." Geneva: World Health Organization. https://www.who.int/publications/i/item /9789240059153.

Xanthaki, Alexandra. (2023). "Message of the Special Rapporteur in the Field of Cultural Rights, Ms. Alexandra Xanthaki on the Participation of Russian and Belarussian Athletes in Sports Competitions." Committee on Culture, Science and the Media, Parliamentary Assembly of the Council of Europe, April 25. https://www .ohchr.org/sites/default/files/documents/issues/culturalrights/activities/message -AXanthaki-CoE-publichearing-25April2023.pdf.

Xu, Guoqi. (2008). *Olympic Dreams: China and Sports.* Cambridge, MA: Harvard University Press.

Zelensky, Volodmyr. (2023). "If Russian Athletes are Allowed to Participate in the Olympic Games, It's Just a Matter of Time before the Russian Federation Forces Them to Play Along with War Propaganda—Address by the President to the Participants of the Summit of the Sports Mini." President of Ukraine, February 10. https://www.president.gov.ua/en/news/yaksho-rosijskih-sportsmeniv-dopustyat -do-olimpijskih-igor-l-80917.

Zhao, Suisheng. (2023). "The Patriotic Education Campaign of Xi Jiaping's China: The Emergence of a New Generation of Nationalists." *China Leadership Monitor, 75* (Spring), March 1. https://www.prcleader.org/zhao-spring-2023.

Zimbalist, Andrew. (2015). *Circus Maximus: The Economic Gamble behind Hosting the Olympic Games and World Cup.* Washington, DC: The Brookings Institution.

Zipp, Sarah. (2017). "Sport for Development with 'At Risk' Girls in St. Lucia." *Sports in Society, 20*(12): 1917–1931.

Zirin, Dave, and Jules Boykoff. (2020). "Racist IOC President Avery Brundage Loses His Place of Honor." *The Nation*, June 25.

Index

Note: page numbers in *italics* indicate textboxes and figures.

Sport for Development and Peace
(SDP), 4, 26, 86, *146*, 196, 198;
action sports as complementing,
169; debating SDP, 155–58; as
development policy, 147; SDP
programs, 145, *148*, 153, 157,
158–59, *172*, 195; SDP sector, *21*,
23–24, 143, 144, *151*, 159–60;
theory of change in, 149; women's
empowerment in, 150–53
"The Sporting Spirit" (Orwell), 19
sport nationalism, *73*, 75, *76*
Sports and Humanitarian Assistance
(SAHA II) project, *174*
sportswashing, *22*, 45, 82–83, 111, 113,
124–25
Steiner, Achim, 7
Stockwell, Melissa, *136*
Stoke-Mandeville Games, 136
Sugden, John, 180
Suleymanoglu, Naim, *129*
Summer Olympic Games: 1908 London,
96, *98*; 1912 Stockholm, 96,
97, *98*; 1920 Antwerp, *94*,
96–97, *98*; 1924 Paris, 97;
1928 Amsterdam, *95*, 97, *99*; 1932 Los
Angeles, 97, *99*; 1936 Berlin, 21, 67,
90, *95*, *97–98*, *99*, 113, 118n11, 123,
137, 193; 1948 London, 67, *99*, 100;
1952 Oslo, *101*; 1956 Melbourne, *99*,
103, 111, 123, 137; 1960 Rome, *99*,
103–5; 1964 Tokyo, *99*, 103, *105*;
1968 Mexico City, *22*, *105*, 107, 123,
126, 127; 1972 Munich, 87, *99*, 107,
108, *109*, 127; 1976 Montreal, *99*,
107, *109*; 1980 Moscow, *99*, 107–8,
113; 1984 Los Angeles, *77–78*, *99*,
102, 107–8; 1988 Seoul, *99*, 109,
129; 1992 Barcelona, *99*, 100, 110,
129, *138*; 1996 Atlanta, *99*, 100, 110,
111, 115, *129*; 2000 Sydney, 39, 91,
100, 111, 130; 2004 Athens, *70*, *100*,
111; 2008 Beijing, 67, 86, 87, 89,
100, 102, 106, 112–13, 117, 118n11,
123; 2012 London, *100*, 113, 155;

2016 Rio de Janeiro, 12, 86, 93, *100*,
114, 130, 173; 2020 Tokyo, 17, 39,
60, *74*, 92, *100*, 110–11, 114, 123,
126, 173; 2024 Paris, 4, 16, 18, 26,
34, *74–75*, 89, *95*, *128*, 129, 193,
198; 2028 Los Angeles, 89
Sundberg, Ralph, 180
Sustainable Development Goals
(SDGs), *45*, 124, 144, 147, 149,
159–60; in Kazan action plan, *148*;
SDP sector, practice-oriented tool kit
for, 159–60; sport's contribution to,
143–45, 194
Svitolina, Elina, 125–26

Thorpe, Holly, 9, 169
Title IX legislation, 130
Tomlinson, Alan, 180
Tong, Allan, *172*
Totten, Mick, 128
Tour de France, 34–35, 57, *152*
transgender athletes, *34*, 92, 130, 132
transnational solidarity, 121, *152*
Tug of War, 32
The Two Escobars (film), *15*

UEFA Foundation for Children, 167
Ultimate Frisbee, 36, *37*, 83, 144
United Nations, 16, 24, 26, 68, 100,
142, 144, *148*, 164, 198; Assistance
Missions, 165, 167; Children's Fund,
43, 141, *146–47*, 159; COVID-
19, on sports' recovery from, 143;
Department of Economic and
Social Affairs, *145*, 160, 171, 198;
Development Program, *6*, 7, 16,
174, 175, *179*, 183, 195; Goodwill
Ambassador program, 173–74; High
Commissioner for Refugees, 168,
173, 178, 188; Interagency Task
Force on Sport for Development and
Peace, 24, 31–32; "New Agenda for
Peace," 24–25; Office of Drugs and
Crime, 14, 171, 188; Our Common

About the Author

Timothy D. Sisk is professor of International and Comparative Politics at the Josef Korbel School of International Studies, University of Denver. His research, teaching, and policy-oriented work focuses on conflict prevention, management, and peacebuilding in fragile and postwar contexts. He teaches graduate and undergraduate courses on comparative politics, politics of deeply divided societies, elections and conflict dynamics, and sport and international politics. He works with fellow scholars, international and regional organizations, and students on international peace and security concerns such as peacemaking, peacebuilding, and inclusive governance and democracy building.

Prior to joining the University of Denver in 1998, Sisk served as a program officer and research scholar in the Grant Program of the United States Institute of Peace in Washington, D.C., and earlier earned a doctoral degree in political science from the George Washington University and an MA in international journalism and BA in international studies and German from Baylor University. Having been "raised on" baseball, basketball, and football, he is an avid cyclist, skier, and all-around outdoor-sport enthusiast. A member of the Professional Ski Instructors of America, he is a certified Nordic/cross-country ski instructor in classic and freestyle subdisciplines.

Book projects are a team sport. This book has its origins in a sport-and-politics course at Korbel School developed in the late 1990s by the author with the late eccentric and enthusiastic historian, Arthur N. Gilbert. The ideas reflected here in some ways constitute a synthesis of the engaging student interests and research over the years, and the author is grateful to have learned from their varied interests and experiences. Participants in the Spring 2023 course contributed to the research in this volume, and the author is especially grateful to those whose research is tangentially reflected in this book. Finally, friends and family have long endured the author's interest in the topic and have contributed immensely to both the theory, case, and life-mattering topics that arise in conversations about sport: physical activity, play and mental health, and its relationship for an urgent need for a better world in today's turbulent times.

www.ingramcontent.com/pod-product-compliance
Lightning Source LLC
Chambersburg PA
CBHW051959270326
41929CB00015B/2717